In the Service of the Peacock Throne

In the Service of the Peacock Throne

*The Diaries of the Shah's Last
Ambassador to London*

PARVIZ C. RADJI

HAMISH HAMILTON: LONDON

First published in Great Britain 1983
by Hamish Hamilton Ltd
Garden House 57–59 Long Acre London WC2E 9JZ

Copyright © 1983 by Parviz C. Radji

British Library Cataloguing in Publication Data

Radji, Parviz
   In the Service of the Peacock Throne.
   1. Radji, Parvis   2. Diplomacy – Iran
   I. Title
   327.2′092′4   JX1853

ISBN 0–4241–10960–4

Phototypeset by Tradespools Ltd, Frome, Somerset
Printed in Great Britain by Unwin Brothers Limited
The Gresham Press, Old Woking, Surrey

To Farhad, My Brother

Introduction

These diaries begin on June 4, 1976, and end on January 26, 1979, covering exactly the period I served as Iran's Ambassador to London. They were originally intended, I suppose, as a sort of introductory guide to the diplomatic life of London for those of my compatriots who would one day be assigned to the London Embassy. If a factual and straightforward account of my working experience could have provided prospective Iranian diplomats with even a moderately improved appreciation of the work involved, my purpose in writing the diaries would have been fulfilled.

As events turned out, however, my tenure of office was to coincide with the unfolding of cataclysmic changes in Iran, changes that I, for one, had certainly not foreseen. As the clouds loomed larger and darker on the political horizon, the initial attempt to pose as a disinterested observer of the London social and diplomatic scene was soon abandoned. Instead, the entries became an emotional and highly subjective account of the developing events as I could perceive them from London, and of the hopes, the frustrations, the anxieties, the fears and the sheer agony that accompanied each successive trauma, leading ultimately to the Shah's departure from Iran and the termination of my own assignment. This book is not a history of the Iranian revolution, but of one individual's experience of it.

My brother and I, the only children of a relatively prosperous Persian family, were born in Iran in 1935 and 1936 respectively. Our father, an orthopaedic surgeon who had received his own training in Toulouse, had somehow developed a predilection to provide his sons with 'an Anglo-Saxon education'. So, in 1950, we were sent off to the Hill School, in Pottstown, Pennsylvania, a smart East Coast private school which prepared its pupils for eventual entry to Ivy League Universities.

1

Neither of us, however, was destined to receive an American education. Political events, as they were to do so often later, intervened to alter the course of our lives.

The year 1951 saw the rise to the premiership in Iran of Dr Mohammad Mossadeq. The nationalisation of the country's oil industry not only ruptured Iran's relations with Britain, but, by temporarily halting the export of oil, created an acute shortage of foreign exchange. The cost of an American education proved prohibitive, and my brother and I were brought over to England. The uncertainties of our financial situation persisted for the next two years, and we found ourselves spending increasingly protracted holidays in Iran. But, with the resolution of the Anglo-Iranian dispute in 1953, the position improved sufficiently to allow us to pursue our secondary education at various cramming schools in England, until 1956 when we both gained admission to university. My brother went to Edinburgh to study medicine; I to Cambridge to read Economics.

I returned to Iran in 1959, brimming over with enthusiasm, impatient to flaunt my newly acquired knowledge, longing to serve the common good of my country. Iran was a land of considerable poverty but of even greater promise. Financed by a growing income from the export of oil, the Shah had initiated a programme of industrialisation, whose aims seemed to me both estimable and attainable. I soon determined that the oil industry, upon which the economy primarily depended, was where I ought to be. My application for employment was accepted, and I was given an administrative job. It was then that I first met Amir Abbas Hoveyda.

Hoveyda was at that time a director of the National Iranian Oil Company (NIOC). He was a career member of the Foreign Ministry, and had last served as counsellor at the Iranian Embassy in Ankara. He was an immensely affable and highly cultivated man, well versed in European history, languages and literature, and with a penchant for mildly flamboyant clothes. He had been brought into NIOC by its Chairman, Abdollah Entezam, another diplomat under whom Hoveyda had served in post-war Germany. Entezam himself had formerly been Foreign Minister and acting Prime Minister, and now presided over the nation's most vital industry.

In an Iran thirsty for trained manpower of any sort, it was not difficult to move quickly up the administrative ladder. Within two years, I had risen from the position of a trainee analyst to that of Hoveyda's private secretary. But, while I respected Hoveyda as an individual and admired him as an administrator, I was becoming

2

disenchanted with my own position in the company. The prospects for someone who wished to rise through the ranks to a position of relative prominence, without a commanding knowledge of the technical aspects of the oil industry, appeared bleak. The top echelon of the company was wholly composed of either professional oilmen or political appointees. In short, NIOC now seemed an unsuitable vehicle for the furtherance of my ambitions. So, with Hoveyda's blessing, I applied for admission to our diplomatic service, and in 1963 entered the Ministry of Foreign Affairs.

As it happened, both Entezam and Hoveyda were soon to leave NIOC as well. In 1963 the Shah launched his much publicised White Revolution, a programme of agrarian and social reform which embodied much that was progressive in outlook and badly needed in practice, but which aroused fierce opposition from the more benighted clergy. The standard-bearer of the religious protest, one Rouhollah Khomeini, was exiled to Turkey, and the ensuing disturbances in Qom and Tehran were effectively but ruthlessly crushed. Entezam, an erudite man of liberal, centrist views, with a towering reputation for personal probity and a Sufi's disdain for the trappings of office, was appalled at the ferocity with which the religious opposition was suppressed, and at one of his weekly audiences with the Sovereign had the courage – or the temerity – to voice his reservations. The Shah, under pressure from the Kennedy administration to present a less feudalistic image, replied that, if Entezam could not align himself with measures that were designed to liberate Iran from the shackles of backwardness, he should make room for someone who could.

Having been given special dispensation on account of his health from attending official functions, Entezam now decided to put in a final appearance at ceremonies that were shortly to follow, marking the day in the seventh century when the Prophet Mohammad, according to Shi'ite belief, had raised the hand of his son-in-law Ali, to proclaim him his appointed successor. As required by custom, the invited dignitaries assembled in order of precedence in the chandeliered halls of Golestan Palace to offer their felicitations to the monarch. The Prime Minister on behalf of the government, the doyen on behalf of the diplomatic corps, the chief of staff on behalf of the military, had had their turn. As the ranking civil servant, it was now Entezam's turn to tender his greetings. 'Now that *for the last time* I have the honour, on behalf of the civil service, to felicitate Your Majesty on this joyous occasion', he began, dropping the first public hint that he had been given his marching orders.

It was not the beginning but the conclusion of his remarks,

3

however, that provoked royal indignation. Entezam, who was known to smoke regularly and drink occasionally, ended his formal greetings by wishing the Sovereign good health and success in the noble endeavours he had embarked upon, and which he, Entezam, hoped 'Your Majesty will pursue with moderation'.

'Moderation?' demanded the Shah, nettled to the marrow, 'Moderation is required in smoking and drinking, not in the pursuit of good deeds.'

Later that day Entezam retired to the privacy of his rented apartment, where for the next fifteen years he remained out of the political limelight. Yet, through an irony of history, as we shall see in these pages, it was to Entezam the Shah would turn in the turbulent autumn of 1978 to form a government, in a desperate attempt to stem the tide of the revolution Khomeini was relentlessly leading against him.

With Entezam's departure, Hoveyda, his acknowledged protégé, did not stay on at NIOC. A man constitutionally incapable of gloom or despondency, he went on leave, and shortly afterwards threw in his political lot with his lifelong friend and Foreign Ministry colleague, Hassanali Mansour, an attractive, ambitious and articulate, if rather glib, son of a former Prime Minister who had just founded the Progressive Centre. This was a political grouping of aspiring intellectuals, teachers, technocrats, journalists and soldiers of fortune whose programmes were well-presented but, on closer scrutiny, indistinct.

The Progressive Centre soon transformed itself into a political party, the Iran-e-Novin, or New Iran, contested the parliamentary elections that followed, and won a sizeable majority. On March 7, 1964, Mansour succeeded Assadollah Alam, the Shah's trusted personal friend, as Prime Minister. Alam was given the influential post of Court Minister, while Hoveyda, now the Secretary General of Iran-e-Novin, was assigned to the Ministry of Finance.

Mansour's premiership did not last long. After only ten months in office, he fell victim to an assassin's bullet, fired by a theology student who had carved the word Allah on the handle of his revolver. Though never publicly admitted, it was generally agreed that the presentation to Parliament by the Mansour government of the Status of Forces Agreement, a bill which granted the American military and their dependents immunity from prosecution under Iranian law, had supplied the principal motive for the assassination. The Shah, to emphasize continuity, reached over the heads of more senior ministers to appoint Hoveyda to the premiership.

It did not take me long to make my mind up, when the Prime Minister's offer came a couple of months later, to join him at his more exalted office. Not that I was unhappy at the Foreign Ministry, where, again because of a scarcity of eligible personnel, I had been assigned to the Minister's private office as his personal assistant-cum-speech-writer in English. But the chance to resume my association with my former boss, now theoretically the second most powerful man in the land, to be the recipient of his confidence, to witness at first hand the exercise of political power, the wielding of personal influence, and the bestowal of official patronage, proved irresistible. And then there was the personality of Amir Abbas Hoveyda himself. It would do his memory an injustice if in death I tried to paint him larger than he was in life; but he was, I always felt, an uncommon man.

Endowed with immense charm and a natural friendliness, there was never about him that arrogance which is so frequently a characteristic of men in power: never the hint of patronage, or the condescension of a *de haut en bas* attitude. He was approachable even if he was not particularly humble, and he had the capacity, virtually unheard of amongst Iranian politicians, to laugh at himself. There was a phrase Mozaffar-ed-Din Shah, the Qajar King, used to employ whenever he sought the frank opinion of his closest advisers: 'You have our permission to be impertinent,' he would say. With Amir Abbas, his close associates could be impertinent, because he saw the disinterestedness of the motives which inspired such comments, even if the manner of their expression overstepped the limits of strict tactfulness. He never pulled rank.

He could also be incredibly clever and cunning. He could impose his views on others even when his reasoning was tenuous at best. He could twist arguments to his own advantage, dissemble or fudge when necessary. He could seize upon one small weakness in his opponent's otherwise valid comments to discredit his views totally; and, while he could at times be ruthless, he was essentially a kind and generous man, devoid of malice.

I remember an occasion in the course of a meeting when he had lost his customary cool and had subjected a subordinate to a barrage of verbal attacks, reducing the hapless man to tears. Shortly after the meeting had broken up, Hoveyda summoned the still shaken individual to his office, and threw the curved handle of his ubiquitous walking stick around the man's neck, pulling him gently forward. He then kissed him on both cheeks, expressing regret for his excessive harshness.

He was an educated and highly cultivated man. His secondary schooling in Beirut had provided him with a fluency in Arabic which, as with his English, he spoke well and confidently: he had a

5

smattering of Turkish and German from his diplomatic postings in those countries, while French, over which in some ways he had a more perfect command than over his native Persian, he spoke luminously. He had studied history at the Université Libre de Bruxelles, and political economy at the Sorbonne. He was as familiar with the classics and the history of Europe, as he was with modern trends in literature and philosophy. He was an immensely able administrator, and scrupulously honest.

His detractors would later say of him that Hoveyda's greatest fault lay in lending his first-rate mind to make the Shah's régime intellectually respectable in a manner that none of his predecessors, nor indeed the Shah himself, with his militaristic, disciplinarian approach, could ever have done; that Hoveyda's shrewdness enabled him to recognise in the Shah a weakness for flattery, particularly his wish to be compared to de Gaulle, and that by playing on this trait in the Shah's character he accentuated the Shah's estrangement from his own people; and that, precisely because of his deep immersion in the cultural traditions of Western liberalism, he ought to have known better.

These may be valid criticisms. My own opinion is that, whatever Hoveyda's positive contributions or personal shortcomings, they were totally marginal to the central issues, external as well as internal, that paved the way for the tumultuous changes that were to follow. Nor am I at all convinced that a less intellectually gifted man, a stupid man – and there was no shortage of them – as Prime Minister would have ensured the survival of the monarchy. Between the 1963 resignation of Dr Amini and the advent of the Revolution, no Prime Minister of Iran was ever more than an instrument for faithfully carrying out the wishes of the sovereign. Throughout, the Shah remained impervious to advice – if, indeed, advice was ever offered. The events are perhaps too recent to permit definitive judgment.

From 1965–1969 I remained at the Prime Minister's office uninterruptedly. This was the period of my most feverish activity. I would rise each day at six, be at the office by seven-thirty and stay on generally until nine or ten at night, having had lunch in my office. Hoveyda was both a demanding and a rewarding boss, and I should like to think I learnt much from serving under him. Then one day, in 1969, he told me of an informal conversation he had had at some social function with Princess Ashraf, the Shah's twin sister, whose international responsibilities in the domains of literacy and women's rights were expanding. She needed someone who could handle the growing volume of her work. Did I know anyone I could recommend? In the meantime the Princess was going to India shortly and would I go with her as a member of the delegation to make sure the visit went well?

Though I knew the Princess only casually, I was aware, as everyone was, of her formidable reputation as a woman of enormous power, of dauntless courage, of iron determination, of single-mindedness of purpose, of immense generosity to her friends, and firm opposition to her foes. In the event, the visit, which was to mark the centenary of Mahatma Gandhi's birth, went well: or so, at least, I thought. We were received by President Giri, took tea with Prime Minister Indira Gandhi, participated in a massive commemorative rally, and were wined and dined officially on every remaining free occasion. But the Princess felt slighted by her rather indiscriminate *placement* at the rally, and cut the visit short. We returned to Tehran earlier than expected and soon afterwards the Princess went abroad.

Even though our first working encounter had been less than a resounding success, I felt complimented when asked to accompany the Princess on her annual visit to the United Nations General Assembly. The procedure was for the Foreign Minister to go to New York within, say, the first fortnight of the convening of the General Assembly, to deliver his address, to meet whichever of his counterparts he wished to, to host a few receptions and attend many more. He would then leave, making room for the arrival of the Princess, who would act as Chairman of the delegation for the remainder of the Assembly. The hustle and bustle of New York diplomatic life held much attraction for the Princess. For someone who loved life and lived it intensely, who was unburdened by considerations of money, New York had an infinite variety of choices to offer. The city, in its majestic vastness, also gave her a measure of protective anonymity which she welcomed.

As our contacts continued and I grew to know the Princess better, one particularly important aspect of her character became clear: her entire existence centred on her abiding love for one man whom she adored, and would always adore, above all others, her twin brother. He was the light of her life, the apple of her eye, the blood that flowed in her veins. She loved him with a passion that was both possessive and unsharing. The Shah was one half of the symbiotic whole of which the Princess was the other.

The General Assembly was only one of the Princess's many international obligations. She represented Iran on the UN Commission for Human Rights which met each year alternately in Geneva and New York, and on which she had already served as President. She was the chairman of a literacy committee which Iran co-sponsored with the Soviet Union and which convened annually in Moscow and Tehran. There were innumerable international women's rights organisations over which she presided; and there was never any shortage of invitations to visit other countries in the context of our bilateral relations. It was a gilded existence of much travel and some diplomacy, the work co-efficient of which could be adapted to suit each particular occasion. After a while, however, I realised that it was not for me. It was a life based exclusively on privilege and position rather than on merit. The issues involved seemed never of more than peripheral importance, while the accolades and rewards stood out of all proportion to the effort put in. In 1973, after three years in the service of the Princess, I returned to Hoveyda's office and was granted the title of Special Adviser to the Prime Minister.

The next three years, viewed with the wisdom of hindsight, were crucial for the future of Iran. As the country's oil income grew, so did the Shah's confidence in his ability to lead his people and to fulfil for them his vaunted economic ambitions. Indeed, the Shah saw the 1973 boom in oil prices – for which he was a prime mover – as the moment to realise his grand vision of Iran, as a global force to be reckoned with, economically no less than militarily. Massive expenditures were undertaken well beyond the human or infrastructural capacities of the country. These were the seeds of the gigantic economic dislocation that was to become increasingly apparent after 1976. Even then, it is conceivable that things might not have come to a head so fast had the Shah persevered with his customary iron-fisted policy and stamped out any public discontent that the economic disarray may have inspired. By then, however, Jimmy Carter was in the White House, and the Shah, mindful that respect for human rights had been an important principle of the President's electoral campaign, felt compelled to make concessions in the form of a degree of political liberalisation. This he did at the fateful moment when all the economic indicators were signalling danger.

In the spring of 1976 I began hinting to Hoveyda that I would welcome a change of assignment. He had been Prime Minister for over eleven years, and I had been associated with him for most of that time. As he himself would sometimes admit in private, his approach to issues lacked innovation, his public promises carried little conviction, his political utterances were bereft of credibility. The gruelling routine had taken its toll. He was exceedingly tired, increasingly irritable, and prone to impatience and ill-temper. The pressures on us were in no way comparable, but in my far less exalted and demanding position I, too, was beginning to weary of the routine that had come to dominate my life, allowing little room for imagination or initiative. I wanted a post abroad, preferably in Europe, ideally on the Mediterranean. The Athens Embassy was becoming free and Rome was soon to be vacant. Though I never seriously thought I would be offered it, I was aware that London, too, could be due for a change. The incumbent Ambassador, Mohammad Reza Amirteymour, a career diplomat who had served with distinction in Delhi and Moscow, from where he had been transferred to London in 1974, had incurred massive personal debts at the gaming tables which, according to rumour, ran into seven figures. Under pressure from his creditors, it was said in Tehran, he wished to return to Iran to sell what remained of his properties in Tehran and Khorassan in an attempt to settle his debts.

I consulted my two patrons, the Prime Minister and the Princess. Hoveyda, who supported my request for a post abroad with what I felt was the merest suspicion of good-natured envy, promised to speak to the Foreign Minister and to raise the matter himself with the Shah at an opportune moment. The Princess, who was as fierce in her loyalty as she was adamant in her demands, dismissed Athens and Rome out of hand, and declared that I ought to be posted to London. She would speak to her brother at the first opportunity, obtain his consent and convey the royal instructions to the Foreign Minister.

With a characteristic display of gumption and decisiveness, the Princess did precisely as she had promised. The Shah, whom I met frequently but never knew intimately, agreed to the appointment readily, and the rest was mere formality. Hoveyda, visibly surprised by the speed of the Princess's move, expressed his delight, and the Foreign Minister, Abbasali Khalatbary, a distinguished man of a calm and kindly disposition, promised the fullest co-operation.

Thus in the early summer of 1976, a few days before the Princess herself was due to visit London, I arrived to take up my assignment.

I present the diaries as they were written day by day. Many entries which seemed to me of insufficient general interest have been omitted, and I have tidied up the language where I thought this was needed for the sake of clarity. But in no case have I changed the sense of what I wrote. It was tempting to endow myself with greater wisdom and foresight than I possessed at the time, but it is a temptation which I have resisted.

1976

Wednesday, June 16

The last days have been something of a nightmare. I arrived in London on the 4th. On the evening of the 5th, a Saturday, Behnam, the Number Two, telephoned at about 10 p.m. to convey 'tragic news'. I immediately asked whether Amirteymour[1] had met with some misfortune. Behnam replied that he was dead.

From Abbas, the butler, I obtained the number of Amirteymour's flat and spoke to the policeman now on the scene – not believing, not wanting to believe, the finality of Amirteymour's death. I asked if he was sure the former Ambassador was dead. 'Oh yes, sir,' he replied. 'He's cold.'

A thousand thoughts rushed into my head. After a moment's reflection I calculated the time difference with Iran, nearly 1 a.m. by then, and rang Hoveyda. Shaken by the news, he muttered something about its being too late to wake up HIM[2] and said goodbye. I then went to Amirteymour's residence round the corner in Ennismore Gardens. Behnam and his wife, Fereshteh, were there, weeping and lighting one cigarette after another. Others from the Embassy and the Consulate arrived, as did eventually the coroner, an East European judging from his accent, who gave an opinion that death had occurred at least six hours previously.

The next morning I called on my predecessor's sister, the Begum Eskandar Mirza, to express condolences.

The prospective arrival of Princess Ashraf and attention to the details of her programme kept me busy during the next few days.

Anthony Crosland called on the Princess on Tuesday, June 8. A handsome and intelligent man, I thought, but not very good at small talk. He spoke about the Cold War, the Chinese withdrawal from Africa and the importance of Nato and Cento. Mrs Thatcher came the next day, having lost the previous night a motion of censure against the Government. She looks a little like a priest's wife, conveying an impression of physical innocence. She said she was for the restoration of the death penalty in England, favoured more severe measures against terrorism, and believed in the need for a strong military posture by the West; none of which struck me as very priest-like.

By 6.30 that same day, and two hours before the official Embassy dinner for the Princess, from thirty to fifty people had gathered on the pavement opposite the Embassy Residence and were shouting: 'The Shah is a murderer ... The Shah is an American puppet ... Ashraf out ...' They were brandishing placards showing people

[1] My predecessor, still in London then.
[2] His Imperial Majesty (The Shah).

13

alleged to be political prisoners bound to stakes, their bodies riddled with bullets.

By the time Princess Margaret arrived at 8.40 the demonstrators were still there, slogan-chanting as tirelessly as ever. I apologised for the 'reception committee' outside, but the Princess said she was quite used to this sort of thing herself, as every time she was in the United States the pro-IRA Irish-Americans mounted similar performances, and that it wasn't to be taken seriously. Then she added, to my astonishment: 'But, of course, you have torture, which we don't.' I replied that I was amazed how misinformed Her Royal Highness was about Iran.

Throughout the evening Princess Margaret smoked constantly, coughed frequently, and showed no great interest in conversing with either Princess Ashraf or the other guests. After dinner, I took her upstairs and showed her my living quarters. She agreed that some radical surgery was required and that in particular the pink porcelain in the bathroom would have to be changed. The Princess was apparently now in a good mood and stayed till after midnight.

On Saturday, June 12, suitably attired, I attended the Trooping the Colour ceremony, received King Constantine and Queen Anne-Marie of Greece for lunch with the Princess at the Embassy, and left immediately afterwards for Oxford, where Princess Ashraf was to inspect the library whose construction cost she had financed.

Our arrival at Wadham College proved a disastrous occasion. To avoid the demonstrations, we were to be smuggled into the College through a back entrance, but there were demonstrators there too, and in the alley leading to the back gate cars had been deliberately parked in such a way as to prevent the passage of ours. While at least a hundred people, some with hoods on, chanted the most ferocious obscenities and pelted our car with eggs, we were obliged to sit where we were, feigning nonchalance as we awaited the arrival of reinforcements.

· Arrive they did, at last, as did a worried looking Stuart Hampshire, the Warden of Wadham. Some unconvincing pleasantries about 'students always being students' failed to relieve the embarrassment of the occasion. We were taken to the Warden's Lodgings where, with maps and architectural drawings spread out on a table, a thickly Scottish accented Professor McMillan explained the library project, while the deafening chants of the demonstrators outside seemed to shake the entire room. Warden Hampshire looked distinctly unhappy, afflicted, as it were, with a social responsibility from which he couldn't rid himself soon

14

enough.

We were given dinner in Hall, which had been emptied of undergraduates, presumably to prevent a repetition of the afternoon. The saying of grace was dispensed with as in the circumstances inappropriate, and the whole wretched meal was rushed through.

Eprime Eshaq, an Iranian of Assyrian origin and for many years a don at Wadham, appeared to be the only person enjoying himself, and he did so hugely. More abuse was shouted at us by the demonstrators at our departure. The Princess looked quite shaken by the day's experience. She left the next day.

Monday, June 28

Lunch with David Spanier, the Diplomatic Correspondent of *The Times*, at PG.[1] I know him from Cambridge, though I believe he had already gone down when I went up. Four years ago, he and his wife, Suzy, who writes about fashion for the *Evening Standard*, visited Iran, on my suggestion, as guests of the Government. He is, I believe, slightly right of centre.

I raise with him the 'image problem' that I maintain Iran suffers from 'in certain sections of the British Press'. If we are going to be judged at all, I say, we must be judged within a frame of reference that has some bearing on our particular circumstances. The Shah is dragging Iran out of the Middle Ages and catapulting it into the twentieth century. There are bound to be some growing pains; there is a need for discipline; there must be certain limitations on individual freedom. At this stage of Iran's development, our concept of democracy must be to feed, house and educate people, not to give them a licence for political permissiveness that would inevitably lead to anarchy.

David agrees that there is an image problem. He says he thinks a lot more contact with the Press is essential, citing the Israelis as a successful example of this. He says there are about fifteen to twenty people who are the opinion-makers in the British Press and suggests I establish regular dialogues with them. And he warns against attempts to woo *Private Eye*, who have been calling HIM 'The Shit of Persia' for something like three years; he doesn't think they can be 'bought'.

There is, he explains, such a thing as journalistic conscience and unless an article is 'balanced' it would suffer from what he called

[1] Princes Gate, the Ambassador's residence.

15

the 'Chalfont syndrome'.[1] He thinks that we in Iran should be more thick-skinned but also more open and more honest. 'Give the number of your political prisoners,' Spanier recommends, as an example of what might be done.

I send a cable to Tehran giving the gist of our conversation, noting particularly Spanier's suggestions for greater openness and honesty in dealing with the Press. Await the reply with some anxiety.

Thursday, July 1

I receive HIM's reply to my 'image' cable to the following effect: 'Do what you can to change the attitude of the Press, but it might be useful to remind them once in a while that Iran can always diversify her sources of supply, but Britain can't very well do without Iran's market.'

I return to Tehran tomorrow. My departure from Tehran, put forward so that I should be in London in time for the Princess's arrival, had been too hurried to allow me to see some of those I certainly ought to have seen. I came away with no specific instructions, no briefing to speak of, indeed with little information on the various aspects of our relations with the Brits.

First impressions of my new job have not been at all encouraging. The Princess's Oxford reception and three weeks in London have been quite sufficient to confirm the magnitude of our image problem, and I am not at all sure whether my superiors in Tehran fully appreciate the extent and gravity of this particular difficulty.

Friday, July 9

The past week in Tehran has been most interesting and marvellously enjoyable. Friends have not been in short supply and everyone has been immensely kind. Cyrus Ghani[2] gave a dinner to which the Prime Minister came. Hoveyda was in one of his more

---

[1] Lord Chalfont, Minister of State at the Foreign Office 1964–70, and before that Defence Correspondent of *The Times*, who had written a number of articles in support of the Shah's régime in *The Times* and elsewhere.
[2] A prominent international lawyer who represented numerous UK and US companies in Iran and who possessed considerable knowledge of the American political scene.

16

jovially sadistic moods and made everyone, including the stuttering Cyrus, stand up and make speeches. He himself spoke last and said at one point, 'No matter who says what about Parviz, I haven't yet been able to find a successor to him at the Office,' which I found most flattering.

On Monday, the PM gave a dinner for Prime Minister Bhutto of Pakistan and on Wednesday we lunched tête-à-tête. I told him of the need to establish some sort of dialogue with Amnesty International and to take a less hawkish approach to the British press. He replied that I ought to put down my suggestions in a memo which he could discuss with HIM

In the evening, Parvine Farmanfarmaian entertained in her usual lavish way. An incredibly shy Andy Warhol and some of his friends provided a measure of additional attraction. He looked bleached, as if at some stage of chemical decomposition. I understand they are here to do a portrait of the Empress.

With growing alarm I read an article in the July 7 issue of the *International Herald Tribune* by Bernard Nossiter, the paper's London Bureau Chief, which seems to impute a role for Savak[1] in Amirteymour's death. My name is mentioned, with sinister-sounding connotations, claiming that I had invoked diplomatic immunity on instructions from Tehran to prevent an autopsy.

Monday, July 12

Lunch with Hushang Ansari.[2] He says that HIM, having a sense of history and an eye to posterity, cannot bring himself to issue instructions that may appear to compromise his firm stand on policy matters, but that I should, as HIM has instructed, establish a meaningful dialogue with the British Press, and that HIM tacitly approves. He agrees there is a problem with Amnesty, as standing instructions forbid any form of contact.

I see Tony Parsons[3] at Alireza Arouzi's. He reveals that I have made my debut in *Private Eye*. They have reprinted the *Herald Tribune* article, only their figure of £1m. as Amirteymour's gambling losses is closer to the truth than Nossiter's more modest figure of £100,000.

[1] The State Intelligence and Security Organisation which combined the functions of the secret police with those of overseas information gathering.
[2] Minister of Finance.
[3] Sir Anthony Parsons, British Ambassador in Tehran, later British Representative to the United Nations.

He asks, anticipating the kind of reaction to be expected from HIM, whether we have looked into the possibility of suing them for defamation against a Head of State. I say suing would make a martyr of the *Eye* and probably generate public sympathy for it.

Saturday, July 17

Call on General Nassiri, head of Savak, at his headquarters. His own office is small and modestly furnished. He speaks of lax security at many of our Embassies and Consulates abroad, leading to loss of confidential documents and passports. (The Geneva consulate has just been attacked and occupied for three hours by dissident students.) He says it would be a valuable service if dissidents living abroad could be persuaded to make public confessions of guilt and express contrition. He says all they have to do is to tell the authorities everything about their past activities and contacts.

There are some, I say, who are willing to renounce their past and undertake not to engage in anti-Government activities, and simply want to live and ultimately die here, if we guarantee them safe conduct. He replies: 'Surely, the least they can do is to tell us about their past actions and associates. Otherwise, they can live, and die, in whatever hell they have been living in all along.'

The General is courteous and, despite his age, lucid. I then go and see Parviz Sabeti, Savak's Chief of Operations. He says inspection of cells and interviews with political prisoners can be arranged with prior notice, but for Amnesty to conduct such visits would require the green light from above.

Monday, July 19

With Princess Ashraf I fly to Nowshahr on the Caspian where Their Majesties are staying. Fereydoun Hoveyda,[1] is at the airport to greet the Princess. She and the Prime Minister, never the best of friends, have recently had a row over the PM's refusal to give an official appointment to one of the Princess's aides, so I expect embarrassing snubs. On the quay at Nowshahr I bow to HIM, to King Hussein and King Constantine, and kiss the hands of the Empress, Queen Alia [of Jordan] and Queen Anne-Marie [of

[1] Iranian Representative to the United Nations and brother of the Prime Minister.

Greece]. The Prime Minister is there, too, as are one or two of the more pretentious members of the Empress's entourage. Fereydoun and I are invited to join the royal table for lunch. The conversation is mostly about the physical unattractiveness of Andy Warhol.

I drive, after lunch, with the Prime Minister to the Foreign Minister's villa, about 20 kilometers away. After a brief discussion of the Embassy's situation in London and about who I should take as my new Number Two, now that Behnam is leaving, I refer to the two subjects I want to raise with HIM later in the afternoon. Both Hoveyda and Khalatbary[1] urge me to proceed with extreme caution, and emphasise that HIM is very sensitive about both the British Press and Amnesty International. The PM's driver drops me back at the quay, where I find Fereydoun and the Princess in conversation before their respective audiences with HIM. I put on my tie and jacket and wait quite nervously for my own.

Princess Ashraf is summoned first, then Fereydoun, and finally it's my turn. As I enter the room, HIM's great dane leaps at me, with a bark, then hears his master's command and resumes a watchful seated posture next to a white leather armchair.

'You have had an eventful start,' says HIM, after I have bowed and kissed his hand. He is standing in the middle of a large rectangular cabin which serves as the Royal couple's living area. As I begin to mumble my reply, he starts pacing from one end of the cabin to the other, and I find that I have constantly to turn on my ankle on the spot so as not to present my profile to him, which would be regarded as disrespectful.

I reply to the effect that my predecessor's sense of timing was somewhat unfortunate. I then say that, since my departure from Tehran had been in haste, I had sought the honour of an audience in order more closely to familiarise myself with HIM's general thinking, and to seek instructions on two specific points.

'The first is the question of *Private Eye*', I hear myself saying. 'Every other Thursday, when the magazine appears, I suffer from attacks of anger when I read their references to Iran.' HIM interrupts to say he quite understands that every patriotic Iranian must feel insulted by the magazine's offensive comments.

Would he permit it, I go on, if some trusted friends arranged an 'accidental' meeting on neutral territory so that some kind of dialogue might be established with some of the editorial staff? Not, I hasten to explain, that one could realistically expect to convert them overnight or to persuade them to sing our praises, but one might perhaps hope for a toning down of the language, and even ultimately for an end to their offensive allusions to HIM. I admit

[1] The Foreign Minister.

19

there is a danger that the whole thing might backfire – *Private Eye* might claim that the Iranians had appealed to them on bended knee. I add that I am convinced that to try to 'buy' them would be disastrous, because 'they seem to adhere to *some* principles'.

'Principles?' asks HIM angrily, with an expression of bewilderment on his face as he turns on me the full glare of his wrath. 'Principles?' he repeats. 'They even attack us for wanting to buy their own Concorde. Principles?'

HIM continues to pace the room in ruminative silence. After what seems to me an indecent interval, with his face averted, he says in a soft voice, void of anger, 'It's not worth it.'

A few moments later I speak again, 'I also wish, with your Majesty's permission, to raise the subject of Amnesty International.' I say that existing instructions proscribe any sort of contact, verbal or written, with the organisation, the consequence of which has been that Amnesty's sole source of information about Iran is now confined to our political opponents. I add that I have already spoken to Parviz Sabeti and that he felt – subject, it goes without saying, to the approval of HIM – that we could allow certain individuals from Amnesty, acting purely in their own private capacity and not as official representatives of the organisation, to come and visit prisoners in specific instances.

'Their demands would grow,' HIM replies, 'if we show them an open door.' I say: 'We can do for Amnesty International what we did for Eric Pace.'[1]

'And where did *that* get us?' he answers.

More silence on my part in the face of HIM's rhetorical question.

At length he says that a group of Iranian jurists should reply to Amnesty's accusations, and that he will issue the necessary instructions to the Prime Minister. I am offered his hand, which I bow to kiss, and retreat from the cabin.

'I have seldom seen you in such a preoccupied mood,' says Princess Ashraf, as, with Fereydoun Hoveyda, we fly aboard the Mystere 20 back to Tehran. I hate myself for my attitude of complete sycophancy throughout the audience.

Dinner at Amoo [Uncle] Abol's, spoilt somewhat by an unseasonable downpour. Both he and his wife, Shamsi, tell me that an autopsy had been performed on Amirteymour in Tehran which showed he died of a heart attack. He had formed the habit, they tell me, of writing a farewell note to Roya, his daughter, after a drink or two each night and then simply sleeping it off. Only the last attempt had proved permanent.

[1] A *New York Times* reporter, who was allowed to visit a number of prisoners, and later wrote an article about it.

20

Wednesday, July 21

My stay in Tehran comes to an end tomorrow. In the course of the past ten days, apart from the audience with HIM and conversations with the PM, I have managed to learn something about the less contentious aspects of our relations with the UK. I had a longish session with Hassanali Mehran, Governor of the Central Bank, who briefed me on the state of the various loans we have extended to the British Water Authority. Those discussions were followed by a luncheon at his office with the directors of those Iranian banks that have branches and offices in London.

I have also paid courtesy farewell visits to Amir Assadollah Alam, the Court Minister, and Nosratollah Moinian, HIM's Private Secretary, rituals that one is expected to observe by tradition. And, while no spectacular discoveries about the attitudes of my superiors were made during the visit, I now have a firmer grasp of what is, and is not, acceptable to them. On the whole, the trip has been illuminating.

Thursday, July 22

Fly off to Nice, and from there drive to Juan les Pins to stay at Princess Ashraf's stately and empty villa for three days of swimming, reading, and tennis.

Friday, July 23

Behnam telephones from London to say that *The Times* and *Guardian* carry reports that Savak is said to be keeping a couple of British MP's, who are in contact with dissident Iranian students in the United Kingdom, under surveillance. The BBC have been on to him for comment and he has categorically denied the allegations. The MP's in question, Messrs. William Wilson (Lab. Coventry, South-East) and Stan Newens (Lab.-Co-op., Harlow), are to raise the matter with the Home Secretary at Question Time.

Monday, July 26

Return from Nice. There is an invitation to a Garden Party at Buckingham Palace in the afternoon. The invitation says 'morning dress or lounge suit'. Turn up in the latter, only to discover that in the Queen's tea tent I am a sartorial catastrophe, as everyone else, including the Prime Minister [James Callaghan] is wearing morning dress.

Sunday, August 1

I make my second appearance in the *Sunday Times* after an interview I gave to one of their reporters, James Fox. It is a denial of the allegations of that brace of MPs about Savak keeping an eye on them. Apart from one fairly complimentary piece in the *Financial Times* of June 4, 1976, the day of my arrival in London (by Robert Graham, the FT Man in Tehran), every time my name has appeared in the papers it has either been in connection with someone's suspicious death, the sinister circumstances of my appointment to London, or Savak's skulduggery. How depressing.

Monday, August 2

Pay a courtesy call on the Pakistan High Commissioner. One down and 149 more Heads of Mission to go.

Wednesday, August 4

I take Hossein Eshraghi[1] with me to dine with the Anglo-Iranian Parliamentary Group at the House of Commons. Eldon Griffiths is the Chairman and a chum of Ardeshir's.[2] Peter Temple-Morris, married to Tahereh, Khozeimeh Alam's daughter, is the Secretary. Both are Conservatives and exceptionally friendly. Amongst those present, I recognise Julian Amery and Reginald Maudling. After an enjoyable but undistinguished dinner, I am formally introduced

[1] Iran's Ambassador to Mexico, then passing through London.

[2] Ardeshir Zahedi, Iranian Ambassador to Washington, former husband of the Shah's elder daughter.

by Eldon Griffiths. I speak for five minutes, after which I offer to answer any questions they may wish to put to me. It all goes quite well, I believe.

Thursday, August 5

I lunch at PG with Abbas Aram, a former Foreign Minister and Ambassador to London, under whom I served at the start of my career in the Foreign Ministry in 1963. He says HIM has bestowed a very great honour on me by appointing me to London and would, in turn, expect quite spectacular results. When I say that a slightly less hawkish image than has been struck from that Olympian coign of vantage would make my job in London easier, he replies that, despite any inner reservations he may have held at certain times about aspects of HIM's policies, in the end they have always proved correct, and that his trust in HIM's leadership is complete.

Sunday, August 8

Go to the airport to see Hossein off to Mexico and to receive Hushang Ansari, Minister of Finance and Economic Affairs. He briefs me on his talk with Kissinger and says HIM fears that Jimmy Carter may have 'Kennedy-type pretentions' and would much prefer to see Ford re-elected.

A letter of thanks from Peter Temple-Morris follows one from Eldon Griffiths in which he says, 'You were quite magnificent [at the Anglo-Iranian Parliamentary Group dinner], and we appreciated your humour and frankness very much indeed.' The praise is not, however, universal. It seems that, in the course of our discussions, I had at some point expressed the opinion that the re-emergence of the Kurdish independence movement through Russian intrigue seemed for the moment unlikely. Not so, says HIM through Khalatbary, after reading an account of the dinner discussions in my cable. 'Your opinion on this point is incorrect', was the laconic comment.

Friday, August 13

Call on the Moroccan and Syrian Ambassadors. The latter, Adnan Omran, a seemingly intelligent and well-informed man, is somewhat persistently interested in the size and content of our arms purchases. I send a cable to Tehran about my conversations with the Syrian Ambassador, pointing out that the meeting took place during my courtesy call on him, and explaining that new ambassadors, as 'recommended' by Foreign and Commonwealth Office protocol, are expected, on their appointment to London, to call on their more senior colleagues.

I lunch with my cousin, Nader, who says that, lovely as life is in London, 'the whole attitude of the British is wrong' and this accounts for all their troubles.

Sunday, August 15

With Belinda Cadbury, I go to Denis and Iona Wright's[1] house – Duck Bottom near Aylesbury in Buckinghamshire. When we are alone, Denis recounts some of his experiences in Tehran. He relates how Ernest Peron, the Shah's boyhood friend at Le Rosey, and a certain Bahram Shahrokh, had gone to see him on HIM's orders shortly after he had arrived in Tehran in 1953 to re-establish relations, broken off during the Mossadeq crisis. They had told him that HIM had instructed them to inform Denis that he wished all matters relating to oil to be conducted, through them, by the Shah himself, and not through the Foreign Minister. Denis, with authority from London, had reported this conversation to the then Foreign Minister, Nasrollah Entezam, who had subsequently checked with HIM to see whether these were indeed the Shah's instructions. HIM had been furious with Denis for having exposed this manoeuvre.

'Things are very different now in Tehran, of course, and although charges of torture have damaged Iran's international standing, the overall balance is favourable,' he says.

I ask Denis if, during his days in Tehran, he ever kept a diary. He says he did, but always wrote things knowing – or, at least, allowing for the possibility – that his servants might photograph them.

Denis, as Chairman of the Iran Society, has invited me to

[1] Sir Denis Wright, GCMG, British Ambassador in Tehran from 1963 until his retirement from the Diplomatic Service in 1971.

24

address the Society's annual dinner to be held in November. 'For God's sake,' he warns me, 'don't start rattling off endless statistics about your achievements as your predecessors have done.'

Monday, August 16

Lunch with Mostafa Fateh, one of Father's oldest and dearest friends, and one of the dissident Iranians the Shah most intensely dislikes, at L'Ecu de France. Mostafa tells me he is convinced HIM is no longer a sane man and believes his *folie de grandeur* will ultimately bring about his downfall. Mostafa boasts that his sexual powers – he is 70 plus – have lost none of their fervour.

I give a cocktail party for Cyrus Behnam, my departing Number Two, and later dine with him and his wife and a rather nervous and hopelessly over made-up Embassy secretary at the Mirabelle.

Tuesday, August 17

Receive an angry cable from Tehran. HIM demands an explanation of the phrase 'recommended by the FCO' in my cable about my conversations with the Syrian Ambassador. HIM wants to know whether I am here to *carry out his instructions*, or do what the *FCO recommends*. I reply that the choice of the word 'recommend' was unfortunate and that the paying of courtesy calls was only the observance of accepted diplomatic practice. Await reaction nervously.

Wednesday, August 18

My cable of explanation 'has been perused by His Imperial Majesty' and there are no comments, which means that my solecism has been forgiven – until the next time, I tell myself.

Monday, August 23

Edward Heath having invited me to drinks, I punctually present myself at his Wilton Street house, and am shown upstairs by a

25

middle-aged woman secretary. He greets me with his beaming smile. He is dressed in an open-neck shirt and slacks. He looks suntanned and well. The room is L-shaped, has a wooden floor and is sparsely furnished. A picture of Broadstairs hangs on the wall, while the smiling faces of the Iranian Royal Family appear on a porcelain cigarette case placed on a side table. A gift from Ardeshir [Zahedi], I suspect.

I am a little uncertain what it is that Mr Heath wishes to discuss with me and so am politely reticent, to allow him to broach it in his own good time. But after an hour in his interesting and pleasant company, in the course of which I am served two cups of China tea, I come to the conclusion that his reason for asking me is a gesture of kindness to HIM's new man in London.

Heath speaks of his experiences in China and the great respect and affection shown him there. Reverting, finally, to the domestic scene, he says it is difficult at present to be optimistic about the future of Britain.

Wednesday, August 25

Go to Rudi Alam's elegant house in Brompton Square for dinner. Harriet Crawley, whom I vaguely know from Tehran, is there, as is a Victor Lownes, an American who runs the Playboy gambling club. Victor tells me that Amirteymour owes his establishment £170,000 in gambling debts and wonders whether he can recover the money. 'I am very doubtful that you can,' I tell him, 'but don't you think the poor man had been milked enough already?' 'Yes,' Lownes replies, after a moment's reflection with a disarming smile, 'probably.'

An incredibly attractive Swedish girl reads my palm and tells me I shall die with a smile on my face. At dinner, I sit between Rudi and Kirsty Macleod, who has just published a book on Downing Street wives. She sounds enormously intelligent, if a little chippy. Soon, with Victor now participating, the conversation turns to women's mammaries and American presidential politics. I wish I could remember the Swedish girl's name.

Friday, August 27

It rains ... after 38 days of continuous drought. London looks becoming in the rain, more so than any city I know.

On HIM's instructions, I call on his Highness Shaikh Zaed al-Nahyan, Ruler of Abu Dhabi and the current President of the United Arab Emirates, at his recently acquired London pied-à-terre at No. 11, The Boltons. As it is the month of Ramadan and the Sheikh is fasting, I have been asked to turn up at 8 p.m. as hospitality can only be offered after 8.15 when the daytime fast can be broken. An enormous house, it is lit to a dazzling brightness, furnished in early Frankenstein and brim-full with children of all ages.

Promptly at 8.15 his Highness appears, and with his Foreign Minister acting as interpreter we engage in diplomatic small talk. His Highness enquires after HIM's well-being and I say that I am here to convey the Shah's good wishes to his Highness. Shortly afterwards, we move to the dining-room where a long rectangular table-cloth has been spread on the floor and plates and cutlery laid to accommodate about 40 people. Rice and kebabs and all kinds of meat are brought in by bare-footed servants, and non-alcoholic drinks abound.

Some, like the Foreign Minister, eat with their hands. Others, like myself, use the Mappin and Webb silver cutlery. Mindful that I have guests coming to dinner at the Embassy, I eat little and slowly. No doubt impelled by a wish to be helpful and to remedy the situation, the Foreign Minister picks up a mutton leg. As it is poised tentatively over my plate, completely forgetful of the ordinances of Ramadan, I politely reject the offering, saying I really can't eat it as I have already had dinner. The stunned expression of the Foreign Minister jolts me into awareness of my gaffe.

Saturday, August 28

Three American civilians working for Rockwell International have been murdered in Tehran. Prepare myself to make reassuring noises to my staff and, should they raise enquiries, to the newspapers.

Tuesday, September 14

Call on the Soviet Ambassador, Nikolai Lunkov. Curiously, we talk American presidential elections.

Lunch at the BBC with Gerald Mansell[1] and several of his colleagues. I take one of my staff along, for moral support. The discussions are, to say the least, spirited, with neither side mincing its words. But I am happy that, even though no concessions were made, our dialogue with the BBC, interrupted some time ago, has now resumed.

In my boiled shirt, I go to Mansion House for the Lord Mayor's reception for Nikpay.[2] As the procession enters, we clap rhythmically. The Lord Mayor of London reads a couple of sentences from his speech in Persian, which tickles my pride.

Friday, September 17

The Foreign Minister and Mrs Khalatbary stop in London on their way to the General Assembly in New York. He is in a good mood and implies all is well with me in Tehran. The account of my BBC luncheon had been particularly interesting, he says.

Monday, September 20

Gordon Richardson, Governor of the Bank of England, comes to lunch. He is understandably optimistic about the future of the British economy, minimising the dangers of devolution. He speaks well of Heath and ill of *Private Eye*.

Wednesday, September 22

Some fifteen ambassadors, myself included, have been asked to drinks at the Foreign and Commonwealth Office to pay a collective courtesy call on the Foreign Secretary. The reception, if one can call it that, is held in the Ambassadors' Waiting-Room. Wine and spirits are served from a table placed at the end of the room. Crosland, followed by a number of aides, comes in, shakes a few hands, stays about twenty minutes and, pleading Rhodesia, leaves. A most unsatisfactory arrangement.

[1] Managing Director, BBC External Services.
[2] Gholam Reza Nikpay, Mayor of Tehran.

Monday, September 27

Lunch with Sir Denis Hamilton and the Board of Directors of *The Times*. Denis Hamilton tells me privately that he is a friend of Iran and knows a lot of people there, such as Hushang Ansari. But he thinks the Shah can no longer be spoken to. Every time a reference is made to some of the more contentious issues of his rule, there is a display of clout from the Court, threatening a unilateral break in economic and commercial links. 'I've seen,' he goes on, 'how his ministers treat him – all that bowing and hand-kissing ...'

I respond by speaking of different customs in different countries, and of the essential paternalism of oriental societies, but I feel a mounting sense of anger at the same time.

I send a cable to Tehran, retaining most of Denis Hamilton's observations but omitting the reference to the Shah's treatment of his ministers.

Wednesday, September 29

In the evening I go to Combermere Barracks, Windsor, to dine with the Life Guards. The dinner is in honour of Prince Kamyar Pahlavi, a nephew of HIM. I had at first turned down the invitation, but after Kamyar had apparently complained to Tehran, I had received a mildly worded cable from Alam, the Court Minister, asking me to attend and saying it would please Prince Abdol Reza, Kamyar's father and the Shah's brother. My entire conversation with the Prince consists of two phrases: 'Good evening', and 'Goodbye'.

Thursday, October 7

To Mrs Anne Armstrong's, the American Ambassador, to watch, in the company of a large invited audience, the second Carter–Ford debate – a most unedifying performance by Ford, demonstrating his lack of grasp of rudimentary issues. Iran is a major topic in the debate. As with every presidential candidate, much sucking up to the Jews, the Catholics, the Poles, the Blacks, big business, small business, etc. I feel vicariously embarrassed for Mrs Armstrong, who is high in the councils of the Republican Party.

Wednesday, October 13

Lunch with Fred Warner[1] and his chairman, Lord Kissin, at Guinness Peat [the merchant bankers]. I speak in general terms about prospects of increased trade with Iran.

Since Roberto Campos, the Brazilian Ambassador, has personally rung to invite me, I drop by for drinks at some address he has indicated, ostensibly to introduce a Japanese–Brazilian painter. Many painted ladies are present.

Thursday, October 14

Princess Shams[2] arrives aboard the Falcon aircraft of the Red Lion and Sun Society,[3] of which she is the President. I am given two hours notice of her arrival, but manage to be at the airport in time. She has forgotten to bring her passport along, but the airport authorities are flexible and understanding. After a visit to her son, Shahbaz, who lives in London, and a call on her oculist in Bond Street, she leaves early in the evening.

I go to Shusha Guppy's[4] for dinner. Lord Kaldor, whose lectures I used to attend in Cambridge without understanding much of them, is there with his wife. By chance, I sit next to a woman named Sonia, and conversation veers somehow to Byron. I say I think his kind of romantic Englishman is probably a rare bird nowadays. She disagrees. All Englishmen, she says, are, and always have been, romantics at heart. I say that, as far as I know, only twice did the British go off to fight in wars out of conviction rather than compulsion. I cite Greece, during the struggle for independence, and Spain in 1936, adding that while the Empire was founded by men whose adventurous spirit led them to distant shores, a clear distinction could be made between the war in Spain and the motives of such British participants as Orwell, and those Englishmen who tied Indians to cannon.

[1] Sir Fred Warner, GCVO, GCMG, former diplomat, director of Guinness Peat, and Member of the European Parliament since 1979.
[2] Elder sister of the Shah.
[3] Iranian equivalent of the Red Cross.
[4] An Iranian folk singer living in England.

30

Friday, October 15

I ring Shusha to thank her for the party and it is only then that I discover Sonia is Orwell's widow!

Tuesday, October 19

I dine with Jacob and Serena Rothschild. I sit on Serena's right and have Peggy Ashcroft on my right. Talk turns to the British Cultural Festival in Iran next year. Peggy Ashcroft says a suitable play to perform in Tehran would be *The Hollow Crown*, with sketches of the beheading of Charles I and Mary Stuart suitably included. My goose pimples are instantaneous. 'Aren't you being a little mischievous?' I ask, and her lovely face breaks into a delightful smile.

Wednesday, October 20

Lunch with Majid Rahnema[1] at Princes Gate. Khatib Shahidi, the Embassy's Cultural Counsellor, is also there. Majid's latest obsession is with a book written by one David Cooper, a South African doctor, called *The Grammar of Being*. Nothing would please him more, he says, than a chance to meet the author.

Thursday, October 21

I call on the Honourable Paul Martin, the Canadian High Commissioner. As a matter of courtesy, my *curriculum vitae* has been sent to him in advance. We reach one another in the middle of his enormous office and, as we shake hands, he says, 'You're a young man for an ambassador. Born in 1936, I see.'

Mr Martin is a short, stout man, bespectacled and with a squint,

---

[1] A former Minister of Education whose differences with the authorities over the running of Iran's universities had led to his dismissal.

31

who was formerly Canada's Foreign Minister, and was assigned to London after a heart attack. As I sit facing him across his desk, he says, 'I was in your country just after the revolution in '58. Kassem was alive still.' I say nothing, allowing him to sink in deeper, deriving a mildly sadistic pleasure from his solecism. But, once he launches on his recollections of Baghdad, I interject to say that, close though we may be to the Iraqis, 'they are our *neighbours*', and then sit back to savour his attempt at extrication.

For a fraction of a second, I think Mr Martin is about to suffer his second heart attack but he recovers gallantly. After a couple of syncopated and deeply-felt 'ohs', he says, 'Of course, you're the *Iranian* Ambassador. The Iraqi is coming to see me in the afternoon, hence the confusion.' The Shah and Tehran now become the subjects of our conversation.

Tuesday, October 26

HIM's birthday. Roger du Boulay, Vice-Marshal of the Diplomatic Corps, suitably accoutred in morning dress, calls to present Her Majesty's felicitations. We clink champagne glasses and nibble caviar sandwiches. At lunchtime I host a reception for about 300.

Polly Garnett and Sonia Orwell come to PG for dinner with me and Cyrus. Cyrus's mention of George Orwell evokes sentimental reminiscences from Sonia on their life together, bringing at one point the merest glisten of a tear to her eye. Polly is sharp, quick, intelligent and erudite. Talk inclines to the state of the British economy, the need for greater austerity and the uncertain prospects ahead. When Polly and Sonia both say their life styles have changed little, 'except for eating a little less meat', I feel a twinge of guilt at the caviar and champagne that are being lavishly served.

Thursday, October 28

Lord Drogheda and David Cotton[1] come to lunch at PG during which the declining pound again dominates the conversation. After

[1] An aide at the Rothschild Bank.

lunch, Lord Drogheda brings up the British Cultural Festival, due to be held in Iran next year, asks a few rather annoying questions about the lagging organisational aspect of the project and is terribly vague about the extent of British financial participation. The cost of the festival is supposed to be met jointly by British industry and cultural organisations and the Iranian government.

Monday, November 1

Lunch with David Holden and Frank Giles [of the *Sunday Times*] at PG. They are both well-informed and percipient about Iran, and, what's more, not hostile.

Tuesday, November 2

Am invited to dinner by an American, Mrs Ellsworth Donnell. She says she is a friend of Ardeshir's, and dabbles in journalism. The Harold Levers and the Michael Heseltines are there amongst a group richly sprinkled with bankers.

Lever says that, despite all the talk about industrial unrest, Britain's diminished world role and the falling pound, life in this country is still very pleasant, the people are highly civilised and 'all economic difficulties are ultimately surmountable'.

Heseltine intervenes to say, 'I wouldn't include that last comment in any despatch you may wish to send to Tehran.'

Mrs Donnell entertains elegantly.

Thursday, November 4

Carter is in, and I wonder what my superiors in Tehran think about it. I really do wonder.

Go to a mammoth reception at the Soviet Embassy to mark the October Revolution. Under enormous Soviet pressure, we have recently handed back a defecting Russian pilot, and the Ambassador is full of smiles and speaks of 'lots of co-operation' between the USSR and Iran.

Proceed to the Savoy for the Iran Society's annual dinner. Princess Anne is the guest of honour, Lord Carrington the

President, Sir Clive Bossom the retiring Chairman, to be succeeded by Sir Denis Wright. Mr Anwar, the Egyptian Ambassador to London, a friend from Tehran days, and his charming wife are my personal guests.

Carrington delivers an amusing, joke-ridden speech, while Princess Anne sips Coca-Cola, and with her left thumb cracks the bones in her right palm. When she speaks, she reminisces about her trip to Iran to attend the celebrations marking 2,500 years of the Persian Monarchy.

Finally I stand up and read my text.

Friday, November 5

Lunch at White's with John Russell, now with Rolls Royce and once number two at the British Embassy in Tehran. He says that, while in Iran, he once asked HIM 'whether you have forgiven the British for having deposed your father'.

'Forgiven,' the Shah had asked, 'forgotten, or do you mean do I understand?'

Monday, November 8

Lunch with Michael Weir[1] at Walton's, and congratulate him on his acquisition of a new wife. Talk generally about Iran–British relations, but he does say that if I should ever want to see the Prime Minister for a tête-à-tête all I need do is to ask, which puzzles me somewhat.

Thursday, November 11

Lunch with Chapman Pincher at PG. He speaks about an interview granted him by HIM five years ago which Lord Rothschild had arranged, and which Sir Shapour Reporter[2] had attended. Pincher says he was surprised at the closeness between HIM and Reporter, and at the role Reporter's father had played in

[1] Sir Michael Weir, K.C.M.G., British Ambassador in Cairo since 1979, formerly Assistant Under-Secretary of State at the Foreign and Commonwealth Office.
[2] Consultant on arms sales to the British Defence Ministry.

pointing out Reza Shah[1] as someone suitable to found a new dynasty. Pincher had put all this information in an article in the *Express* and had obtained HIM's clearance through Lord Rothschild for its publication.

I feel hurt and humiliated by Pincher's account, and long to do or say something that might salvage a modicum of national pride. But the facts are indisputable and, in any case, they had been cleared by HIM himself.

Saturday, November 13

Have lunch with my newly arrived Number Two, Mr Meshkin-poush. I am grateful that he has at last arrived and my first impressions of him are highly favourable. He is a dignified, cultured man who loves Persian music and the writings of Bertrand Russell, some of which he has translated into Persian. He seems to know far more than I do about the running of an embassy.

Monday, November 15

Lunch at *The Times* with Denis Hamilton, William Rees-Mogg [then Editor], David Spanier and several of their colleagues. The discussions are quite subdued and the tone of my interlocutors is deferential, which strikes me as a little condescending. Their questions seem almost perfunctory and are certainly unprobing. Totally missing is the usual aggressive attitude more often than not characteristic of journalists, with the consequence that, on each topic that is raised, I am allowed to hold my first line of defence arguments – these being always the most banal. Denis Hamilton for one, I know from previous meetings, holds quite strong views on HIM, but even he appears suspiciously quiet. I conclude rather glumly that they are all sufficiently knowledgeable about the workings of the Iranian Government and so consider the role of the Ambassador in London to be simply the faithful echo of his master's voice, which makes him of no significance in terms of real power or authority. I am annoyed at my performance.

[1] Reza Shah Pahlavi, founder of the Pahlavi Dynasty, father of Shah Mohammad Reza. Deposed by the invading Allied armies in 1941, he died in exile in Johannesburg in 1944. He ruled Persia (Iran, as it was to become in 1934) from 1926, when he crowned himself Reza Shah Pahlavi, until 1941.

Thursday, November 18

Go to Buckingham Palace for the Queen's annual reception for the Diplomatic Corps. Arrive at 9.30, as instructed, and chat with my Iranian colleagues, all smartly dressed in their Moss Bros. tails, whereupon Mr Collins of the Foreign Office appears and lines us up according to seniority. At about 10.30 Her Majesty reaches the Iranian contingent. I present Meshkinpoush and the newly-arrived Military Attaché to Her Majesty, who is all smiles but says virtually nothing. Prince Philip follows and is, to my surprise, only marginally more chatty. Princess Anne is next. Have I recuperated from my Iran Society dinner, she wants to know. Princess Alexandra follows and says Elizabeth Balfour – 'my cousin' – is giving a dinner next week at which we shall meet. Angus Ogilvy is next and has a compliment for the Shah's leadership.

We break up after the presentations to drink champagne and eat canapés. Mr Collins, chest bemedalled, champagne glass in hand, ebullient amidst hordes of glittering excellencies, is *dans son élément*.

Monday, November 22

Dinner at Elizabeth of Yugoslavia's. Her brother, Prince Alexander, a huge and jovial man, is there, as is his wife, equally huge but less jovial.

I sit next to Princess Alexandra at dinner. Her husband, she says, is attending a stag dinner and she is here alone but for her detective. 'Is he bigger than I am?' I ask. She thinks he is. She won't come and have a drink with me at Annabel's[1] because 'Angus, being basically tribal, is quite jealous'. At some stage during the dinner, the Prince finds a particular remark so amusing that he falls off his chair from laughter. At another moment after dinner, Elizabeth's two Filipino maids rush to pose between Alexander and Alexandra, and in turn to photograph each other. A most amusing evening!

Thursday, November 25

Amnesty International issues a special report on violations of human rights in Iran, and I obtain Tehran's permission to reply to

[1] A night club in Berkeley Square.

their allegations. I deliberately refrain from asking for instructions on what to say in order not to bind myself to Tehran's sterile semantic overkill.

Sunday, November 28

With Meshkinpoush and Kakhi, we agree on a final text of our reply to Amnesty. Prepare 2,000 copies for circulation amongst MPs, embassies, the Press and universities, meanwhile telexing the text to Tehran. I await anxiously for HIM's reaction.

The circular, as far as its contents go, is an exercise in the sort of political charlatanry that all embassies throughout the world resort to. There are, however, two significant extenuating innovations in it which, I say to myself, commit Tehran to new and tenable positions – one, there is, for the first time so far as I know, a condemnation of the use of torture *per se*, albeit before going on to deny it's existence in Iran; and two, it does mark the resumption of the Embassy's, and thereby the Government's, dialogue with Amnesty International.

Monday, November 29

Shams, an Embassy cipher clerk, comes in with a file containing the incoming cables from Tehran under his arm. 'My congratulations, sir,' he says, placing the file before me. HIM has been pleased to express his appreciation of our reply to Amnesty's special report. I breathe a huge sigh of relief. Meshkinpoush, followed by other senior members of my staff, come to offer their congratulations. There is much debate and speculation as to what particular paragraph or phrase must have pleased HIM most.

There is also a cable from Khalatbary stating that the reply to Amnesty is, on HIM's instructions, to be circulated to all Iranian embassies abroad as a model for future dealings with human rights groups. My staff believe my appointment to London over the heads of more senior candidates has now been publicly vindicated. There are telephone calls from our ambassadors in Holland and Belgium with words of praise and encouragement. Smiles are rife.

Monday, December 6

The Amnesty circular seems to have impressed HIM a little too much for my taste. I am now instructed to have it printed in the *Guardian* as an advertisement. I wriggle out of this by pointing out that to do so would, in my judgement, detract from the original effectiveness of the circular; that the circular has been widely distributed amongst those most concerned with such matters in any case; and that, should the newspapers or the BBC in future refer to allegations of human rights violations in Iran, we shall bring pressure on them to refer to the Embassy's reply. Phew!

Friday, December 10

My enterprising secretary, Jaleh Atighi, having located David Cooper in Paris through his London publisher, has spoken to him about my interest in meeting him and has sent him and his girl-friend two Paris-London return tickets, booked them into a hotel for the night and sent a car to pick them up at the airport. Together they come to dinner. Majid Rahnema, thrilled to bits, is there, of course. The rest of us – Khatib Shahidi, Caroline Dawnay and Elizabeth of Yugoslavia – have done our homework and read Cooper's *Grammar of Living*, a book which, I must confess, I did not find all that inspiring. They arrive – he a tall, bearded, balding figure with a protruding paunch and an apparently timid nature; she petite and not very attractive.

It takes a while to break the ice, as Cooper is at first understandably suspicious of the motives of his unknown host and treads cautiously. But the tempo picks up, due principally to Majid's enthusiasm for Cooper's writings. Cooper, who chain-smokes, has the habit of listening for long periods to what's being said without making any interruptions or revealing gestures, then heaving an enormous sigh and emptying his chest in rapid-fire monologues about his particular brand of philosophy. 'Love' and 'revolution' seem to form the premises upon which his theory rests.

Majid is the most impressed, Elizabeth the least. I feel it has been an evening on which opinions could well differ.

Monday, December 13

One remark, one article, one TV or radio broadcast which depicts Iran in an unfavourable light is sufficient to ruin my political day, so morbidly sensitive have I become about the less seemly aspects of the system I represent. The remark or the article need not be couched in scurrilous or vitriolic language to plunge me into the most awful despondency. The symptoms are even worse when the criticism emanates from a friend.

For example, yesterday I drove down to West Byfleet for lunch with mother's old and dear friends, the Pattinsons. It was a perfectly friendly and charming occasion with many reminiscences from the Pattinsons' long association with Iran. All was going well until the moment of parting, when Pattinson, speaking as much to himself as to anyone else, quite innocuously observed, 'The Shah is on *Panorama* tonight,' adding, 'I expect he is going to lecture us again on our laziness.' That remark was quite enough to bring on a mood of anger and melancholy that persisted until I switched off the light to sleep.

Watch HIM being interviewed on *Panorama* by David Dimbleby. He comes across all right, I suppose, but I do wish he didn't appear so stiff and humourless. He is at his best on the need for an oil price rise, at his worst on 'terrorists' and human rights violations.

Wednesday, December 15

Partly from a sense of guilt, I suspect, the Hon. Paul Martin, the Canadian High Commissioner, returns my courtesy call and very kindly offers to send a telex to the Premier of St Lucia, whom he knows well and whose country I am about to visit, to extend added courtesy.

Thursday, December 16

Go to dinner at George Weidenfeld's. I am placed between Antonia Fraser on my left and Diana Phipps [a London hostess] on my right, and both ladies assure me *sotto voce* that Professor Kenneth Galbraith, who is ensconced on Antonia's left, is given to interminable monologues at every dinner. It is a very glittering occasion. Antonia speaks to me about her divorce, their estates in Scotland,

39

the stay of the Crown Prince with them, and about the book she is at present writing on Charles II. She has read a nasty article in the *New York Review of Books* recently on torture in Iran. Her demeanour strikes me as quite regal.

Diana tells me that George Weidenfeld is a good friend of hers and she is probably among the very few people whom George might telephone in the middle of the night to pour his heart out to, and that he does so in German.

I then speak to Lady Milford Haven. A few years ago, she had been asked to dine at the Embassy with Mr Hoveyda, the Prime Minister, and she had found him 'simply enchanting'. But then she had been told that Mr Hoveyda was 'a pansy' and her grief had assumed tragic dimensions. I say that, while I never considered the Prime Minister to be oversexed, I know that he is not a pansy. 'How do you know?' she asks. 'Because he was my boss for twelve years,' I reply. 'Oh', she says, demurely, leaving me wondering whether I have convinced her of the Prime Minister's normality.

Friday, December 17

Lunch with Ulrick Amouzegar, Jamshid's wife.[1] She says that, if Jamshid felt he couldn't achieve anything as the newly-appointed Secretary-General of the Rastakhiz Party[2] within six months, he will resign and retire to private life.

Sunday, December 19

[Spending the weekend at Tidcombe Manor, Lord Jellicoe's house in Wiltshire.] To Jacob Rothschild's – or rather, Serena's – nearby estate for drinks. Jacob's French cousin, Eric, is there, sounding impeccably English. There are stables and a swimming-pool, a tennis court, and a covered area big enough to be an indoor arena.

We go on to Henry Keswick's nearby house at Oare. Tessa Fraser (Reay) is there, looking most attractive. She wears her hair short and tidily cut in a page-boy bob, and displays when laughing two rows of pearl-white, immaculate teeth. Dr David Owen, of the Foreign and Commonwealth Office, is also there with his American

[1] Jamshid Amouzegar, Minister of the Interior and Iran's chief negotiator at OPEC.
[2] Sole legal party in Iran, created by the Shah in 1975.

wife. At lunch, when David brings up the subject of his boss, **Tony Crosland**, I mention the unfavourable impression I formed of his overbearing attitude during the meeting to which I and other ambassadors had been invited to pay our respects to the Foreign Secretary.

Tessa tells me her brother Simon's cattle business in Iran, which he formed in partnership with the Shah's mother, had just folded 'because of the Queen Mother's greed', and my lunch is ruined.

Friday, December 31

[After a week's holiday in the Caribbean I returned to London via New York.] Two events during my stay in New York stand out in my mind. One is a luncheon at Lutèce Lizzie Spender[1] arranged, at my suggestion, with Bob Silvers and Barbara Epstein of the *New York Review of Books*. They turned up half an hour late, which was sufficient to put me in a bad mood. I began by asking, perhaps a bit too casually, which of them was responsible for the nasty things the *Review* had printed about Iran.

Barbara pointed a finger at Bob, who then began talking about Baraheni, whose book about the Shah, *The Crowned Cannibal*, had just been reviewed in NYRB, describing him as 'a bearded poet, a teacher at Indiana University, a learned man'. He says the savage and barbaric treatment Baraheni was subjected to during his detention and torture are all perfectly true. When Frances Fitzgerald (an American journalist) was in Tehran, she had met Baraheni and was shown the stigmata on his body. In any case, he adds, there are the reports of the League of Democratic Jurists and of Amnesty International, complete with names of detainees and dates of their arrests. 'Torture,' he says, 'is practised by little groups of people who want to hang on to their power.'

When talking about a point of Baraheni's article, where he argues the need to respect local languages and customs, Bob says that in Switzerland and Canada minorities are permitted to speak their own languages, and that what has happened in Puerto Rico, where the population is now 'ashamed of speaking Spanish', is tragic. I point out differences between Iran, on the one hand, and Switzerland and Canada on the other; the dangers of irredentism, and the need for cohesion in an ethnically diverse society. But I sense the gap between us is too wide, and our respective points of view too divergent, for there to be any common ground between us.

[1] The daughter of Stephen Spender, the poet.

I am horrified at the ease with which he finds analogies between totally different situations, and the arrogance with which he seeks to apply his universal remedies to them. But his more or less documented references to torture have dented my pugnacity and I am robbed of the wish to win the argument – if winning in such circumstances is at all possible.

The other event concerns Fereydoun[1], and the psychological torments I see him undergoing on account of Iran's human rights record. He is probably more exposed to virulent attack in New York than I am in London. Given his artistic temperament, and considering the left-wing intellectuals he associates with, he is presumably more vulnerable.

With HIM's permission, he has arranged a meeting with Martin Ennals, Secretary General of Amnesty International, and we spend several hours discussing the most appropriate strategy for him to adopt. We decide that his best way of approaching HIM would be to put the case in logical sequence; 1) no one who takes on the Western press comes out a winner; it is an institution that has to be lived with and respected; 2) the general tendency of the press is to be left of centre – and Iran's image in the Western press could not be worse; 3) the one single factor most responsible for that image is the practice of torture, which, for bureaucratic as much as for moral reasons, ought to be summarily stopped.

And, as for Ennals, we decide to say to him that, if Amnesty is genuinely interested in the fate of individuals and not merely obsessed with bolstering its own sedulously cultivated image as a bastion of fearless liberalism, it should submit a confidential list of those detained in whom it is interested. We could then arrange for Amnesty to send people out to Tehran – as private individuals – to interview as many of these detainees as Tehran might allow. Amnesty could then say, or be persuaded to say, that, while there remained enormous room for improvement, things were not as bad as sometimes supposed. Finally, Fereydoun and I decide to meet in London on his way back from Tehran.

There are at least fifty smartly dressed people at Fereydoun's elegant New Year's Eve party at his official Fifth Avenue residence. As I sip champagne and survey the gaiety before me, I reflect that 1976 has been a mixed year. It has, of course, brought high honour in my appointment to London, but along with that the responsibility for defending the régime's more reprehensible practices.

While I have become increasingly confident of my ability to handle one end of a continuous cable colloquy with HIM, there is

[1] Fereydoun Hoveyda, brother of the Prime Minister and Iran's ambassador to the UN.

42

always the worry that something said or written by me with the best intentions might be taken by him as offensive, and so terminate my appointment, and even bring my career to an end in disgrace.

The New Year arrives as I sit on a sofa holding Lizzie's hand. Seated opposite me is a disconcertingly attractive New Zealander named, I am told, Patricia Dow.

1977

Wednesday, January 5

A devastating leader in *The Times* blackens my mood. It says, in part, that:

'... even sympathetic Western observers are not convinced that internal threats are such as to justify the degree of repression used in Iran. Indeed, could any threat justify the systematic torture, executions and other violations of human rights chronicled in the briefing paper recently published by Amnesty International? Economic growth is certainly desirable, but it should be accompanied by progress towards a more humane and tolerant society. Otherwise the tensions that it generates must sooner or later erupt in violent form and carry away the regime that has presided over it.'

I cable the text of the article to Tehran, drawing to it the Foreign Minister's 'special attention'. I wonder what effect the article will have on HIM, knowing how susceptible he is to even the slightest criticism. He will certainly instruct me to reply, and that will be difficult enough, but I hope he doesn't dictate a text from Tehran.

Thursday, January 6

There is a telephone call from Tehran. It's the Prime Minister, who says; 'There is absolutely no reason for this call other than to tell you that my heart has become a little tight for you and I thought I'd ring and say hello.'

I lunch with Andrew Duncan at PG. He is a *Daily Telegraph* reporter who is writing a book on the Middle East oil countries for Doubleday. During lunch he mentions 'full, documented proof of the existence of torture in Iran', expecting, no doubt, a resounding rebuttal by me. I become morose and struggle through the lunch, doing casuistically what I can, but I suspect that Duncan's journalist's acumen has seen through the transparency of my mood.

Friday, January 7

Ostad Meshkat, a turbanned, octogenarian Professor of *Fiqh* (theology), and several other male Iranians come to lunch at PG.

Out of respect to him no alcohol is served. Despite his advanced years, the Ostad is remarkably lucid and impressively progressive in most of his views. He has bought a house in London and now lives here in retirement so as to be near, he says, to good oculists, for his eyes are in need of constant attention.

He insists on eating all courses on the same plate, and when after the middle course his plate is inadvertently changed, we try, but fail, to find his original plate. He feels a need to explain the fuss: 'It's less wasteful and more prudent to eat one's meal from the same plate than from three or four'. He has never craved luxury and, anyway, never understood protocol. Moreover, not knowing what 'unclean' hands have washed the dishes, he could commit the sin of eating from an unclean plate but *once*, if he stayed with the same plate throughout.

Go to the airport to meet Hushang Ansari. I have had a telephone call from Hushang to say he's coming, and been told nothing else, but since Parviz Mina[1] is also in town, I suspect that, in the aftermath of the collapse of our OPEC position[2], they are here to concoct some sort of oil-for-goods and/or arms deal again. Tête-à-tête, we drive to Claridge's. Hushang says he had fore-warned everyone about the untenability of our stance at Doha, and predicts that the next six months will be particularly difficult economically in Iran . . .

I say I wish to compound those difficulties by speaking to him about our deteriorating position on human rights, attention to which is long overdue. He agrees to come to dinner to listen to my difficulties.

At dinner, I speak about the emergence in America of a post-Vietnam, post-Watergate consciousness which, especially through the media, is having its impact on the Europeans. It involves a return to basic human values of decency, openness and honesty, not least in public administration. I say there is no reason on earth why we, of all nations, should come second only to Chile in violations of human rights. Our uncompromising 'no contact' policy on Amnesty, at a time when every accusation they make against us is being elevated to the level of biblical truth, I describe as risible, and I reveal to him Fereydoun's and my joint plan to obtain HIM's permission to establish a dialogue with Amnesty.

[1] A director of the National Iranian Oil Company.

[2] During the Opec Conference at Doha, the Saudi Arabians and the United Arab Emirates successfully resisted pressure from the other producers to raise the price of crude oil, with the consequence that a two-tier price structure came into operation under which Saudi and UAE oil was available at a considerably cheaper price. The other producers were forced to sell their oil by allowing secret discounts.

Ansari wants to know how ideologically left-wing Amnesty is, and whether 'we could ever place any trust in an institution like that'. I say that as an organisation they are 'serious', and that in any case there is no alternative.

As I see him to the door, he turns to me and says: 'You should know that HIM likes fighters.'

Monday, January 10

I ask Parviz Mina to come to lunch. Normally a quiet, reserved and soft-spoken man, I now see him in a state of some agitation over the outcome of the recent OPEC meeting in Doha.

'The calculations were that with a 15 per cent price rise in OPEC's overall production, there would be a 10 per cent decline in exports, of which Iran's share would be about 300,000 barrels a day, and which would be compensated for by the price increase,' Parviz tells me. 'But in reality,' he goes on, 'the situation is totally different. Venezuela has its own markets. Libya and Algeria, being in the Mediterranean zone, will have an unchanged demand for their particular quality of oil, with its specific sulphur content. Iraq will under-sell, whatever the price, and Kuwait doesn't need the money. So all the reduction will be Iran's. And yet the situation is being presented to the Iranian public as a great victory. Goodness knows what will happen when the bills start rolling in for payment.'

He says he had been in the process of writing a report to HIM about the whole affair when Hoveyda called him in to say HIM was so annoyed he didn't want to hear another word about it. When Majidi had raised the subject with HIM he was told to shut up.

Mina says he is, of course, going to stick to the official line, which is that our prices have shot up by 10 per cent and anyone who doesn't want to buy can go to hell. But he wonders what will happen when BP's negotiator, Sutcliffe, visits Tehran shortly. He fears that his instructions will be to throw the man out of the room if he should even breathe the word 'discount'.

Tuesday, January 11

Lord Longford, Chairman of the publishers Sidgwick & Jackson, Ali Shapurian, of the Ministry of Information, Khatib Shahidi, the

Cultural Counsellor, and Margaret Laing, the writer and biographer, come to a lunch, arranged by Shapurian in a final attempt to twist Miss Laing's arm to agree to a number of 'corrections', in the book she has written on HIM. It was to have been called *The Shah – Shadow of Allah* but Shapurian has succeeded in getting her to change this to simply *The Shah*.

Margaret Laing, a quiet, timid and rather unassuming creature, sports a Davy Crockett fur hat to cover her striking silver-blonde hair. After two sips of wine, I notice that she turns the colour of a boiled shrimp. She bites her nails and notices that other people notice she bites her nails. When Shapurian eventually steers the conversation to the subject at hand, Lord Longford suggests that the first step towards solving Iran's 'bad press' must be to change the name Iran back to Persia. He also wants to know whether press criticism is mainly directed against 'an individual' or against the Government as a whole. He is keen for them to be invited to go to Iran to publicise the book, a suggestion of which Miss Laing, who explains her intense dislike of travelling, does not entirely approve. She is most comfortable in the security of familiar surroundings, she confesses. For myself, I strive to steer clear of someone else's pet project.

Saturday, January 15

Lunch at PG with Meshkinpoush and Amir Taheri, an Iranian journalist who is here to counter Amnesty's 'campaign of vilification' against Iran. He is planning a reply to the *Times* leader. From him I learn that we are about to pull out our troops from Oman and establish a dialogue with the South Yemenis through the good offices of the Egyptians, and perhaps also with the Libyans, through the good offices of the Iraqis. I express my points of view to Taheri, but make clear that since Tehran has sent him on an apparently *ad hoc* mission, he must do as he sees fit.

Monday, January 17

Princess Ashraf telephones from Tehran to say HIM has given absolute freedom of action to Fereydoun to speak with Amnesty International, and that I can do the same.

Go to lunch with King Constantine and Queen Anne-Marie at

their house in Hampstead. I am the only guest. His Majesty says, *inter alia*, that Karamanlis's[1] position 'is a little delicate' and that, if clashes should break out between rival political factions, 'it is possible that the Army may step in' and invite the King back.

Meet Fereydoun, just in from Tehran, at the Embassy. He says that, while HIM has permitted contact to be made with Amnesty, there are to be no concessions and no compromise. We go over what he has said to HIM and what he and I had agreed he would say to HIM. As we talk, it becomes clear to me that some notable omissions have occurred during the audience.

The Tehran press has been instructed to mount a counter-offensive against Amnesty – and I am to coordinate that campaign from London!

Mount a campaign against Amnesty? What utter nonsense! We had been seeking to do the very opposite – to establish and engage in a dialogue. Fereydoun, I suspect, changed his mind at the last minute and back-tracked in the presence of HIM. But I don't blame him, I tell myself. I would have done exactly the same, in the circumstances. Fear, rather than rationality, fear rather than commonsense, fear rather than patriotism, seems the governing force in the life of an Iranian public servant.

How infuriating and frustrating. For a while, I shall do nothing, I tell myself.

Tuesday, January 18

Another long meeting with Fereydoun, who is lunching with Martin Ennals. In the evening, a little before the other dinner guests arrive, he comes to give an account of his talk with Ennals. He – Fereydoun – had stuck to his guns tenaciously, he says, as had Ennals; and again I wonder if anything is to emerge from our newly re-established dialogue, whether some kind of concession, some gesture of conciliation, would not have been appropriate from our side.

Wednesday, January 19

Fereydoun has arranged that I should drop by at Claridge's in the evening for an introductory meeting with Ennals. Apart from

[1] The Greek Prime Minister.

51

Ennals's wife, there is a Professor Blain there from New York University who is connected with Amnesty's activities in America, also an English woman named Ann Birley, a researcher on Iran. Ennals says the most obvious objection to the military tribunals in Iran that are condemning people to death is that they blatantly disregard the legal procedures clearly laid down under current Iranian law. He refers, I am made to understand, to the provision that allows appeals to higher civilian courts once the death sentence has been passed. I stick to a firm but low-key, explanatory attitude. I pick up Cyrus Ghani at the Dorchester and we go to Pamela Egremont's. After dinner, many others come, including Claire Hollingworth, the Defence Correspondent of the *Daily Telegraph*. She says she is an old and good friend of the Shah's, having first interviewed him when the Allies invaded Iran during the war. She says corruption in Iran has reached colossal proportions and did I know that it was corruption and moral turpitude that had finally brought about the defeat of South Vietnam? She recounts a story of petty bribery at Tehran Airport that I find somehow humiliating.

As I drop Cyrus off, he says the next time he is in London he wishes to see no one and do nothing so long as he can sit next to Sonia Melchett at dinner again!

Am I, I ask myself, basically a weak and impressionable person? Am I an alarmist, a poltroon who would desert the field at the first sound of gunshot? A panicker, terror-struck at the first sight of blood? Why is it that, when Claire Hollingworth speaks about corruption in Iran, there is a sudden release of adrenalin, and I am made damp with perspiration? Why is it that when people talk about torture by Savak or bribery in high places, I feel humiliated to such an extent that I am robbed of any will to answer back? Such iniquitous deeds have been going on for a long time and, what is more, I have known about them all along. Why then this sudden feeling of revulsion? Is it because I was for many years so cocooned by my superiors in Tehran that it is only now, when I am exposed to the front line of attack, that my protective armour is shown up as vulnerable and totally inadequate?

Is it that I just don't know the rules of the game, that along with the lavish house, the Rolls Royce and the Dom Pérignon comes the responsibility – bureaucratic rather than moral – to defend the system, willy-nilly? Are public officials meant privately to have morals? And then, such evil practices go on all over the world. What does any Chilean or South African envoy do, not to mention an Israeli Ambassador? What sort of individuals were people like Ron Ziegler, or Alexander Haig, who, at the height of the Watergate scandal and in the face of insuperable odds, stood their ground with resolute firmness, courage and loyalty right to the end? Is it, indeed, courage and loyalty to turn a blind eye to systematic barbarity and to go on enjoying the innumerable charms of London life?

Or is one not, on the contrary, simply being a compassionate and humane person if one shows genuine – indeed understandable – revulsion when confronted with any form of brutality? Ought one's conscience not to revolt when certain principles of what is generally regarded as common decency are transgressed? Where, I ask myself, is the point when the seismograph begins to agitate, showing that one is suffering from a regular *crise de conscience*?

I put these thoughts to Hossain Eshraghi at lunch today, adding that I thought I lacked the courage to resign.

'Don't,' he said emphatically, 'make yourself the laughing-stock of the Foreign Ministry, especially when you know damned well nothing is going to be changed.'

Friday, January 21

Lunch with Jamshid Ashrafi, the Under-Secretary at the Ministry of Economy, and here to sign a 500 million dollar syndicated loan. He speaks about the chaos our mindless expenditures have created, noting that when our foreign exchange earnings were 26 million dollars, we had a deficit; when they were 46 million dollars, we had a deficit. Last year Iran's foreign exchange earnings were *20 billion dollars* – and we still had a deficit.

Alexandra 'Gully' Wells is an improvised guest to dinner with Hossein arranged by Lizzie. Gully confesses to being a socialist who doesn't like the 'crudeness' of the Arabs, and thinks that Enoch Powell is mad to say the blacks should be deported from England. Quite an outspoken girl, I reflect.

Saturday, January 22

I read with something akin to horror a story in today's papers about two Iranian men who, walking in Hyde Park after a dinner party, are said to have decapitated a swan in the Serpentine. The details are gruesome. There is a poignant reminder to readers that swans mate for life and that the dead swan's mate will now pine away in its wretched loneliness until it, too, dies.

Tuesday, January 25

Partly as a reaction to Amnesty's working paper on Iran, the non-Iranian employees of Iran Air's offices in London have gone on strike to protest, among other things, against the non-recognition of the right to strike in Iran.

Mark Dodd, head of BBC's Eastern Services, is shortly to visit Iran. I had sent a cable to Tehran saying that 'Mr Dodd has shown a measure of good will' by informing the Embassy of the BBC's impending broadcast of Amnesty's report on Iran, and inviting the Embassy's counterbalancing comments. I had asked for special treatment of Dodd during his visit. There is a terse reply from HIM: 'What good will?'

Dinner at Mrs Anne Armstrong's in honour of a Mr W. Clements, an Under-Secretary of State in the Defence Department during the Ford administration. I sit between Mrs Winston Churchill and Mrs John Davies, wife of the Shadow Foreign Secretary. Others at our table include Mrs Armstrong, Fred Mulley, the Defence Secretary, Mr Clements and General Alexander Haig, who says, 'I know your counterpart in Washington well.'

The General says he first met the Shah in 1962 when President Kennedy was in power. Kennedy and the Shah had disagreed openly about Iran's arms requirements, and the Shah had walked out, saying he would get his arms from the Soviet Union. 'No love was lost between those two,' General Haig emphasises. It was then that Kennedy had asked Haig to go to Iran to report, not only on Iran's arms needs, but on the social conditions of the country as well. It was that visit, the General makes it abundantly clear, that led to the launching of the Shah's reform programmes. Mrs Churchill wants to know whether we have 'the third or the fourth largest army in the world'. When I reply that I am sure her husband, as an expert on defence matters, could easily clarify that matter for her, she says, 'You must be the cleverest man in Iran', and then, as an afterthought adds, 'The *second* cleverest, after the Shah.'

Diana Phipps is there, looking lovely but a little lost.

Wednesday, January 26

Lunch with Afshar, who has been entrusted by Alam with the success of the Laing book. He says that if Alam, who is hospitalised in Paris with some form of cancer, should die, the only remaining person who could still permit himself to speak openly to HIM on all subjects will have been removed.

On instructions from Tehran, I give a reception for some 50 selected Iranians to mark the 14th anniversary of the Shah-People Revolution, during which I speak for about five minutes.

Hassan Kamshad, an old friend from my university days, says to me on his way out: 'This was the first speech by an Iranian Government official I have heard in which no mention was actually made of the Shah's name!' Good Grief!

Thursday, January 27

The Times publishes a letter purporting to be from two Iranian journalists in reply to their editorial. It appears to me a credible reply, particularly as its tone is moderate. There's a good deal of adverse mail on the killing of the swan, with some describing it as 'an act of mindless brutality', others calling Iranians 'scum'. One writer asks what would happen if 'an Englishman did the same to one of the Shah's swans'.

A call from Fereydoun from New York. AAH [Prime Minister Hoveyda] has rung him to say HIM will see Ennals if he goes to Tehran as a '*simple citoyen*' and not in his official role as Secretary-General of Amnesty International. I am elated, and feel what we should now do is to ensure the meeting's success by telling Ennals to limit his demands to a minimum, if he wants to get anywhere, and impressing upon Tehran, through Princess Ashraf and/or AAH, the need for a measure of flexibility.

I send a five-page cable to the Foreign Minister on this second point, saying in effect that rather than leaving it to the Embassy in London or the newspapers in Tehran to claim that things have improved in Iran, the opportunity should be given for Amnesty to say it. If we create the circumstances for them to say this just *once*, then the dam will have been breached and other benefits will follow. More than anything else, I say, what is needed is a statement renouncing the use of torture. At the same time, I have the Press Section circulate a release to MPs, trade unionists, academics, student unions, industrialists and the Press, explaining Iran's terrorism problem and calling Amnesty's campaign against Iran unmerited.

Saturday, January 29

There is a telephone call from Farhad Nikoukhah in the Prime
Minister's office to say that the PM himself has been put in charge
of our 'image' campaign and that someone would soon be visiting
me in London for consultations.

Monday, January 31

The 'swan' mail continues unabated.

My two cables, one on the need to establish and maintain a
dialogue with Amnesty, the other detailing our counteraction
against Amnesty in the form of the distributed circular 'have been
seen by HIM' and there are no comments. Meshkinpoush says
HIM cannot be displeased with my suggestion for a dialogue with
Amnesty; if he were, I would have been told to mind my own
business in no uncertain terms.

There is another call from Nikoukhah: the Tehran papers will
have articles tomorrow condemning the practice of torture as
involving acts of inexcusable barbarity. Will the condemnation, I
wonder, be in identical language in all the papers?

Their Imperial Highnesses Prince Gholam Reza and Princess
Manijeh, plus entourage, come to dine at Princes Gate.

Tuesday, February 1

Accompany the royal couple to the Duke and Duchess of Kent's for
drinks. The Prince and the Duke talk about tanks and the
Princesses about their children's schools, while I small-talk with
the Secretary and a lady-in-waiting. Dine later with the royals and
entourage at Les Ambassadeurs.

The Prince, the Princess and I retire early. The others go
upstairs to gamble.

Wednesday, February 2

There is a report in *The Times* about the release from Ghasr Prison
of some 65 political prisoners, including some who had been

accused of plotting to kill the Shah. Towards the end of the piece, I read the following:

'Amnesty International has accused Iran of the systematic torture of prisoners. Today, the Tehran newspaper *Kayhan* said in a leading article the Shah had ordered the practice to be abandoned.'

Further on, there is a longish reference to the Embassy circular claiming to have irrefutable evidence that Iran had been made the target of a world-wide campaign of denigration by Amnesty International. Passages accusing Amnesty of political bias against Iran are quoted.

There is also an article in the *Daily Express* speaking about 'the shame of the men who broke a swan's heart', and a letter from my Press Attaché expressing 'regret' for the 'beastly act' of the Iranians concerned. Telephone calls pour in from animal-lovers expressing their satisfaction at the Embassy's condemnation of the swan-killers.

An impressive volume of post arrives commending us for our circular on Amnesty; most letters take the view the organisation is riddled with Communists. I am immensely pleased with my morning.

At 5, we take the train to Newcastle, where Princess Manijeh is to launch a ship. The arrival is very ceremonious, with Sir James Steel, Lord-Lieutenant of Tyne and Wear, in full dress uniform, and a posse of others – the Mayor, the Chairman of Swan Hunter, the shipbuilders – waiting to receive the Prince at the station. The route to the hotel is lined with what would seem to be every available policeman and policewoman. Policemen with dogs haunt the grounds of the hotel.

Thursday, February 3

We are given lunch at the Gosforth Park Hotel. I sit between Lady Hunter, wife of the Chairman of Swan Hunter, and Lady Steel, wife of the Lord-Lieutenant. Lady Steel is a colourful, amusing and quite forthright character, who speaks in an accent I can't place. She has a son in Tehran who is 'doing business' there. Lady Hunter is more reserved and discerning. After lunch, the Lord-Lieutenant and his wife drive me in their car to the dockyard for the launching ceremony. Lady Steel asks the driver, 'who has been with us for 25 years', whether he has had lunch.

57

'Yes,' says Albert laconically.

'And did you find someone congenial to have it with, Albert?' she persists.

'Yes,' says Albert, with a nice economy of words.

'So did we,' observes Lady Steel, 'so did we.' Lady Steel also notices that there are many more policemen covering the route than there would be 'for our own Queen', and Sir James replies diplomatically that it's all a sign of respect for visiting dignitaries.

The launching ceremony itself – my first – is most watchable. A mullah had been flown over from Paris especially for the occasion to bless the ship, as none could be found in London, and the champagne has been deferentially replaced by rose water to avoid causing offence.

The mullah recites some passages from the Koran which, of course, neither the Persians nor the Brits understand. The Princess then pulls a handle and the vessel, I/S *Kharg*, a 35,000-ton supply ship, glides gracefully into the River Tyne.

Sunday, February 6

Lunch with Richard Kershaw, a BBC journalist, at Burke's. He says he wants to go to Tehran to do a 15-minute interview on OPEC with Amouzegar. He seems to know quite a bit about Iran, the activities of Savak, Princess Ashraf, etc., and generally reinforces my favourable impression of him.

Tuesday, February 8

Lesley Blanch comes for a drink. She has been commissioned to write a biography of the Empress and is full of genuine and high praise for her. She expresses her fear that the book may make for rather tedious reading as it is all complimentary. She does say, however, that whenever the subject of the book is mentioned amongst her friends, the first thing they want to know is 'why are you saying nice things about a régime that ties people to electrically heated iron beds and roasts them'.

With a surge of fresh confidence, I say that, while excesses may have been committed in the past, torture no longer exists in Iran, and that she can proclaim that fact with impunity. I send a cabled account of my conversation with her to Tehran, making sure that both her remark about the 'iron bed' and my assurance that torture is no longer practised come out in high relief.

A stag dinner with Peter Walker at the Turf Club. His guests comprise a number of Tory MPs and Young Conservatives. The conversation is fast-paced and lasts about three hours, ranging in subject matter from the single party system in Iran and our armaments policy to OPEC, student surveillance in the UK, and – inevitably – torture. Walker himself strikes me a bit too strongly pro-Shah.

Saturday, February 12

In my cable to Tehran after the Walker dinner, I had said something to the effect that it took nearly 200 years for democracy to evolve in its present form in Britain and that, admirable as this system was, it would be wrong to think that its importation by other countries whose history and society had followed a totally different course would be universally felicitous. Khalatbary cables: 'His Imperial Majesty asks whether you think democracy really exists in the West?' Meshkinpoush assures me the question is rhetorical and that there is no need for a reply.

Tuesday, February 15

The other swan dies.

Lord Drogheda stops by for a drink before flying out to Tehran. I tell him all will be well if he just doesn't try to intimidate everyone. He takes that good-humouredly.

Dinner at Vane[1] and June Ivanovic's in honour of Prince Rainier and Princess Grace of Monaco. I am seated between the Princess and the hostess. I tell the Princess that I find her as beautiful off as on screen. She blushes visibly, mumbles inaudibly and eventually produces a muted 'Thank you'. Her favourite film of herself is 'the last one – *High Society*'.

She speaks about her trip to Iran in 1971 to attend the 25th centenary celebrations of the founding of the monarchy, and recalls the nastiness of the French press's coverage of the ceremonies. 'The Shah,' she says, 'should have received members of the invited press on the first rather than the fifth day of their stay.'

[1] The Consul-General of Monaco.

When June Ivanovic mentions that she finds smoking soothes her nerves, and I put in that I suffer from a skin rash, Princess Grace recommends us both to take regular doses of apple cider vinegar, and goes on to explain at length that there is in the body an excess of alkali that needs to be counterbalanced by an intake of acid. What I particularly need is yoghurt, wheatgerm, Bircher Muesli, boiled eggs, powdered milk, yeast, honey (instead of sugar), brown rice and no alcohol – all of which remedies she kindly and patiently writes down on my menu. She promises to send me a book about it and asks me to let her know how I get on.

The following item, along with a photograph of Lizzie, is in the *Wednesday, February 16 Evening Standard* Diary:

'Considering the poet Stephen Spender's Thirties' enthusiasm for Left-wing causes (Spanish Civil War, etc.) I had rather imagined that he might be considering his daughter Lizzie's current friendship with the Iranian Ambassador, Parviz Radji, with a somewhat jaundiced eye. But not a bit of it. The other night he gave a dinner party for Lizzie and Mr Radji at which all the horrid rumours about the Shah's beastliness to his Leftward subjects were not even mentioned, and they all got on splendidly.'

I conclude that no occasion is too private for gossip-column spies, and no opportunity missed for a stab at our human rights shortcomings. I see Lizzie in the evening and say nothing until she asks if I have seen the paper. 'I have,' I say, 'and I'm not accusing anyone.'

Thursday, February 17

Lunch with Harold Evans, Editor of the *Sunday Times*. David Holden, Keith Richardson and one or two others also present. A spirited session at which I repeat my by now well-practised arguments in defence of our policies.

Bob Pomeroy, a friend from San Francisco, stops by on his way from Tehran where he and his firm are assisting the [Imperial] Navy in its construction programmes. The Chah Bahar[1] project, he says, has been postponed for lack of funds and he cannot imagine where we are going to berth the three Spruance Class destroyers and submarines we have bought and which are due for delivery next year. He speaks affectionately and admiringly of the Shah, but wonders why even the least important of decisions need his personal attention.

[1] A huge air and naval base on the Gulf of Oman then under construction.

Sunday, February 20

Lunch with an old and extinct flame who now lives in Italy. She says she had had dinner the other night with Prince Abdul Aziz of Saudi Arabia and that when the Prince learned she was Persian he wanted to know why, when Prince William of Gloucester and Mrs Armstrong, the American Ambassador, had gone personally to sign the visitors' book at the London hospital where King Khaled was being treated, 'His Excellency The Iranian Ambassador had seen fit to send only a Third Secretary'. (Actually Meshinpoush, the No. 2.)

Monday, February 21

Rush to Wellington Hospital to sign the book, and chat with the Saudi Ambassador and the Chief of Royal Protocol.

My cable on the *Sunday Times* lunch hasn't gone down all that well, and I am reminded that I should refer to my directives – the one on Iraq, on this occasion. However, the more delicate luncheon talks with Ennals produce no royal comments.

Dr David Owen is appointed to succeed Anthony Crosland as Foreign Secretary. He is 38, intelligent, good-looking, and a friend. I am pleased, but also somewhat surprised.

Wednesday, February 23

Ann Birley, Amnesty's researcher on Iran, telephones to say Martin Ennals has agreed to go to Tehran *à titre privé*, which pleases me.

The Government's budget is announced in Tehran. Defence expenditure has been slashed by 3 billion dollars. The pity of it is, of course, that this will be interpreted as a gesture towards Carter's presidency.

Go to Homayoun Mazandi's for dinner. Simon Fraser and his pretty wife, David Frost and Lady Milford-Haven are amongst the faces I recognise. An enormous house, opulently decorated, tons of caviar and rivers of Dom Pérignon. At dinner, David Frost speaks to me about his love for Iran and admiration for HIM. I leave early.

Saturday, February 26

Edward Heath, who has come to lunch, notices Margaret Laing's book on the Shah on my desk. He says she once did a biography of him that he didn't much like, and asks my opinion of the book on HIM. I say I haven't read it, but that, judging by a review of it in the *Spectator*, I thought it '90 per cent favourable, but uncomplimentary when speaking about our human rights violations'.

Later, because of the personal prestige of Edward Heath, I send a cable to Tehran saying he had come to the Embassy on a social occasion and that politics were not discussed, but I do recount our brief exchange on the Laing book.

Sunday, February 27

From the press cuttings on my desk I see the two books on HIM – Margaret Laing's *The Shah* and Gerard de Villiers's *The Imperial Shah* – have been widely reviewed. The *Guardian* carries an interview with Margaret Laing, and gives the picture of the Shah as a man with immense and absolute power, ruthlessly, and often brutally, exercising that power.

The *Sunday Times*, in a piece by Woodrow Wyatt, provides, for me at least, a much more intelligent and sympathetic assessment of the situation, and is quite complimentary. A review in the *Observer* by Gavin Young is fair and better, i.e. more favourable, than I had dared hope.

Monday, February 28

Dinner at the Dennis Walters's. Peregrine Worsthorne, the elegant right-wing elegiast who is Deputy Editor of the *Sunday Telegraph*, is amongst the guests, who include Henry Keswick, Ariana Stassinopoulos and Edwina Sandys. After dinner Henry, who owns the *Spectator*, refers to Roger Stevens's review of Margaret Laing's book and asks my opinion of it. I say that what people say about Iran is generally complimentary, apart from the human rights albatross that hangs round our neck. I go on to say that, while some of Iran's human rights detractors may be justified in their criticism, they often fail to take into account the complexities of the issues involved. By now in full spate, I need no encouragement to denounce the practice of torture, while at the same time upholding the need for strict discipline in a time of social transition. Perry Worsthorne says he is surprised to hear me applying nineteenth-century English liberal standards in my defence of Iran, when *no* defence is necessary. Quite the contrary, praise is due. I say that, if I use the language of nineteenth-century English liberals, it is because we are constantly being judged by those standards, and that, if the criteria for judgement were to be standards formerly prevalent in Iran, there would be no problem.

Wednesday, March 2

There is a furious reaction from HIM to my comments to Heath on Margaret Laing's book. It is lucky indeed, says the cable, that I hadn't read the book, which is 'inaccurate and frivolous'. Since in his review Roger Stevens has described the Shah's reforms as 'moderate'[1] I am instructed to take a refresher course on the 17 points of the 'Shah–People Revolution', so that I can appreciate their just worth. The whole tone of the cable is unmistakably minatory.

I call in Meshkinpoush, show him the cable and ask his opinion. His advice is that, while HIM's anger lasts, it would be best not to send any reply, which might be interpreted as impertinence. I say I definitely want to reply, and together we draft a cable which says: 1) that I am sorry I commented on the contents of a book I had not read, but had supposed – in the event, foolishly – that, since the book had been inspired by the Imperial Court and the text had been sent to Tehran, it bore official approval; 2) that while 'moderate' may not have been the *mot juste* to describe HIM's revolutionary transformation of Iran, Stevens does refer in his article to HIM's personality as 'truly remarkable by any standard, one of the success stories of the century', and elsewhere states that the Shah has 'brought his people a measure of respect and prosperity hard to conceive even two decades ago'; 3) that, nevertheless, to have aroused HIM's displeasure is a matter that weighs on my mind and pains my conscience.

The cable goes, as Meshkinpoush and I exchange apprehensive glances.

Dinner at Princess Margaret's.

[1] The Foreign Minister's cable incorrectly uses the word 'mild'.

Thursday, March 3

Receive a long letter from Gully Wells, who had recently been my guest at the Residence, ostensibly 'a very belated thanks for that delicious and enjoyable lunch', but which quickly goes on to say that she found the letter I gave her as she left, explaining my government's position, 'very unimpressive and totally unconvincing'. She asserts that Amnesty does not defend terrorists but is 'only concerned with non-violent prisoners of conscience'. She claims that the disparity between the official figure for the number of political prisoners in Iran and unofficial estimates made by 'foreign journalists and Iranian exile groups' is so great that it 'would seem to me to indicate that there are too many things going on in Iran that the government wants to conceal from the rest of the world'. She concludes in a high moralising tone: 'It seems to me that nations, like individuals, should always try to behave better, and not worse, than the lowest common denominator if they have any regard at all for moral and human values.'

Lunch with Afshar at the Guinea. I tell him about HIM's reaction to the Laing book. Afshar was one of the two senior officials who, according to Laing, had read the manuscript. I am surprised, I say somewhat maliciously, that he and Shapurian, the other official, spent so much time trying to get Laing to minimise the number of houses she says the Shah owns, while nothing was done to persuade her to tone down her entire chapter on Savak's activities. I leave him a worried man.

Friday, March 4

Receive HIM's much-awaited reply. The Foreign Minister says HIM's displeasure was aroused by Stevens's description of Iran's fundamental and radical reforms as 'mild' (wrong word again!). The tone of the cable, a smiling Meshkinpoush assures me, is clearly conciliatory.

Monday, March 7

Attend a memorial service at Westminster Abbey for Anthony Crosland. Lord Donaldson delivers an honest, appreciative and yet not uncritical eulogy of his 'friend of 30 years'. Susan Crosland is flanked by two young girls, one on either side, and followed by a tall young man wearing his hair in a Chinese pigtail.

I see an article in the *Kayhan International*, alongside a huge photograph of Roger Stevens, attacking his review of Margaret Laing's book. Again, the term 'mild reforms' is used. I send a cable to the Foreign Minister drawing his attention to the fact that the word Stevens had used was 'moderate'.

Hossein comes to dinner. He says:

1. Savak has been reporting favourably on the way I have been handling my assignment.
2. There are rumours in the Ministry [of Foreign Affairs] that since Ardeshir [Zahedi], with his lavish life-style, is not expected to get on well with an austere, pious Carter administration, he and I will shortly swap our posts in London and Washington.
3. Tehran has become totally unlivable in.

Tuesday, March 8

Lunch at Claridge's with Martin Ennals, who is going to Tehran on the 14th.

Friday, March 11

Lunch with Cyrus Ghani, who is back in London again. He says the Empress comes out far better in television interviews than does the Shah. He had been approached to take a legal interest in some of the artistic activities of the Empress, but had declined because, as he said, 'he didn't want to get involved'. I say that in different ways we are all, to use a favourite expression of AAH's, making 50 per cent profits with 50 per cent efficiency, and yet none of us wants to get involved. Drive to Oxford to attend the final session of a seminar on Iran at the Centre for Middle Eastern Studies. The Jellicoes, the Denis Wrights, Roger Stevens, Professor Marbro, Derek Hopwood, Professor Ferrier are amongst those present. Dr Mohammad Yeganeh[1] delivers a respectable discourse on the future of the [Iranian] economy.

Roger Stevens says he is under attack in our Press for words he never used, and says that Tony Parsons has written about it to

[1] Iranian Minister of Commerce and Industry.

Kayhan International but he doesn't know whether the letter will ever be published[1].

After dinner, which struck me as mediocre, we move to another room for port and madeira, swapping places yet again for nuts and fruit. I shall never understand the ways of the Islanders.

Sunday, March 13

A well-written and powerfully argued article in the *Sunday Telegraph* by Peregrine Worsthorne entitled 'The Human Right that Matters Most', in which there is a reference to Iran. It begins thus:

'The most important human right is to live under a Government strong enough to maintain law and order. Nothing causes human beings so much misery as anarchy. The worst of tyrannical governments is better than no government at all.'

It ends by saying:

'Machiavelli is responsible for much less bloodshed than Christianity; *Realpolitik* for far fewer wars than religion; strong government for much more human happiness than weak. And anarchy is the worst enemy of civilisation, even if freedom is its best friend ...'

Lovely! I have supplied myself for a long time to come with what I feel is a well thought-out body of arguments which I can use in defence of strong government. From now on, I shall sing Perry's kind of tune, with no regret, remorse or recrimination.

Monday, March 14

I send off a letter to Gully Wells, using my personal writing paper rather than Embassy stationery.

My principal motive for replying – and in unequivocally aggressive language – is my expectation of a violent reaction from Tehran. I very strongly suspect that Gully's reply, with its researched information and moralising tone, is intended for a wider audience than just myself. If her reply should somehow, somewhere, be published, Tehran would certainly take me to task for leaving 'such blatantly false allegations' (as they would surely term them) unanswered. It is a possibility I must guard against.

[1] It was – on March 15.

66

Tuesday, March 15

Drive to Cambridge in response to an invitation jointly from Graham Storey, my tutor at Trinity Hall, and Peter Avery[1]. I am excited by this first visit after 18 years. To Peter Avery's rooms at King's. Graham Storey is there, and we greet each other cordially. Max Jaffe, the Curator of the Fitzwilliam Museum, and Professor and Mrs Gershevitch are amongst those to whom I am introduced.

Shortly afterwards we move to other rooms, this time the Vice-Provost's, for more drinks. A Mr Burbridge rather directly asks for money for a Persian-English dictionary the Cambridge University Press hopes shortly to publish. We move again, this time for drinks with the Provost, Sir Rodney Leech, and Lady Leech, to whom Peter presents me as 'the youngest ambassador you've ever met'.

Dinner in Hall at King's is an elegant, sumptuous occasion with much fine silver on display. The food is superb. Sit between Peter Avery and Professor Jasper Rose, who, I suspect deliberately, strikes what seems to me a mildly provocative pose.

We move back to the Provost's room for more drinks, and after a brief exchange with Sir Kenneth Berrill, head of the Government's Think Tank, I make my farewells and return to London.

Thursday, March 17

The Prime Minister telephones from Tehran to say: 1) Ennals's audience with HIM had gone well; 2) his own conversation with Ennals had been constructive also; 3) Ennals had asked for literature on the legal aspects of the courts' handling of the terrorist trials, and for observers to be allowed to attend the trials, to both of which requests the Government had given its consent; also that a delegation from Amnesty International, acting as private individuals, should be allowed to look into the conditions of the prisoners. To this latter request no clear reply had been given, it having been pointed out to Amnesty that the International Red Cross, in whose objectivity the Government placed greater confidence, was currently doing precisely that, so that there seemed little point in duplicating the work.

[1] Lecturer in Persian at Cambridge University.

Sunday, March 20

About 200 Iranians – Embassy colleagues and dignitaries among the resident community – come to a Now Ruz (Iranian New Year) party. Towards the end of dinner I steal upstairs to watch the Lyle-Bugner fight and lose £20 for backing Bugner.

If there is one wish I have for the new year of 2536, it is that my intolerable skin itching should be cured.

Monday, March 21

To Admiralty House for a luncheon hosted by Frank Judd, Minister of State at the FCO, in honour of Bayulken, Secretary-General of CENTO.[1] Judd, who sits on my left, asks what I think of CENTO. I say that, while the organisation does not send waves of fear down the spines of the men in the Kremlin, it is a measure of its success that not an inch of the territory belonging to its member states has been lost to the Ruskies. I add that the experience of Pakistan has nonetheless led HIM to place even greater faith in self-reliance, given that Pakistan, in spite of belonging to two military pacts, was dismembered by an invading foreign army.

Judd makes a speech offering what strikes me as half-hearted support for the organisation. In his reply Bayulken says the regional members are always sensitive to, and sometimes bemused by, criticism which castigates them for spending their own money to protect their own interests. He cites the example of Iran, confessing not to understand how the Press could interpret Iran's expenditure on arms as a source of instability when, in his view, the opposite is the case. On the way out, I thank him warmly for his 'realistic observations'.

Attend a reception given by the Foreign Secretary at the Banqueting House in Whitehall. As my turn comes to shake hands with him and his pretty wife, David Owen says I must soon come and 'have a bowl of salad' with him.

[On March 22 I flew to Malta, to which country I am also accredited, to present my credentials. I returned via Rome and Paris.]

[1] Central Treaty Organisation

Monday, March 28

Arrive in Paris to dreadful snowy and windy weather. I go to see
Princess Ashraf at her Avenue Montaigne apartment. She looks
serene and relaxed, and tells me about her visit to Mecca, which
now seems to have complete hold over her emotions.

Wednesday, March 30

On a friend's recommendation, I go to see Dr Grupper, the famous
dermatologist. He is a short and somewhat stoutish man, with an
excellent command of English, who exudes self-confidence. He
listens to my medical history and says he knows Dr Calnan and Dr
Domonkos, his British and American colleagues, when I mention
their names, but he clearly regards himself as their superior. He
asks me to take my shirt off, runs his nails on my body, which in his
under-heated room causes instant waves of goose pimples. With
apparent astonishment he repeats over and over again, 'Mon
Dieu.'

Topsyn gel, a strong fluoro-cortisone, is recommended for external
application, and Atarax 25 mg tranquillisers, three times a day, are
prescribed. 'I am the busiest man in France,' says Dr Grupper, 'but I
should like to see you for two minutes tomorrow evening.'

Thursday, March 31

Afsaneh Jahanbani, with whom I have shared seven years of the
Prime Minister's office, comes to see me at my hotel. She says
Hoveyda is indescribably tired, incredibly bad-tempered and quite
genuinely fed up, all of which, after his twelve years in that
demanding job, I can well understand. 'He is very, very fond of
you,' she tells me, 'and never misses an opportunity to sing your
praises to one and all.'

In the evening I stop by to see Grupper. The Topsyn gel has
brought improvement. Grupper is overjoyed. He dictates to his
secretary a report on my condition in which he uses the phrase, *'une
amélioration spectaculaire'*. Perfectly true, of course, but the *'amélioration'* would probably have occurred anyway with the application of
a less potent hydrocortisone, I tell myself. He says I should see him
again in two weeks' time.

Friday, April 1

I return to a cold and rainy London.

Sunday, April 3

Drive Hushang Ansari, who has been in London again and is leaving today, to the airport. On the way to Heathrow, he says: 1) all the talk about our cutting down on our arms purchases is 'nonsense'. He explains that towards the end of last year General Toufanian,[1] expecting a drop in oil revenue and a possible change in the US Administration, placed all his orders well in time; 2) that HIM appears satisfied with my performance because, whilst he is not in the habit of complimenting people, he does refer frequently to the 'London Embassy reports'; 3) he agrees that our change of policy on human rights issues can be described as a '180-degree turn'.

I see an article in the Atticus column of the *Sunday Times* with a rather complimentary photograph of Gully Wells, entitled 'Gully and H.E.' It reads:

'To all those invited to accept hospitality at the Iranian Embassy in London, I offer a cautionary tale.

'Early this year, a party at the Embassy was attended by Alexandra Wells, 26-year-old rising star of the publishing world, daughter of the novelist Dee Wells, and step-daughter of the philosopher Sir Freddie Ayer. Ms Wells (known to her friends as Gully) got on so well with the Ambassador, Parviz C. Radji, that she accepted his subsequent invitation to lunch. Late in the lunch, which was thoroughly enjoyed by all, Gully paid a "compliment" to the "democracy" now obtaining in Iran. Her remark was noted by Mr Radji, who presented her as she left with a printed letter – then being circulated to MPs, Lords, journalists and other interested parties – defending Iran against Amnesty International's recent charges of political torture.

'Gully read the letter, brooded about it and decided to reply, which she did at length, concluding: "The fact that one is surrounded by evil is absolutely no justification for following that path oneself."

'Ten days later, she received the following reply from His Excellency.'

[1] In charge of military purchases for the armed forces.

The article ends by quoting my reply to her in full.

I ask Meshkinpoush to draft a cable to Tehran, explaining the circumstances of this rather embarassing private affair.

Wednesday, April 6

I send a reply to the *Sunday Times* re Gully. In answer to a complaint from me about political bias in a *World At One* interview, I receive a letter from Sir Charles Curran, Director-General of the BBC, in which he agrees that Brian Widlake's introduction 'did include some editorialising phrases ... in an otherwise unexceptionable interview'. He concludes by hoping 'that we will have an opportunity to meet before long, and, perhaps, to discuss the BBC's policy and practice in its News and Current Affairs programmes'.

Lord Barnetson, Chairman of Reuters, and Donald Trelford, Editor of the *Observer*, come to lunch at Princes Gate. Trelford tells me his paper is considering sending someone to Iran – perhaps Katharine Whitehorn – to take a fresh look at things. I promise co-operation from the other end, adding that I recall the *Observer*'s having had the same idea a few months back but that it had been shelved after the takeover of the paper by the American oil company, Atlantic Richfield, headed by Robert O. Anderson. His connections with Iran, it was thought, might have laid the paper open to the suspicion of having some ulterior motive.

Trelford strikes me as a perceptive, intelligent individual with a probing mind and a generally sympathetic disposition. He says he knows Gully Wells and asks what I thought about the article. I say I felt that I had to reply to her letter, but that I have no quarrel with Gully.

Thursday, April 7

Lunch with Martin Ennals, Ann Birley and a young lawyer named Wrobel, who is going to Tehran tomorrow in a 'private capacity', to cover the trial of eleven anti-State activists. I am Martin's guest at a Bangladeshi restaurant in Soho whose food he likes.

Wrobel, who sounds unmistakably American, has been to Iran in 1962, presumably on a similar mission. Lunch, despite the circumstances, is agreeable, with Martin quite pleased with his audience with HIM.

Sunday, April 10

The *Sunday Times* has printed my reply to their Atticus piece.

Thursday, April 14

Sir Keith Joseph comes to lunch with me at PG. He is undelightful company, a bit wooden and without much humour. Throughout lunch, whether he is speaking or I am, his gaze is directed towards the window, as if pondering some insoluble problem physically located in the middle of Hyde Park. I am also rather surprised he is not better informed about Iran.

To the airport to receive Prince Gholam Reza who has flown in on HIM's instructions, specifically to pay a visit to King Khaled. We drive to his Cadogan Square house and I pick him up an hour later to go to the King's house in Hampstead. I wonder to myself whether this surely excessive display of friendly attention to the King is somehow related to my initial insensitivity, perhaps since discovered, in sending Meshkinpoush to sign the book at the hospital.

On arrival, we are led into a ground-floor drawing-room at the end of which stands a tall and distinguished man in traditional Arab dress, flanked by a number of aides amongst whom is the Saudi Ambassador, Alheglan. The Prince walks up and shakes hands with a slight bow, and so do I, recognising the King from his photographs, one of which hangs on the wall behind him. Talk is about Islamic unity, the ideological impeccability of the tenets of Islam, and, as the King sees it, the twin dangers of Zionism and Communism.

Monday, April 18

Mr Mehrdad Rambod, a member of the Majlis [Iranian Parliament], drops by for a courtesy call. He speaks about developments in Iran and says, amongst other things, that he is against the one-party system and has publicly said so. He adds that while a little mustard enhances the flavour of meat, a spoonful on a transparent slice ruins the taste – by the mustard, meaning our press and television propaganda.

Tuesday, April 19

Lizzie rings up to say a reporter from the *Daily Mirror* has been pestering her and would I see the reporter? I do. She concentrates on Lizzie's and my marriage intentions. I'm very dubious about the outcome of the interview.

I stop by at the preview of Jessica Gwynn's[1] paintings and proceed to Sonia Melchett's for dinner. Dominique de Borchgrave says the eccentricity of the English is a defence for their timidity in communicating. Charlie Douglas-Home says I was stupid ('too kind' are his actual words) to have spoken to the *Daily Mail* and that if one doesn't speak to gossip columnists one can't be quoted. Sonia says, 'You are a bachelor ambassador from a rich and important country which is also facing great difficulties, and that's why people are making a fuss over you. Take it in your stride.'

Thursday, April 21

Peter Walker drops in for a chat. His book, *The Ascent of Britain*, which contains references to Iran, has just been published. He has been invited by Hushang to go to Tehran. Whilst there, he would like to see HIM, the PM and someone in the military. He would prefer to stay with Hushang rather than at a hotel.

The *Daily Mail* article appears. It is silly and politically innocuous, but it does say I have no intention of marrying.

Hushang Ansari descends on London again. I send Bahar, my Economic Counsellor, to greet him at the airport, and I go to Claridge's to see him later. He says HIM had disliked the passages on Iran in Peter Walker's book and asks whether I think 'we can now cancel the planned Walker visit'.

I ask which passages had been deemed offensive. 'For one thing,' Hushang says, 'Walker takes a lot of credit for suggestions others have made. For another, he says HIM admired Heath as about the only one who could save Britain from her industrial troubles, and this is going to land us in trouble with the Labourites'. Moreover, Hushang goes on, 'Walker describes Iran, along with Brazil, as countries that suffer from balance of payment deficits'.

I say that, whatever view one may take of the historical accuracy of certain passages in Walker's book, he speaks respectfully and admiringly of the Shah and is sympathetic to the régime's accomplishments. 'Peter Walker,' I say with deliberate emphasis,

[1] The wife of Charles Douglas-Home.

'is friendly to our cause, and there is a conspicuous scarcity of valid and significant political voices which are willing to stand up in support of Iran.'

'HIM doesn't like the passage where Walker says HIM admires things British.'

'Perhaps HIM should commission Savak to write a book on him,' I say. I sense from Hushang's stare that I have gone a little too far.

He says finally: 'Think about the Walker visit for twenty-four hours and let me know your answer tomorrow.'

'My mind is made up. The visit should go ahead as planned.'

'Think about it with an open mind.'

I know that I have lost, as I suspect Hushang's mind is already – perhaps was already – made up.

Wednesday, April 27

Go to Claridge's to take Ansari to the airport. In the lobby I meet Mr Brown, the manager. 'Mr Ansari has been having high-powered meetings with Dr Kissinger and all, hasn't he?' he says. I suppress any sign of surprise at this intelligence. Feigning knowledge, I smile sagely.

In the car, I mention off-handedly my having heard about his meeting with the ex-American Secretary of State. Ansari, whose bluffing postures I know from our poker-playing days, replies with a curt 'yes', keeping a cool, unperturbed exterior. But a moment later, in a tone of mixed annoyance and curiosity, he asks: 'But who told you?'

'*Kallaghe*,' I reply. (The word means in Persian, 'a little bird'.)

'I see', he says. Long pause. Then, frantically, 'But how could Callaghan know?'

'*Kallaghe*,' I repeat, 'not *Callaghan*.'

'Good,' he says, obviously relieved by the correction, 'because HIM wouldn't want the British to know about the meeting.'

Having regained his composure, he then tells me that, since Walker's visit to Tehran might be interpreted as our endorsement of what he has said about the Labour government, Hushang had rung him to say HIM's previous commitments wouldn't allow an audience, and had also hinted at royal displeasure with the book's contents.

In the afternoon, I go to the House of Commons for a meeting of the Anglo-Iranian Parliamentary Group. Stan Newens, a vocal and extreme anti-Shah left-winger, is there among some 25 to 30 other

MPs. Newens raises questions about human rights – as a regular reader of *Kayhan International* he is *au courant* with the latest developments in Iran – and refers to the ending of torture, asking pertinent questions about the International Red Cross Commission which is inspecting the conditions of 'political prisoners' in Iran.

I reply that I accept his questions are asked in good faith and that I will reply to them in good faith, at the same time commending his up-to-date knowledge of current developments in Iran. I say wherever terrorism exists, violations of human rights seem a regrettable but inevitable concomitant. Stan Newens is not the only one who is restive about our human rights record.

Nicholas Bethell[1], whom I suspect I first met at Shusha Guppy's, also speaks at some length about Iran's shortcomings in that respect. He points out that allegations of torture, repression, arbitrary arrest, and people's disappearance, whatever their truth may be, are now invariably associated with Iran in British minds. Other MPs try to be helpful by asking why the Embassy doesn't go on the offensive and deny the many untruthful allegations that are made about Iran.

Meanwhile, I send a cable to the PM, emphasising the extreme importance of publishing the Red Cross report on the prisoners, whether the contents are favourable or unfavourable.

Friday, April 29

I am filled with self-reproach, bordering on disgust, for my half-hearted, unconvincing, totally wet defence of Iran's human rights record at the House of Commons two days ago. I have been arrogant enough to think that my personal honesty and credibility are more important than the instructions I am given by Tehran. I must present the official line, whether I find it convincing or not, and it is stupid and pretentious of me to try single-handedly to change the rules. I haven't received a single word or letter praising my defence of Iran. It must have been a pathetic performance.

Saturday, April 30

My cipher clerk, Shams, telephones me at the Residence to say there is a cable, 'that I must hand to you personally, sir'. I ask him

[1] Lord Bethell, author and, since 1975, Member of the European Parliament.

to come over at once, thinking that my Red Cross cable must have so angered HIM that I have been summoned back to Tehran. Instead, there is nothing more than an instruction to pay another visit to the valetudinarian King Khaled. My Red Cross cable 'has been seen by HIM', and there are no comments.

Monday, May 2

My cable re the Irano-British Parliamentary meeting at the Commons has evoked a royal response, and the decision whether I should meet Stan Newens, the Left-wing MP, has been left to me.

I watch *Panorama* in the course of which David Dimbleby grills Carter on human rights violations in Iran. I decide to protest to the BBC.

Charlie Douglas-Home says he has spoken to William Rees-Mogg about my suggestion that he (Charlie) should visit Iran as a guest of the Government, and because there was thought to be an implication in the invitation that he would be expected to report favourably the visit has been ruled out. He also tells me that Kissinger had been to lunch at *The Times* recently during which he had professed to be a greater admirer of Assad than of Sadat[1], and had said that the Israelis had unsuccessfully during the Middle East negotiations played on his being a fellow Jew, but nonetheless his commitment to the existence of Israel was total. He thought the real danger for South Africa, as far as American public opinion was concerned, would come when Americans, as in the case of Vietnam, could see whites shooting blacks daily on their television screens.

Tuesday, May 3

Naseer Assar, an Under-Secretary at the Ministry of Foreign Affairs, has been removed from his job after an interview in which he spoke about Iran's foreign policy. I feel intensely angry – and not from any great love I have for Assar. But everyone is capable of making mistakes, and, after all, public statements can be retracted, corrected, explained, denied, and the errant official can be reprimanded, over-ridden, or sent to Coventry. But you can't just remove people after years of loyal and honest service because of one unintentional slip. And what infuriates me even more is that, apart

[1] Presidents of Syria and Egypt.

76

from guesswork, there is no clear indication which of Assar's remarks has incurred HIM's displeasure. I am certain we shall never be told of the nature of poor Assar's peccancy.

Wednesday, May 4

Westminster Hall, in morning dress, for an expression of thanks to the Queen for her reign of twenty-five years. In a ceremony which I find replete with pomp and pageantry and little else, the Queen, with an eye to events in Ulster, says she can't forget she was crowned Queen of the United Kingdom of Great Britain and Northern Ireland.

There is a Nordic-looking man in the front row occupied by the Diplomatic Corps wearing a curious, dark blue, semi-military uniform with a flamboyantly embroidered cap. I ask de Perinat, the Spanish Ambassador, who is sitting next to me, who he thinks the man is. He doesn't know, and asks Fack, the Dutch Ambassador, sitting next to him. 'The ticket collector on the Orient Express,' he replies.

Friday, May 6

Lunch at PG with Saideh Pakravan. Seven years ago we were colleagues in the Prime Minister's office. She now lives in Paris and says she has severed her political ties with Iran. Though she doesn't say so, I suspect she disapproves of the Shah's régime. What she does say is that she believes materialism has become the only motive inspiring Iranian society. She was always a somewhat emotional person, and hasn't changed much.

Monday, May 9

An article on Iran in *The Times* by Lord Chalfont, called 'The Double Standard of Human Rights,' in which he refers to the current presence in Iran of the Red Cross team, and recently of a representative of Amnesty International, both looking into different aspects of our human rights violations.

I send off another letter to the Director General of the BBC, complaining about the Dimbleby interview with President Carter on *Panorama*. 'My complaint in this case,' I say, 'is not the "editorialising" of this interviewer, but rather his insistence, not once but three times, in pressing for some sort of condemnation of Iran, and of Iran alone, out of the American President's mouth.' I claim that this 'provides yet another instance of the BBC's undisguised, not to say gratuitous, hostility towards Iran'.

Tuesday, May 10

There is quite a remarkable article in the *Financial Times*, referring to an even more remarkable article in Tehran's *Kayhan International* which quotes from a letter written by Ebrahim Khajenouri [an Iranian author] calling for a discussion of the failure of the single-party system. 'It is too early to judge,' says the *Financial Times* article, 'whether the authorities are trying to give a greater appearance of liberalism, or whether disgruntled intellectuals are seeking greater freedom. It could be a combination of the two.' The article goes on to say that Iran seems to be improving its human rights image, and refers to the admission of foreign observers to a recent political trial and to the Red Cross visit to prisoners.

I am terribly excited by all this. As far as I know, this is the first instance of public dissent, if it qualifies as that, since the Amini Government in 1963. I call in Meshkinpoush, who has already seen the article and who shares my enthusiasm. He tells me another letter, addressed to the Prime Minister (the Khajenouri letter was addressed to Jamshid Amouzegar, Secretary General of the Rastakhiz Party) but as yet, at any rate, unpublished, speaks even more critically of the way Iran is going, both politically and economically. [The *Financial Times* article referred to a 200-page letter 'sent recently to the court for the Shah's attention, written by a former editor of *Kayhan*, Sadr Haj Seyyed Javadi', which was said to be 'similar in tone' to the Khajenouri letter.]

Meshkinpoush says the sudden appearance of these articles in the Iranian press ineluctably leads one to believe they form part of an orchestrated campaign. From Washington?

Friday, May 13

A reply from Sir Charles Curran on the Dimbleby interview, in which he asserts that 'it is entirely normal practice for an interviewer to follow up a question to which he feels he may have received an incomplete answer, and the amplifications given by the President in his subsequent answers seem to me justification for Mr Dimbleby's pursuit of the matter'. I judge this reply quite unsatisfactory and decide to answer it immediately.

In the evening, I go to Hassan Yaseri's house for dinner. He is the NIOC[1] man in London. Kamshad, just back from Tehran, is there, bubbling with gossip, speculation and enthusiasm about 'the Letters'. He says the second letter, written by Haj Seyyed Javadi, is seventy pages long, and that it expresses deep concern over HIM's 'unconstitutional' acts. His motive for writing the letter, Haj Seyyed Javadi says, is so that the contents 'may be recorded for history'. Kamshad says Khajenouri's letter is also an invitation to liberalisation and that the Carter imprint on these documents is 'quite obvious'. Reza Baraheni, says Kamshad, has now achieved the status of a demi-god amongst Iranian dissidents in the United States, and is constantly surrounded by some twenty student bodyguards. The Shah, he concludes, is so powerful that he can afford to loosen the screw a bit and let people say what they want.

Sunday, May 15

A reporter from the *Sun* rings up to say that a number of English girls have been made pregnant by Iranian naval cadets, who are returning to Iran [following completion of their naval training in the United Kingdom] and what do I think should be done with the children they leave behind? I say that, while I know nothing about the matter, the Embassy would be pleased to look into the problem with understanding and, where necessary, to provide a measure of assistance on humanitarian grounds.

Monday, May 16

The *Sun* story produces the expected ripples and both the BBC and Capital Radio telephone to ask for interviews. I call in Captain Fiuzi, my Naval Attaché, and we speak to the interviewers together. It all goes smoothly.

Lunch at PG with Lord Chalfont, Eldon Griffiths and Peter

[1] National Iranian Oil Company.

Wilsher of the *Sunday Times*. Somalia, Ethiopia, Jugoslavia, the Persian Gulf, Peter Jay, the European Parliamentary elections, Gully Wells and Margaret Thatcher are the topics touched upon. Chalfont says the Conservatives will get in at the next general election in Britain and stay in power for two parliamentary terms (ten years). He wants to know if I can tell him the contents of the Red Cross report on prison conditions in Iran. I reply that I don't know what it says, but that I have asked Tehran to publish the findings, whatever they are. 'That would be absolutely right,' he says. Meshkinpoush, who drafts the cable to Tehran, suggests that I leave out the last bit. I agree.

Tuesday, May 17

David Owen and his PA were to have lunched with me and Meshkinpoush today before their prospective visit to Tehran for the annual CENTO ministerial conference. His office rings up at eleven to say that 'because of the illness of someone close to the Foreign Secretary', he must cancel the luncheon. Since I had asked Tehran for instructions about what to discuss at the lunch – and hadn't been given any – they would have expected a report about it. So I send a cable saying it was cancelled for the reason given.

Wednesday, May 18

Tehran wants to know how I interpret the Owen luncheon cancellation and whether I think the excuse given was genuine. I say I have no way of knowing, but that unless I receive some sort of apology, the cancellation could be interpreted as a slight.

Thursday, May 19

Send off another letter to Sir Charles Curran to keep the BBC on its guard, in which I say: 'I am sorry that you felt unable to address yourself to an explanation as to why Iran was isolated for a series of questions on human rights which, by their nature and the persistence with which they were put, were palpably intended to

80

taint Iran's image before millions of viewers.'

Tehran wants to know why, in the course of the interviews about the pregnant English girls, we had said there were no religious or national barriers to marriage between the sailors and the girls, but only a contractual undertaking on the part of the cadets not to marry for the first five years of their training. We reply that the Press might have interpreted the other restrictions as evidence of religious or racial prejudice.

Meet Ansari again briefly at Claridge's. He says HIM is in a contemplative mood these days and admits that his (Ansari's) meeting with Vance[1] could have gone better. HIM, he tells me, will be going to Washington in November.

Friday, May 20

A letter arrives from David Owen explaining that his son – who, I remember, is suffering from some dreadful disease – had collapsed and was taken to hospital, and expressing regret over the cancellation of our scheduled lunch.

Sunday, May 22

President Carter makes a speech at Notre Dame University and says America must abandon its inordinate fear of Communism and its attempts to contain it world-wide. That policy, he says, led America to embrace any dictator who opposed Communism. Vietnam is cited as an example. Bloody hell! What does HIM think of these remarks, I wonder?

Tuesday, May 24

Messrs Stan Newens and Ken Fletcher [Labour MPs] come to the Embassy 'with open minds' to discuss the situation in Iran. Stan Newens, who leads the discussion, is courteous and seems genuinely concerned about torture and human rights violations. We agree to disagree, but a dialogue is established and I am thanked for talking to them.

[1] Cyrus Vance, American Secretary of State in the Carter administration.

Ahmad Ghoreishi[1] comes to lunch. He is highly sceptical about the prospects of any change in Tehran and believes that, while the Americans are the only people the Shah will probably listen to, Carter can't do anything to liberalise Iran. He dismisses the importance of 'the Letters' out of hand.

Wednesday, May 25

The Foreign Secretary, back from the CENTO meeting in Tehran, wants to know whether, despite the very short notice, I am free to lunch with him today. My inclination is to say no, but Meshkin-poush says I must accept. David Owen receives me, all smiles and a warm handshake. I hand him the plastic tube containing 2cc of North Sea oil which he had admired on Hoveyda's desk in Tehran. 'The Prime Minister had promised me that,' he says. I ask about his son, who suffers from a form of leukemia. 'Before his last relapse', he tells me, 'I would have said his chances were 50–50. Now I think they are considerably reduced.' I am surprised at his calm and apparently detached way of speaking. Talking about his training as a doctor, he says that one day, while in the office of a leading neurologist, he had decided that a concern with macro-humanity was more rewarding than one with individuals, and had consequently turned from medicine to politics.

At times, he says, he has despaired of the Labour Party because of the domination a number of 'lunatic extremists' exercised over it, but somehow he had stayed on. Harold Wilson he describes as a conservative with radical ideas. President Carter comes in for a great deal of praise for his 'honesty, simplicity and bright mind'. Carter's attachment to moral values is quite sincere, says Owen.

I say I subscribe to his moral principles, but, referring to Carter's Notre Dame speech, add that a country which shares a thousand miles of common border with the Soviet Union, and whose history for the past sixty years has largely consisted of an attempt to resist Soviet expansion, overt or covert, will find his advice about 'not having an inordinate fear of Communism' hard to swallow.

Owen says Carter is a flexible man and that he has demonstrated that flexibility with Chancellor Schmidt on this particular issue. He then moves on to his visit to Iran and his audience with HIM.

[1] Chancellor of National University and member of Rastakhiz Party's political bureau.

82

Human rights were discussed and Iran's present efforts to improve its image noted. Owen is full of praise for Tony Parsons and speaks warmly of Ramsbotham[1], his predecessor.

The atmosphere at our tête-à-tête luncheon is remarkably friendly and informal. We dine at the conference table in his room. The napkins are paper and the food satisfactory. He says I can ring his office and come to see him whenever I want to.

In the evening, Princess Margaret comes to dinner. On her way up to the drawing-room, she inspects the Blue Room, now redone by David Mlinaric – 'It's much better now' – and peeps into the ballroom. 'She looks nice,' says the Princess, nodding towards the portrait of Empress Farah on the wall, 'but he always looks so gloomy.' In the drawing-room, there is a photograph of me being presented to Mrs Gandhi, flanked by Their Imperial Majesties. 'Is that Mrs Gandhi?' asks the Princess and, when I agree that it is, she looks thoughtful for a moment, then 'Dick-tay-ta,' she announces, leaving me wondering who in the picture she really has in mind.

Sunday, May 29

Lunch at PG with Mohammad Safa, former colleague from the PM's office. He speaks about 'the Letters', but says that Haj Seyyed Javadi is a perfectionist who thinks in terms of Utopias. He speaks at length about the crying need to ensure a 'minimum of democratic freedoms', but is rather vague about the limits of the 'minimum'.

I ask him whether he thinks it might help if I wrote a formal letter to the Prime Minister – one that he could show to HIM – about some of the more pressing political problems that really could be quite easily defused. Safa says that, on Hoveyda's specific instructions, he had spent several days concentrated work preparing a 30-page memorandum on the possible role of Iranian youth in the Rastakhiz Party. He made an appointment to see the Prime Minister, and presented his memorandum with a mixture of pride and expectancy. 'This is the memo you asked for, sir,' he said.

'On what?' the Prime Minister asked, fingering the thick bundle with obvious apprehension.

'On Iran's youth and its role in the Rastakhiz.'

'Tell whoever wrote this thing that I want a half-page summary. Idiots!'

[1] Sir Peter Ramsbotham, GCMG, GCVO, Ambassador in Tehran 1971–74, and in Washington 1974–77.

Monday, May 30

I have a long conversation with Meshkinpoush, asking him whether he thinks it would be a good idea if, in keeping with the current fashion, I too wrote a 'Letter' to the Imperial Court pointing out, in view of HIM's forthcoming visit to Washington, the usefulness of observing a set of rudimentary guidelines that would, in my view, make for a more successful royal visit. These guidelines would include condemning the use of torture; presenting a more modest picture of our accomplishments and aspirations, and abandoning our more turgid propaganda; and showing respect for the ways of the Western democracies rather than attacking what HIM sees as their shortcomings. Finally, we should try to explain opposition movements in Iran not simply in terms of Communism, but also in terms of religious fundamentalism.

After listening with ill-concealed irritation, Meshkinpoush wants to know why I regard it as necessary constantly to 'push' Tehran. 'You've already taken what the Ministry considers to be courageous initiatives,' he tells me. 'Be content with that. The Shah's patience is not inexhaustible and continual harping on one or two issues will only anger him.' When I reply that this régime is the only one I want to see in power in Iran and that consequently I want to try to persuade it to get rid of its uglier manifestations, he reminds me, almost wearily, that thousands of others have thought they could change things by the bold expression of their views. 'Remember the Entezams?'[1] he asks. I ask him, in turn, to ponder the problem – not to dismiss it lightly, and to begin thinking about the kind of language which, while conveying the sense of my thinking, would be least likely to be judged offensive.

Tuesday, May 31

Moinzadeh, my head Savak man just back from Tehran, comes to see me. He has seen Nassiri, Sabeti and others and says they all consider me as the initiator of the massive changes of policy that have been forced upon them. To my utter amazement, he says Nassiri had told him that I had direct contact with HIM on a number of sensitive political issues and had been given *carte blanche* by HIM for the handling of all human rights questions. He

[1] Abdollah and Nasrollah Entezam, distinguished Iranian diplomats, both of whom had incurred HIM's wrath by counselling a more 'moderate' approach in the 1960s.

confirms that the change in the treatment of political detainees in Iran is 'beyond belief'.

Thursday, June 2

In two days' time, I begin my second year in London. My thoughts revert to my arrival at the airport and being greeted by the immaculately attired Mr Collins, to unpacking my bags with the sinister Ramyar[1] lurking in the wings and to Amirteymour's *felo de se*. It has been a richly eventful, immensely instructive, if also a deeply worrying time.

My primary preoccupation – indeed, obsession – has been the defence of the reputation of the country I represent from a constant barrage of attacks on it. Though only tentative steps have been taken by Tehran to make my task easier, I am delighted to detect a noticeable change in HIM's attitude, a realisation on his part of the immense damage inflicted on Iran's name abroad as a result of the quite needless excesses of Savak, and I am able to sense the awakening of a more tolerant acceptance of dissent, however vestigial its dimensions. All this is to the good.

Socially, it has not been an unsuccessful year. In spite of a spate of snide paragraphs in the gossip columns, the invidious 'playboy' label has mercifully eluded me. On the whole I think I have managed to persuade my colleagues and associates that I approach my mission with seriousness and diligence.

Tuesday, June 7

Dinner at Diana Phipps's. After dinner Mark Boxer and Barbara Walters come in – Barbara is here to telecast the Jubilee celebrations. She speaks of some notions she has about HIM. The Shah, she says, is his own worst enemy in interviews because he is too honest. As an example, she cites his admission that Savak operates in the United States, his 'male-superiority' attitude on women, and his remark about the influence of Jews in the media. 'She [Empress Farah], on the other hand, is marvellous.' I ask her if she thinks our case is beyond redemption, as far as the American media are concerned. She ponders this for a long time, and finally mumbles, 'No.'

[1] The previous Ambassador's valet.

Thursday, June 16

A certain John Bulloch, reviewing Margaret Laing's book in the *Daily Telegraph*, writes that there is a 'royal (Iranian) connection' with the drug traffic. It's a statement that can't be allowed to stand. At the same time, I certainly don't want to antagonise the friendly *Daily Telegraph*.

Friday, June 17

The Spenders and the Berlins come to dinner with Lizzie and me. Isaiah is for me, of course, the star of the evening. The conversation ranges far and wide. Isaiah says Nehru, whom Field Marshal Alexander, a contemporary of his at Harrow, had described as the 'nicest chap among his school-friends', really hated the Indian masses. They then speak of a certain individual as the fourth man in the Philby affair. Isaiah says he had met Donald Maclean in Moscow in 1956. Maclean, pointing to the KGB agent keeping an eye on them from a respectable distance, had asked ironically: 'Where in England can you have such a free conversation?'

He asks what he should talk about when he goes to Iran shortly in connection with a British Institute library project in Tehran. I meekly suggest the dilemma facing nations which pursue higher material standards at the risk of losing their own cultural identity. '*Zend-Avesta*,'[1] he says, 'might be a safer subject.'

After dinner we all go to John Gross's.[2] Stuart Hampshire is there and wants to know whether the Ashraf Pahlavi Library can be inaugurated without the Princess's participation, in view of what happened during her visit to Oxford a year ago. 'For a long time now,' I reply, 'I have been looking for the person who suggested the idea of a library in the first place – with a gun.' I shall ponder the problem, I tell him wearily.

Wednesday, June 22

Lunch with Ebrahim Golestan.[3] He says when Jacques Chirac[4] was

[1] Zoroastrian scriptures.
[2] Then Editor of the *Times Literary Supplement*.
[3] A left-wing intellectual and perhaps Iran's foremost film director.
[4] The then French Prime Minister.

visiting Tehran recently, he (Golestan) had been invited to a dinner for Chirac given by Hoveyda at the Foreign Ministry. Hoveyda had introduced Golestan to Chirac with the words: 'He is our foremost writer and director, but we ban all his works in Iran.' A few nights later, he had been arrested at his house, his books and papers confiscated and he himself taken to the Central Police Station. There he had been subjected to humiliating treatment and, while he had not himself been physically molested, he had been made to watch another man being beaten up. The next day, after his wife had spoken to the Empress, he was freed, together with profuse apologies for the 'mistake'. Shortly afterwards, while spending a few days at the Caspian, he had been invited to the Palace. HIM had remarked on his sun tan, adding, with a knowing half-smile: 'I didn't know sun-bathing was allowed where you've just come from.'

He says that while both the Shah and the Empress are intelligent, well-meaning, dedicated and personally kind and humane, a 'courtier mentality' with a sub-culture of its own has now come to prevail over the whole system, and this is infinitely more damaging than the deliberate brutality of any single individual. Anyone who doesn't comply, socially or politically, with these obsequious standards is liable to be accused of being at least lacking in respect or, worse, unpatriotic. So deep is this mental affliction, Golestan says, that it is quite beyond all redemption.

Dinner at Diana Phipps's. The David Bruces[1] are amongst the guests. At dinner Diana says, quite out of the blue, that some of the people she has asked had actually refused to come because I, the Iranian Ambassador, was to be present. She adds that the Bruces had experienced similar treatment during the Vietnam war. My goodness! Such monumental tactlessness from so sophisticated a woman!

Saturday, July 2

Shahryar Shafigh[2] comes to see me. He says the Imperial Navy has been assigned two roles, one to protect the Persian Gulf, and the other to safeguard the oil lanes, neither of which is it in any way equipped to do. Disclosures of corruption and the subsequent arrests and dismissals have frozen everyone into a state of inaction.

[1] David Bruce was a former American Ambassador in London.
[2] Princess Ashraf's son, and Commander of Iran's Hovercraft Fleet in the Persian Gulf.

He adds that Habibollahi, the present naval commander, while a good man, is terrified of taking any decisions. Much of the equipment the Americans are flogging us we could never use, he says, citing as an example the Spruance Class destroyers. He says an added problem is the difficulty the Americans are creating about the training of Iranians in the United States, because so many naval cadets had opted to stay there after completing their training. From now on we are going to rely more on the British for the training of our people. I wonder if he says these things to his uncle.

Monday, July 4

Lunch with Ahmad Ghoreishi, just back from the States. He says so many problems relative to Iran's image in America could be easily solved but for Ardeshir (Zahedi, the Ambassador) whose passion for entertainment shows quite clearly that he is not the person to solve them. He says he spoke to groups of Iranian students at Berkeley and Colorado Universities where Baraheni's name had been invoked like that of a saviour. 'Nobody in Iran knows this man or a line of his poetry,' Ghoreishi had reminded them.

I wonder, after Ahmad is gone, whether he wouldn't make a good Iranian ambassador in Washington. But I reflect that the question is an academic one because, in view of HIM's manifest distrust of thinking people, he would never be offered it. The thought is really quite appalling.

Tuesday, July 5

Go to Edward Heath's for dinner. Anthony Royle[1] and his pretty model wife, the Rees-Moggs, Pamela Egremont and a lovely-faced creature called Gillian Widdicombe, are there. Throughout dinner, the lovely-faced creature is content to say nothing and just flash her beautiful eyes in different directions.

When the ladies withdraw, Ted asks about the state of 'our mutual relations'. I explain that all – well, *nearly* all – is well, that our bilateral trade is flourishing, that we share an identity of views on the need to keep the region free from subversion and to contain

[1] MP for Richmond and a former Junior Minister at the Foreign and Commonwealth Office.

Communism, and that we value Britain's participation in the economic development of Iran in a partnership that is 'rewarding for you and beneficial for us'. Where our metaphoric swords have crossed in the past, I tell him, is over the treatment we receive by sections of the media for our shortcomings on human rights. Some of that criticism has been tendentious and exaggerated, some of it perhaps justified. But Tehran has now shown a realistic understanding of the problem and has taken sincere and effective steps to put an end to excesses, and I am sure that that problem, too, will in time be resolved.

Mr Heath thinks my analysis a fair one. In his view, Carter's human rights campaign stems from the post-Vietnam, post-Watergate isolationism that grips America, and because the issue of human rights can be applied equally to 'Left' and 'Right' countries Carter can hide his real isolationism behind this banner. Rees-Mogg agrees. He says the Russian leaders are old men and their age would tend to dampen their enthusiasm for involvement in foreign adventures.

We join the ladies, drink a little more, admire some of Ted's pictures of his Broadstairs home, and eventually take our leave.

Wednesday, July 6

Lunch with Mostafa Fateh at Mark's. He says that before Vance or Sullivan[1] went to Tehran, the American Embassy had sent a translation of Haj Seyyed Javadi's letter to Washington, and that when Vance spoke to HIM, he repeated more or less verbatim the points made by Haj Seyyed Javadi. In unexceptionably courteous language he referred to HIM's arbitrary rule as violating every single provision of the Constitution of 1906. I ask Mostafa how sure he is of the accuracy of this version of Vance's exchange with HIM. 'One hundred per cent,' he says. 'The Shah is more insecure in his relations with the Americans than ever.' 'And the British?' I ask. 'The British,' says Mostafa, 'are concentrating on only one thing in their relations with Iran and Saudi Arabia: money.'

Thursday, July 7

Lunch with Charlie Douglas-Home. He asks about the Red Cross

[1] The American Ambassador.

report. I say that as far as I can gather, without having seen it, the number it gives for political prisoners in Iran is much closer to what we say it is, and their treatment less harsh than what is claimed by Amnesty.

Tuesday, July 12

Mrs Thatcher and her husband Denis come to dinner at the Embassy. Mrs Thatcher knows about the Empress's current visit to the United States and the noisy demonstrations her visit has inspired. She asks about Iran's oil figures and shows herself informed and interested on the subject. Both husband and wife strike me as very pleasant, but I notice that every time Mr Thatcher tries to say something she interrupts him to say, 'But *dahling*, the Ambassador already *knows* that.' No potentially contentious issues are mentioned and the evening passes agreeably but uneventfully.

Wednesday, July 13

I am astonished to read in the *Financial Times* that Amouzegar, in Stockholm for the OPEC Conference, now says Iran is *against* a rise in the price of oil, and is *against* the indexing of the price of oil to that of the so called 'basket' price of industrial goods and services. Referring to comments made by Sheikh Yamani[1] he says he is in total agreement with 'His Excellency'. Until yesterday the official line was to dismiss Yamani as a lackey of the Americans, who kowtowed to their every whim as far as Saudi oil policy was concerned. And now suddenly this! There are many calls from friends and colleagues to enquire about our 'new oil policy', and, being unable to elucidate, I dissemble. What a sudden and abject reversal!

Meshkinpoush comes to see me in the afternoon, wanting to know my opinion about recent developments in Iran. He confesses to being confused and worried. I say I firmly believe that, while the Americans may be preaching liberalisation to the Shah, it is inconceivable that they would want to go any further. 'Far too much is at stake for them to want a more fundamental change,' I tell him. 'For anything more drastic to happen, they would need the tacit approval of the Russians.'

[1] The Saudi Oil Minister.

90

Charlie rings in the evening to say *The Times* will be publishing an article in tomorrow's paper in reply to a recent pro-régimes piece by Alan Hart. He adds that the writer, Fred Halliday, is a regular contributor to the *New Left Review*. A worrisome, confusing day.

Thursday, July 14

The Halliday article is quite nasty, but the stunning news is Robert Graham's[1] revelation in the *Financial Times*. He reports from Tehran that three former associates of Mossadeq, Karim Sanjabi, Shahpour Bakhtiar and Dariush Foruhar, have written an open letter to the Shah in which they say: 'The only way to create new faith in ourselves, to restore a sense of individual liberty and a spirit of national co-operation in order to come to terms with the problems threatening Iran, is to end despotic government, observe the principles of the Constitution and the Universal Declaration of Human Rights, forego a one-party system, allow freedom of the Press and of association, release political prisoners, permit exiles to return and establish a government based on Majority representation.'

No such letter could have been written, says Graham, if it were not for the protective umbrella of President Carter's stand over human rights, and he asks, rhetorically, whether HIM will suppress these new tendencies or allow genuine liberalisation.

Good heavens! What's happening in Iran? How can the Shah have changed so much, so fast? I suspect that the recent power cuts[2] may have acted as the catalyst for greater political tolerance.

Friday, July 15

Lunch with Afshar, newly arrived from Tehran, at the Connaught. He says the odd thing about 'the Letters' to HIM is that Savak knows exactly where they are being produced and how they are being circulated, but does nothing to stop them. He says HIM's mood alternates between depression and exhilaration. He adds that

[1] *Financial Times* Middle East correspondent, based in Tehran, 1975–77.
[2] There had been a number of electric power failures in Tehran and throughout Iran, which over a period of months had caused temporary hardship and much inconvenience to the Iranian public.

Lesley Blanch was paid $50,000 for her book on the Empress, which 'Farah didn't even want', but which Alam (the Court Minister) thought would make a suitable gift to her from the Shah.

Monday, July 18

Chapman Pincher invites me to give an interview to the *Daily Express*. I ask Meshkinpoush what he thinks about the idea. He says he thinks it would be unwise for me to grant *any* interview in the present political conditions. He chooses his words carefully, but says in effect that he considers me 'a patriot serving his country' and fears that, if I should publicly commit myself too strongly to a pro-Monarchist position, I might find myself 'left out' if there were to be any dramatic changes in Iran. I am both puzzled and surprised by what he says. I protest my loyalty to HIM and say that I am already 'labelled' beyond redemption.

Tuesday, July 19

A most damaging letter in *The Times* from the British section of Amnesty International, challenging the assertions in Alan Hart's article and saying that, if lives have been saved, it is because of pressure by important people in the West.

Lunch with George Weidenfeld at PG. After an interesting *tour d'horizon* of the international scene, he speaks about the possibility of doing a book on the Shah – 'a kind of *Red Star Over China* that would put his point of view across as Snow's book had done for Mao.

Thursday, July 21

Lesley Blanch comes to lunch and says: 1) Her book on Farah is finished. She knows she will be accused of having sold her professional reputation for money, but insists that everything she says in the book she means. It had been very difficult to attribute any negative qualities to the Empress, though 'perhaps vanity would be something she could be accused of'; 2) She now has a far better idea of the enormous service which the Shah has rendered to Iran than she had before; 3) The Empress is emerging as a strong and moderating influence in the land; 4) She will not go on television for an interview on the book because before the camera she looks like Einstein, and in any case no woman over forty should go on television.

Friday, July 22

Kenneth Harris, recently returned from attending a seminar at the Aspen Institute in Colorado at which Farah had spoken, comes to lunch. He speaks highly of the Empress, but, under prodding from me, admits that there had been 'no dialogue but a series of statements'. He says Robert Anderson[1] is very keen to send someone to Tehran to do an interview with the Shah, although he (Harris) is too busy with his biography of Attlee to undertake the task himself.

Cyrus Ghani, back in town, tells me the blackouts have proved a colossal embarrassment to the régime and have provided an outlet for everyone's pent-up and long-smouldering discontent. The situation has laid indecently bare the Government's repeated assurances that increased military expenditure would not be at the cost of improvements in people's living standards. Yet now, all of a sudden, people are being deprived of lighting, air-conditioning and refrigeration – and all in the middle of the worst heat-wave for many years. He also says Ardeshir is being terribly tactless in his deliberate courting of Kissinger under the very eyes of the Carter Administration. 'That kind of thing,' he says, 'only antagonises the Carter people.'

Tuesday, July 26

Mark Dodd, of the BBC External Services, brings Andrew Whitley, the new *Financial Times*-cum-BBC correspondent in Tehran, to the office for a chat. Whitley, who says he has an elementary knowledge of Persian, seems bright and intelligent, if somewhat on the defensive. He asks if I think his assessment of Iran's policies, as they appear in his paper, is fair. With an absent-mindedness bordering on dereliction of duty, I say *I* think his assessment is fair but my superiors do not.

[1] President of Atlantic Richfield, then owners of the *Observer*, and founder of the Aspen Institute in Colorado.

Wednesday, July 27

It is astonishing how, all of a sudden, the newspapers in Tehran are replete with criticism of the Government. *Kayhan International* has a front-page picture of Hushang Ansari, and quotes him as asserting, no less, that 'every tongue must speak out, every pen must write as a right under Iranian democracy'.

The *Financial Times* reports from Tehran that yet another letter, this time written by a group of forty lawyers and addressed to Nosratollah Moinian, Head of the Imperial Secretariat, is circulating in the capital, accusing the Government of having used the judiciary for its own purposes and of down-grading it by rushing through half-baked legislation.

Chapman Pincher, with whom I lunch at the Embassy, asks me about these reports. I say that I have seen them but can't comment. He takes my prepared texts, checks some old stories and promises 'a good story' in two or three weeks.

Thursday, July 28

Lunch at Princes Gate with Len Murray, Moss Evans, Meshkin-poush and Bahar. Of my two guests, Murray appears the more confident, the more polished and the more articulate, while Evans seems more friendly and open-minded. Murray refers to 'certain reservations' about accepting his long-standing invitation to visit Iran. The occasion is an exercise in PR, which doesn't go too badly, I think.

Saturday, July 30

Cyrus Behnam, my number two when I came to London, has died in Tehran from a heart attack. He was never a close personal friend but I am sorry he has gone. Whatever his involvements with my predecessor, he did me no wrong. He was witty and amusing, with ready-made solutions for all the world's problems in the shape of tobacco and alcohol.

Sunday, July 31

Pack for my trip to Tehran tomorrow. I am filled with as much anxiety as with hope, as much optimism as fear at the outset of my journey. In the back of my mind lingers the suspicion that I might have pushed things a little too hard. Yet I do feel that my paper for HIM could perform a genuine service for him and, in spite of any comments Hoveyda or Khalatbary may make, it is important that the paper should be handed to him essentially in its existing form. *On verra . . .*

Monday, August 1

The flight is uneventful, which is the best kind of flight. There are elaborate security arrangements at Tehran Airport for Hoveyda, who is returning from a holiday in Corsica at about the same time I arrive. Stop at Mother's to say hello; then drive to the Hilton.

Huge buildings have gone up in a parabola around the airport in the past year. I think Tehran looks a little cleaner, although the traffic is as terrifying as ever. I have, and always will have, a gut attachment to Tehran. The nerve-wracking chaos of this dusty, unlovely city pleases me infinitely more than the serenity of Hyde Park.

Tuesday, August 2

Afsaneh Jahanbani, eight months pregnant, can scarcely accommodate herself behind her desk at the PM's office when I go to see her. She is, as always, in a cheerful mood, even when she says Hoveyda has been written off as Prime Minister by everyone, but that apparently everyone is wrong.

After about twenty minutes, the door of the PM's office opens and out slips Hoveyda, beaming his Cheshire cat smile and teasing me about combing my hair forward to hide my bald patches. Majidi and Asfia, two aides who have been attending a meeting in his room, follow him and we embrace.

Downstairs, I go to see my old friend and former colleague, Mohammad Safa. In the past, he says, each time we opened our mouths to say something about the need to grant a minimum of democratic rights to the people, we were called salon socialists and told to shut up. Now, with Carter in office, all those whose past political associations had discredited them in the eyes of the régime have suddenly become 'beloved of the people'. But he feels the people are too 'spineless' and too apathetic for these new political initiatives to get anywhere.

Wednesday, August 3

Hoveyda is in fine form, jovial and effusive and very confident. Referring to his premiership he says, 'They've buried me alive, but unfortunately for them and me, I am still alive.' He says the recent expressions of dissent and the spate of letter-writing have their origin 'not in Iran'. He says HIM is sincere about wanting to liberalise 'a bit', but we ought to remember that we have never had the tradition or the discipline to enable us to make such moves successfully, and that in any case we lack tolerance. He points to the portrait of the Shah and Farah on the wall and says the family feud is now very serious, and that, if Princess Ashraf should also be brought into the equation, then the complications would become Byzantine.

When I ask whether the Empress isn't a moderating influence on her husband, he says she is surrounded by highly ambitious people who influence her mind. HIM has instructed him, he says, to throw into the waste-basket any letters signed by Nahavandi[1] that deal with subjects other than works of art or the charities under the Empress's aegis. Then, in a phrase I suspect he must have heard from HIM himself, he adds: 'If ever she had to govern Iran, we would disappear in four hours.' The Rastakhiz Party, he says, must be regarded as a complete failure, and Amouzegar readily admits he is not happy as its Secretary-General.

I hand him my paper, which he reads in complete silence, while I brace myself to resist any alterations in form or content that he may suggest. Finally he says that, while he thinks the proposals are 'very sensible', the 'semantics' have to be changed: 'You should say that these are the opinions of public relations experts you have consulted in London rather than your own opinions.' He keeps a copy to think about the 'necessary alterations' and says he'll let me know his views long before my audience with HIM.

I raise the issue of the power cuts. He says: 'Only 30 per cent of development expenditure is in the hands of the Government. The other 70 per cent is in the hands of NIOC, the Gas Company and

[1] Hushang Nahavandi, the Empress's Principal Secretary.

the Armed Forces, and you can't do everything with 30 per cent.' He adds, however, that the electricity blackouts will be ended by October. And the Red Cross investigation of the prisons? 'They will not be published at the request of the Red Cross because it would create a precedent.' When I say that people will find that explanation hard to swallow and press him on the contents of the report, he says: 'They are not very pretty.' He adds that HIM is nonetheless ordering the release of another 1,000 people on the 25th of Mordad and 4th of Aban – 'at considerable risk.' He speaks with a mixture of contempt and disgust about the corruption permeating the upper echelons of Savak, the army generals and some of the Shah's cronies. 'I sometimes feel as if I have lost my bearings,' Hoveyda tells me. An hour and twenty minutes later I come out of his room and into Afsaneh's, where all those whose appointments have been delayed cast hostile glances in my direction.

Friday, August 5

With Fereydoun Hoveyda, I fly to Ramsar to see Princess Ashraf. On the plane Fereydoun tells me HIM has said we should tell the Americans that they can't go on being ambivalent and must clarify their attitude towards Iran. HIM wishes it to be known, says Fereydoun, that political liberalisation has been decided upon 'not because of Carter or Ennals', but because HIM feels the people of Iran have now reached the required degree of political maturity. What an amazing coincidence, we agree.

The Princess's crowd are there in force, occupying an entire floor of the renovated old Ramsar hotel. The men are playing backgammon, as Fereydoun and I enter, interrupting their games for just long enough to greet us politely before resuming the business in hand. At 2, the Princess appears and greets us warmly. I sense that something in my manner, speech or general bearing displeases her, but she remains charming throughout. Majidi and his wife also arrive for lunch, which is served in the hotel dining-room. This has been reserved entirely for the Royal party so that many tables are empty. The waiters, supplied by the European firm that holds the franchise for the casino, are English. The food and wine are superb.

Little conversation of any substance takes place between the Princess and me. After lunch, as we take our leave, she says: 'Today's lunch doesn't count.' She will see me for a long chat when she returns to Tehran. We fly back, and Majidi drops me off at the Hilton.

97

Saturday, August 6

Amir Abbas Hoveyda resigned today as Prime Minister of Iran after nearly thirteen years in office. In spite of all the rumours about its imminence, I must confess the resignation came to me as a surprise. I first learnt of it when the Prime Minister's secretary called at the office temporarily assigned to me in the annex building at 10 to say the PM 'definitely wants to see you at 4.45 today'. I naturally thought this meant he wanted to return my paper, along with his comments. I went to Mother's for lunch. Back at the office I met Farhad Nikoukhah, an adviser to the PM on press affairs, with whom I discussed the total inadequacy of the calibre of the men at our Ministry of Information, while he spoke of Savak's excesses in book censorship.

At 4.40 exactly, I went to Afsaneh's room, and when I saw that she was emptying desk drawers I sensed something was afoot. 'The day I leave this job,' Hoveyda had always insisted, 'I want my drawers emptied in less than an hour,' so that the phrase 'emptying the drawers' had over the years become synonymous with his departure from office.

'Is Hoveyda resigning?' I ask Afsaneh. She opens the door to the Prime Minister's room and, with a cryptic, vestigial smile, she says, 'Please go in.'

I see Hoveyda's profile as he sits behind his huge desk, feet on table, immersed in what I later discover is my paper.

'I see the drawers are being emptied,' I say as nonchalantly as I can. 'Have you resigned?'

'Don't you think it was about time?' he replies, with as placid an expression as I have ever seen him wear.

He had known, of course, about the persistent rumours, he tells me. Then, when he had been received by HIM at Nowshahr on Thursday, HIM had begun by saying: 'I want to have a talk with you today.' Taking the hint, Hoveyda had asked permission to speak first. After ranging over some of the recent political developments in the country he volunteered the view that new blood was needed if new solutions were to be found. The conversation had taken place in a most amicable atmosphere. Then, after about forty minutes or so, the Empress had walked into the room, 'I want you to meet the new Court Minister,' HIM had said to her, at which Hoveyda said he saw a tear glistening in her eye.

Hoveyda says the Empress's bureau had turned into a rival government and that it had become impossible for him to fire some of the ministers he wanted to. He had asked HIM for a year's sabbatical leave, but HIM had told him that, since the more sensitive issues of foreign policy were conducted not through the Foreign Ministry but through the Court Ministry, he wanted Hoveyda in that post. He and Alam, the Shah had told him, were his closest aides, and while praising Alam's loyalty he doubted whether Alam, in his present state of health, could continue for much longer. In any case, Alam had written to say he was too ill to carry on.

Hoveyda went on to say that, while it was right to have a change at the top, 'the problems will remain'. He confesses not to have any illusions about his future assignment. 'If the Government was corrupt, the Court Ministry is a nest of vipers,' he tells me. Amouzegar will succeed him as Prime Minister, although he hasn't been formally notified yet. The door buzzer goes. Afsaneh announces that Amouzegar is there. He comes in immediately and, after shaking hands with the Prime Minister, embraces me.

'Your paper is excellent', says Hoveyda, handing it back to me, 'only, when you refer to HIM, phrase it in the third person.' I stand up to take my leave, tempted to offer felicitations to Amouzegar, but say nothing.

A reporter friend in Afsaneh's room asks: 'Another re-shuffle?'

'Perhaps a little more this time,' I tell him.

Sunday, August 7

The papers are filled with accounts of Hoveyda's stepping down. I put the finishing touches to my paper and spend the rest of the day visiting friends.

Tuesday, August 9

Ahmad Ghoreishi comes to the office to cast a confidential glance over my paper. He pronounces it 'good but daring'. I say that in Tehran one tends to forget the constant flak directed at Iran in London, so that, while the paper may be daring, I intend to submit it, come what may.

'To a rational person', he says, 'it makes perfect sense.'

The change of government in Iran elicits a leader in *The Times*. There is criticism of Hoveyda and Majidi, but it is HIM who emerges as the villain of the piece.

I pick up the Princess in the evening from Sa'adabad Palace and go to Majidi's for dinner. The Hoveyda brothers are among the dozen guests. Amir Abbas oversteps his limited capacity for alcohol, and by the time, after dinner, Majidi's daughter has taken to singing Joan Baez[1] songs, which she does quite beautifully, the new Court Minister's snores become audible. Fereydoun wakes him up and sends him home.

Majidi himself is bitter about the events of the past few days which have cast him as the *mauvais sujet* of the obnoxious power cuts. He feels that, as the former director of the Budget Bureau, he has been made the scapegoat in a situation for which he was never responsible, and that he has been abandoned by all those who should have stood by him. When I say that I hear he may be posted to Paris as ambassador, he says he will 'never again' accept any government job. He smiles understandingly when I suggest that such categorical predictions ought not to be lightly made by politicians.

Thursday, August 11

I am to be received in audience by HIM today.

There is no one else in the Falcon for the fifteen-minute flight to the Caspian. At Nowshahr, an official car drives me to the pier on which the residence of the Royal Family is constructed. In the waiting room I exchange pleasantries with a number of Court officials and Imperial Guard officers. I wait calmly, judging myself to be neither unduly excited nor nervous. My name is finally called.

HIM is standing in the middle of the room, wearing an open-neck shirt and sports trousers. The great dane lies somnolently in a corner, but a cocker spaniel is running about. I bow, kiss his proffered hand and listen.

'What new things, apart from what we read in your reports, have you to tell us?' He turns his stern, unsmiling face away and starts his inevitable walk up and down the room, but this time he remains within my range of vision, so that I don't have to turn constantly to face him. Before I have a chance to reply, he adds: 'I can't understand this blind hostility towards us on the part of the British. Did you see *The Times* article? Do they mean to imply Alsthom[2] is blameless in all this?' He speaks about Iran's economic importance to Britain and, in a tone of injured innocence, asks what benefit the British derive from saying such things. I find myself in the

---

[1] The singer.
[2] The French company that had supplied the electric power generator whose malfunction the Iranian Government blamed for at least some of the blackouts.

thankless position of having to explain the attitude of *The Times*. I say that, while our relations with the Government and the business community are excellent, the Press *is* hostile.

'Westminster-type democracy is not exportable,' HIM intones. 'It can't even work in France.' He refers to some of the progressive legislation he has had enacted in Iran, which he maintains is more advanced than anything in England, or even Sweden. 'Their Western democracy isn't working, not even in England. It's become a degenerate form of government.'

To break the ice and to avoid plunging headlong into the more contentious issues in my 'paper', I mention George Weidenfeld's *Star Over Iran* project, describing George as 'a friend' but adding a caveat that, because of his unreconstructedly Zionist views, perhaps HIM would wish to bear in mind that, if our policy towards Israel should change, so might the book's attitude towards him.

'Our policy towards what kind of Israel?' the Shah asks rhetorically. 'An Israel bent on keeping the lands of others by force? Or an Israel that genuinely wants to live behind secure borders? The former is not acceptable – the latter is.' While I sense that the project of the book both flatters and interests him, he mutters something about a book being already in hand, and I am instructed to refer the matter to Hoveyda.

My information that Tony Parsons would have been sent as ambassador to Washington, had it not been for Peter Jay's appointment, both surprises and pleases him, and I see for the first time since the start of my audience an unfurrowing of his brow. 'It is becoming almost a tradition, with Ramsbotham first, and now Parsons.' 'Tehran has become an important assignment for the British,' he adds with some pride. 'It is as you say, Your Majesty,' I agree.

Striking, as it were, while the iron is hot, I seize the moment of relative good humour to mention my paper, which I describe as a public relations memo. As I am about to explain its contents, HIM interrupts to say I should give it to his Principal Secretary or to Hoveyda. He then mentions many of the human rights measures he has recently ordered and speaks of the Red Cross Commission and his talk with Ennals. I, in turn, specifically request him to read my paper, 'which is only ten pages', and he again tells me to hand it to Hoveyda. Suspecting by now that he may never learn of the contents of my memo, let alone read it in its entirety, I try to bring up some of its more salient features.

It is then that I commit my blunder. I say I hope HIM will forgive my presumption when I say that some of the techniques we

101

employ in our contacts with the media do not endear us to our audience, and add that while it is true, for instance, that the British have grown lazy and lost their former discipline, for HIM to say so on television will lose him the sympathy of his listeners. I know that I have touched a raw nerve, and I try to palliate his quite open irritation by making my remarks more general. 'Compliments,' I hear myself saying sententiously, 'are always more readily accepted than criticisms.'

'Compliments?' HIM repeats, anger in his voice. 'I can't pay them compliments if I don't believe in what I say. Maybe I shouldn't go on TV at all, then. I can't go on TV and praise a people who twice invaded my country and jeopardised its integrity.' He hesitates a moment, and then, as if he has suddenly found the solution, he says: '*You* pay them compliments. That's right – *you* sing their praises. That's what ambassadors are for.'

I stay a minute longer but I know the audience is over. HIM speaks briefly, and in general terms, about the identity of views between Iran and the UK on many issues, after which I am offered the Royal hand, which I kiss. I then withdraw, with a distinctly unpleasant taste in my mouth.

Shortly afterwards I fly back to Tehran wondering what, if anything, has been achieved. At the Hilton, I experience my first Tehran blackout. There is a complete power cut, beginning at 6.30 and lasting four hours. Looking out of my hotel window towards south Tehran, I see a forest of cranes standing idle in the dusk. With the air-conditioning off, the heat becomes oppressive in less than an hour, and there is no radio or television either. From my balcony, I can see an endless queue of cars stuck in a colossal traffic jam, their tail-lights shimmering in the evening heat, their horns sounding in protest against the extinction of all traffic lights. One can't even read. The ice has melted, so I sip warm vodka and try not to lose my temper.

Monday, August 15

Lunch with Khalatbary, the Foreign Minister. The only other guest is Amir Aslan Afshar, soon to be announced as the new Chief of Court Protocol. Afshar says the cause of much of the trouble we face abroad is our own boastfulness and says he regrets that Iran is now inextricably associated in Europe and America with the words 'Savak' and 'torture'. Until a few years ago he was proud to introduce himself as the Iranian Ambassador; now, he says, he is

102

very much on the defensive.

I give Khalatbary, for his information only, a copy of the paper I have given to Hoveyda, and tell him about my none too successful audience with HIM. Khalatbary is concerned about the massive demonstrations planned for HIM's forthcoming visit to Washington.

I see Tony Parsons at Cyrus Ghani's in the evening. He compliments me on my newly-established contacts with the Press in London, and I express the hope that because of the measures taken in Iran the worst of our troubles may be over. Sheila Parsons, next to whom I sit at dinner, admits to loathing Tehran and loving the countryside. She is critical of the policy of industrialisation and expresses her opposition in such strong terms that I interrupt to say at some stage that Iranians can't be expected to weave carpets all their lives simply to please English romantics. I gather from her that Tony may be posted to the UN, and she hates the idea of living in a flat.

Wednesday, August 17

Momentous political changes are taking place in Iran. The importance of HIM's decision to allow a degree of liberalisation cannot be exaggerated. But, as always in such cases, the question is how far to allow the lid to be lifted. Outwardly, at least, the papers are now more critical, and the ministers more open, about their problems. To the extent that the very expression of discontent diminishes its intensity, this is a good thing. The other side of the coin is that, as HIM has been all-powerful for so long, the finger of responsibility points inevitably, invariably and logically at him for every shortcoming.

The Government, and even the Mayor of Tehran, have now been changed. Amouzegar is bound to bring to his new responsibilities a freshness and dynamism which Amir Abbas, after his more than a dozen years in office, could not have been expected to demonstrate. At the same time, Hoveyda's reputation for financial probity will be a greatly needed asset at the Court Ministry.

In the Empress I feel a little disappointed. I had hitherto believed that her humility and human qualities provided a valuable combination which acted as a counterpoise to HIM's stern and arrogant image. I now suspect she is really quite lacking in any political sense and is beginning to show herself unhealthily receptive to the same sort of inordinate flattery that her husband so much enjoys.

I leave Tehran with an uneasy sense of expectancy about what lies ahead. I cannot dispel an almost physical feeling of promise and peril looming on the horizon.

Thursday, August 25

Back in London I lunch with Meshkinpoush, to whom I give a summarised version of my meetings and activities in Tehran. I also ask him to draft a cable to Tehran on Chapman Pincher's interview, which had appeared in the *Daily Express* of August 22 and which, despite Pincher's assurances, had quite annoyed me.[1] I make these points: 1) Rather than being, as he described me, an Anglophile, I would consider it honour enough to be described as an Iranophile; 2) that I had said very little about arms purchases, Pincher having himself interpolated that; 3) that 'power-mad despot' was his, rather than my, phrase; 4) that I had made no references to Pakistan directly. Another thing I hadn't said, but which I make no reference to in my cable, is the description of Amnesty International as a 'Communist-front organisation'.

Monday, September 5

I receive a letter from Martin Ennals about the Pincher interview, asking 'if you actually said to Mr Pincher that Amnesty International has been so penetrated by Communists that it is now a

[1] In his *Daily Express* article Chapman Pincher wrote:
Radji, an athletic, Cambridge-educated anglophile, had reassuring news. 'Iran has no intention of cancelling any orders for Chieftain tanks, Rapier missiles, ships or any other arms. . . . An astute career diplomat – he is the son of a modestly well-off surgeon – Radji seized the opportunity to ask why the Shah's regime is so sharply criticised in Britain when trade and government relations are so cordial.
'The Shah is projected as a power-mad despot when the record proves that no ruler works harder to create a stable, well-fed, well-educated and progressive society' . . .
Like the Shah himself Radji is particularly bitter about Amnesty International, which has singled out Iran for special abuse and he believes that it has been so penetrated by extremists that it is now a Communist-front organisation. . . .
What irritates him is the way that far more barbaric practices in other countries go uncondemned.
'Pakistan has recently introduced the amputation of hands for theft. Where is the uproar? In some Arab countries adulteresses are still stoned to death. Who says anything?'

104

Communist-front organisation'. Rather than reply formally, I ring him up to assure him I hadn't called Amnesty a Communist-front organisation and that I hadn't called them that when I was issuing circulars about them. I add that I had also not referred in the interview to Pakistan, nor had I described HIM as a 'power-mad despot'. Ennals accepts it all good-humouredly.

Tuesday, September 6

Mr Nehru, the Indian High Commissioner, is my guest at lunch. He is soon to retire and wants to drive back to Delhi through Iran. He says for the first few months after Mrs Gandhi's introduction of Emergency Rule things worked out extremely well – industrial production went up, there was greater social and industrial discipline, inflation was reduced and everyone was generally far better off. But then Mrs Gandhi 'lost touch with the people' and became surrounded by a gang of four that did cruel and savage things in her name, people who were 'corrupt to the marrow'. All safeguards against the exercise of arbitrary power disappeared, while the forced sterilisation programme created many instances in which people were compelled to pay exorbitant blackmail to officials.

We speak about Iran and his projected trip, and I say I would be pleased to write and have him looked after by people in Tehran. He strikes me as a highly intelligent, cultivated man, at odds with his bureaucratic-political superiors.

Tuesday, September 13

Mohammad Pourdad, the Iranian television organisation's representative in London, has left a message with my secretary that there has been an attempt on the life of Princess Ashraf in the south of France and that one of her companions has been killed and another wounded. I ring Juan les Pins immediately. Amir Etemadian is on the line, his voice and manner shaky. On the way back from Cannes in the early hours of the morning, he relates, a Peugeot had blocked their path along the deserted road just past Tétou near Golfe Juan. Two gunmen had walked over to their Rolls and fired seven shots at them. By ramming the Rolls into the rear of the Peugeot, he had forced the way open for their escape. He had been hit in the hand and shoulder, but his injuries were not serious. The Princess was now under sedation and the whole place was swarming with policemen.

After lunch I ring Juan les Pins again. The Princess comes on the line herself, her voice deliberately calm. She says the gunmen could not have been professionals, because if they had killed the driver the others in the car would have become stationary targets. She has spoken to HIM, who has asked her to return to Tehran immediately. That she has survived is a miracle, she says.

'I expect you will now say it's your visits to Mecca that have saved you,' I say.

'Of course.'

'Why should the attempt have been made at all if Mecca is so protective?' I ask her.

'Without the attempt, there could have been no miracle,' she calmly replies.

Wednesday, September 14

Go to David Frost's for lunch. We talk about Nixon, HIM and the film, *Crossroads of Civilisation*, that he is doing on and for Iran. He denies some Press reports that already the BBC has refused to show the series and says he hasn't even spoken to them yet.

Thursday, September 15

Today is Eid-e-Fetr, marking the end of the fasting month of Ramadan, and the Embassy is officially closed, which is why I receive Air Vice Marshal Frederick Sowrey, the newly-appointed UK Permanent Military Deputy to CENTO, for a courtesy visit at the Embassy residence. We talk about the impotence of CENTO, the deficiencies of NATO, and social and military priorities. A perceptive, well-informed individual, I think.

Sunday, September 18

Go with Liz to see David Frost's *Crossroads of Civilisation*. We are shown two of the eight-part series, one dealing with the emergence

106

of Cyrus the Great, the other with Safavid Isfahan. There is a lot of
ketchup in the simulated battle scenes in the first one, which makes
it less convincing, and excessive apologising for Western ignorance
of the true grandeur of Iran's civilisation. But it's all rather
beautifully filmed.

Tuesday, September 20

Pay a courtesy call on John Graham[1] at the FCO. He speaks about
Rhodesia, with which he is heavily involved, and of our cooperation
with the Anglo-American initiative. Graham is full of praise for
Tony Parsons and is himself generally very agreeable.

Lunch with Gerald Mansell at Bush House. I explain the recent
relaxation of the political grip in Tehran and, in reference to the
economy, say it was inevitable that we should reach an impasse,
but that from now on our planning will show greater realism, a
more gradualist and, perhaps, a more modest approach.

Mansell makes it abundantly clear that Charles Curran's replies
to my reproachful letters 'were not drafted at Bush House' and 'no
one here was consulted on them'. It is an informative and friendly
luncheon which ends in my extending an invitation to them, and to
their new Director-General, Ian Trethowan, to lunch at the
Embassy.

Wednesday, September 21

Lunch with Martin Ennals at Mark's. Martin likes good food and
enjoys his drink, and I decide to show him some of the advantages
of capitalistic life. But my real interest is to see if I can get some
favourable references to Iran in Amnesty's annual report, due to be
published shortly. Martin says references will be made to the
'positive responses' made by Iran. 'But,' he adds, 'you still won't
like it.'

I launch my attack. I tell him that when dealing with Iran he
should abandon his obsessive attachment to his liberal con-
ditioning and not try to judge a feudalistic Moslem society by what,
after all, are arbitrary standards. I emphasise that proper notice
should be taken of the changes that have been made and credit

[1] Deputy Under-Secretary of State at the Foreign and Commonwealth Office;
British Ambassador to Iran, 1979–80.

given for them. I conclude by telling him, in milder but unmistakably threatening tones, that unless acknowledgement is made of the improvements we may have to warn Tehran that Amnesty is inherently hostile to the Iranian régime, that all attempts to persuade Amnesty of the Government's good intentions are futile, and that we may thus find ourselves back on our old collision course. He promises to bear these points in mind, and I begin to think that I may have made a dent in his armour.

Thursday, September 22

There is a letter from Majidi, brimming over with warmth, understanding, friendship and concern over my own personal security, and lamenting that, after so many years of faithful and devoted service, it is hard to bear such harsh criticism of oneself from HIM

Mrs Amouzegar [wife of the Prime Minister] arrives, with Major Bahrami as security escort. She says she will be leaving on Sunday and is here for a strictly private visit.

Friday, September 23

Mrs Amouzegar telephones to say she's going into the Fitzroy Nuffield Hospital tomorrow and will be operated on on Sunday. It must be serious, I think to myself, if they want to operate so quickly.

Sunday, September 25

Amir Abbas [Hoveyda] rings from Tehran. 'Do you remember once saying that your conception of bliss was to be able to stay in bed until ten in the morning, drinking coffee and reading the *Herald Tribune* of the same day?'

'I remember.'

'Well, I am now in that position – except that the *Herald Tribune* is a day old.'

'I am delighted you like your job in the Court Ministry, Sir,' I say.

108

The Times has not published the letters sent in reply to its critical leader on the power cuts, and he wants to know whether I think it would be a good idea to buy space in *The Times* to state our case.

I say I shall consider carefully his suggestion but that off-hand I don't think it a good idea. There are other things one can do, such as complain to the editor, or to the Press Council, but to buy advertising space would be, in my view, 'to emulate Kim Il Sung'.[1] I promise to send him a memo as soon as I can.

Tuesday, September 27

Dr John Anderson, the specialist, tells me tests show an alarmingly high degree of calcium in my blood and that the condition can cause stones and permanent liver damage. He suggests I go in for two days of tests.

Pay a call on Mrs Amouzegar at Claridge's. While I am there her husband rings from Tehran and I am put on the line to speak to him. He wishes to thank me 'for all your help'.

An early night, with my stabbing back pain acutely present.

Wednesday, September 28

Peter Thorneycroft, back from a Cretan holiday, comes to lunch. He says: 1) The Tories are much encouraged by the public response to Mrs Thatcher's proposal to 'go to the people' if confrontation with the unions should paralyse the country; 2) Mrs Thatcher has asked Ted Heath to make an important speech on foreign policy at the Conservative Party Conference in a fortnight's time. This is a gesture of conciliation and 'if Heath says something positive, he can have almost any job in her [next] government'; 3) Ted now wants the Chancellorship of the Exchequer, though it is unlikely he will be given it; 4) A general election is unlikely until next year.

Friday, September 30

There is an article in the *Guardian*, front page, no less, suggesting

[1] President of the Republic of North Korea, much given to promotion of his policies through lavish full-page advertisements in the world Press.

that British Government policy with regard to violations of human rights by certain countries is under review, and that Amnesty International has submitted a report to the Foreign and Commonwealth Office about it. Iran, the article says, will be an important test case, as Amnesty has reported that 'incidents of capital punishment there have been on the increase in recent years'. I am absolutely furious. After all the steps that have been taken to bring about a genuine change of policy in the field of human rights in Iran, such statements from Amnesty are bound to be seen in Tehran as deliberately provocative, and so highly counter-productive. Before Tehran has time to issue me with impossible instructions I cable them the text of the article, and add that I shall immediately speak to Ennals and ask for the allegations to be either substantiated or withdrawn. To hell with Amnesty and its so-called objectivity!

Princess Alexandra comes to dinner. The evening has been arranged by Elizabeth of Yugoslavia, even though it is to mark what I suppose is Princess Alexandra's semi-official trip to Iran for the festival. Princess Alexandra says she has been briefed about Iran and knows 'all about Savak, which is your KGB'. She is, otherwise, easy, warm and delightful.

Sunday, October 2

Come across a phrase by Robert Lowell that seems appropriate for some reason: 'The light at the end of the tunnel is a locomotive coming in the opposite direction.'

Monday, October 3

See Princess Alexandra and the Duke of Kent off to Tehran.

Meshkinpoush is back, which is timely because of my hospitalisation on Wednesday. He will be leaving permanently in two months' time, he tells me.

I receive instructions from HIM to tell Ennals that 'since the re-establishment of contact with Amnesty, the organisation has been lying more and more about Iran'.

At the Korean National Day party at Claridge's John Leahy[1] tells me Tony Parsons had been summoned to the Iranian Foreign

[1] Head of Chancery, Tehran, 1965–68. Ambassador to South Africa since 1979.

110

Ministry about the *Guardian* article and that he had subsequently 'telephoned London', which I suppose is something extravagant for a British diplomat to do. I say I am amazed at Amnesty's stupidity in committing such a blunder just when Tehran was showing signs of flexibility.

Tuesday, October 4

Ian Trethowan, the new Director-General of the BBC, comes to lunch, bringing with him Gerald Mansell, Robert Gregson and Mark Dodd. A friendly and, for me, informative lunch in the course of which we discuss Rhodesia, South Africa, national liberation movements in and out of power, and Iran's infrastructural and manpower inadequacies.

Trethowan strikes me as a gentle and prudent individual to whom Mansell is an intellectual superior. I recount the *Guardian* – Amnesty episode. Mansell says if it gets taken up nationally he doesn't see how the BBC can stay out of it. Dodd says the BBC needn't stay out of it, but that if they should decide to give the matter coverage the views of the Embassy should also be expressed. I say that I ask for no more. I then say that, on my arrival in London, I had found three main problem areas: the BBC, Amnesty International and the Press, and that until this latest episode I had thought that the first two had begun to show signs of a turn-around. Dodd says the improved relations with the BBC owe much to my personal initiative, which pleases me enormously.

Wednesday, October 5

A strongly-worded cable arrives from Tehran instructing me to raise absolute hell over Amnesty's provocations and to write to all the papers about the organisation's unremitting and biased campaign against the Iranian régime. It also orders me to have the letters published as advertisements if the papers should refuse to allow them the light of day. Good God! My whole trip to Tehran, I now see, was an exercise in futility.

I ask Meshkinpoush to put his prudent prose to work to seek permission from Tehran to limit our counter-offensive to putting pressure on Amnesty to issue a retraction of their most recent allegations; to be allowed not to publish advertisements since

Amnesty's credibility is greater than ours; and permission to attack Amnesty when the 'natural occasion' – i.e. the publication of their annual report, due soon – presents itself.

Tehran's intemperate 'all-out war' response is typical of the mindless impulsiveness with which decisions are made and instructions issued. I ask Meshkinpoush to ring Ennals and put pressure on him to retract their allegations, seeing that as the easiest way out of the impasse.

I then go into hospital for tests.

Thursday, October 6

I see Meshkinpoush at 4 with the draft of the cable to Tehran. I make a number of suggestions, making the message stronger on the whole, but another meeting tomorrow is indicated.

Friday, October 7

Meshkinpoush comes over again in the evening to read me the revised cable. He warns me that he thinks it too strongly worded and says that what we are doing, in effect, is lecturing HIM on the human rights-dominated climate of opinion in the West, with the all too clear implication that for him to try to swim against the current is unwise. Meshkinpoush says that, since Tehran will probably again leave it to my discretion to take whatever action I think appropriate, I should leave out a certain controversial paragraph from the cable. I agree.

There is an article in the *Guardian* by Liz Thurgood in Tehran in which she says that a group of lawyers have written to the Government to protest against recent arbitrary changes in the Judiciary. They claim that, contrary to what is laid down by the Constitution, the Judiciary has been converted into an emasculated agent of the Executive.

Saturday, October 8

Meshkinpoush rings to say he spoke to Ennals yesterday, and that he (Ennals) had maintained it was impossible that anyone in a responsible position at Amnesty could have supplied the information to the *Guardian*. In reply to Meshkinpoush's insistence on Amnesty's issuing some form of denial, Ennals had replied that the Press was not above misquotation and had referred to my interview with the *Daily Express* as an example. When Meshkinpoush urged that this sort of behaviour endangered our dialogue, Ennals had promised to look into the source of the leak and to let us know. All this goes to Tehran in a cable, and I can only hope the issue is by now defused.

Monday, October 10

HIM replies, re the *Guardian*-Amnesty issue, in the following terms: 'Radji's reasoning is appropriate from the London point of view. In any case, he can do what he thinks fit for the moment. We shall wait and see.' I am not sure I understand fully what he means, but I am pleased. Meshkinpoush says HIM has obviously reached the absolute limit of his patience with us, but still appears, for all that, good-humoured. I should be relieved to have been given a free hand.

Amnesty International, I learn on the news, has been awarded the 1977 Nobel Peace Prize. Bloody hell! Maybe now Tehran will realise the pointlessness of taking on an organisation which, whether one likes it or not, is highly enough considered to get this sort of kudos. On the other hand, I suspect that from now on the degree of respectability in which Ennals is robed will border on the divine, and that it will be a brave man indeed who tries to challenge him.

Tuesday, October 11

Meshkinpoush, sporting a huge smile, walks into my office to say I did well to resist HIM's instructions to raise hell with Amnesty. Together we ponder our future strategy vis-à-vis Amnesty, and decide to reply to the contents of their forthcoming annual report with reason, information, statistics and, if possible, credibility.

Moinzadeh, Savak's representative in the Embassy, is my only guest to lunch. Even though he is on the same side I have an intrinsic distrust for someone engaged in his kind of work. The conversation is pretty bumpy, with me constantly reining in my true feelings behind a contrived façade of bureaucratic indifference. He says I must trust him as a friend, that he wishes me well, that he wants to help me in any way he can, and that he has told his superiors in Tehran that I am performing a truly valuable service to Iran. I embrace him as he leaves.

Wednesday, October 12

General Fereydoun Jam is my guest to lunch. It very soon emerges that his life is burdened with the tragedy of his only child – currently a drug addict.[1] Now twenty-one, his son 'has squandered his own youth and ruined his parents' lives', the General confides to me. The General himself appears mentally and emotionally ill-equipped to come to grips with his problem.

I try to steer the conversation away from his son's addiction. He gradually reveals the events that led to his dismissal as Chief of the Supreme Commander's Staff, and his being made ambassador in Madrid. He says the American military in Iran always spoke highly of him to HIM, and that one day the Chief US Military Adviser in Iran, General Seitz, had smilingly told him: 'I have just given you the kiss of death.' When Jam enquired what he meant, Seitz replied that he had just had an audience with HIM in the course of which he had said that Jam was the best general in the Shah's army. From then on, Jam said sadly, it seemed he could do nothing right. HIM was always finding fault with his performance, and yet, whenever a particular instance was investigated, it would be seen that Jam had acted properly, or had done something only after having first obtained the approval of HIM himself. But the unease and tension had persisted.

Then there came a day when, in the course of a meeting with the other service heads, General Jam had spoken of HIM's displeasure with the performance of certain sectors of the armed forces, adding that such observations on the part of HIM pained him not only professionally but also emotionally, because he 'not only respected HIM as his commander, but also loved him as a brother'.

That remark – patently innocuous, if not honest – had sealed his fate. Shortly before being received by HIM at one of his regular weekly audiences, Alam (the then Court Minister) had asked to see him. HIM was displeased, the general was told, with his 'impudence' in having spoken about the Shah 'as a brother'. He was not being asked to resign, the Court Minister had told him, but if he wished to do so his resignation would be accepted.

[1] The General's son has since been cured of his drug addiction.

114

A few days later, Ardeshir [Zahedi], then the Foreign Minister, had telephoned him at his home to say HIM had indicated that he should be posted to France as ambassador, or to any other country he wished. Jam had eventually been persuaded to ask for Spain, a post then vacant. He says his loyalty to HIM will never be in question and that he is deeply grateful for HIM's generosity. 'But I still don't know what I did wrong', he insists.

Thursday, October 13

Michael Conroy comes to lunch and brings with him Bernard Nossiter, the *Washington Post* bureau chief in London and author of that *grand guignol* article on Amirteymour's death. The luncheon is meant to be a reconciliation of sorts.

Nossiter's belief in the need for press freedom is his alpha and omega, as is his absolute conviction about the supremacy of the American way and its values over all others. He is a man for whom Truth has been revealed for all time; all that remains to be done is to universalise it. When I say – remonstrate, to be more exact – that I believe, honestly and with sincerity, that in a society like Iran's there ought to be certain constraints on individual freedom he stares at me blankly, making me feel – and say – that his mind is no longer open to argument. So we stick to neutral subjects. He says he had asked a prominent British banker about the enormous borrowing requirements of the British economy, and had been told that there was absolutely no cause for worry. 'Don't you see that when a country's debts have reached the level of ours, it's the creditors that have to worry?' he had been told.

Then there had been an episode when, as his paper's correspondent in Paris at the height of de Gaulle's *tout-azimuth* foreign policy, he had quizzed one of the President's tame *fonctionnaires* during a private luncheon about the French *force de frappe*. 'How', Nossiter had enquired sarcastically, 'do you intend to get your Mirages back once they have dropped their bombs on Moscow? Will you refuel them over Poland, for instance?'

'Haven't you understood, Monsieur Nossiter,' the French official had replied, 'that all the Mirages need do is to get to *Germany* and back?'

Nossiter speaks of Robert McNamara in the most scathing terms. 'He's a three-time loser – at Ford's, at the Pentagon, and now at the World Bank. To him, everything is a statistic.' McNamara had gone to the World Bank with a brief to do something to alleviate world poverty. Typically, he had placed the world's available food supply above the line as his numerator, and the world's population beneath it as his denominator, immediately concluding that if you cannot increase your numerator you must decrease your denominator. The whole exercise had collapsed around him in a shambles, of course, says Nossiter, because as everyone but McNamara seemed to know, the birth-rate is only reducible when living standards are raised considerably.

Is there anyone, I wonder when he is gone, that Nossiter really likes?

Friday, October 14

There is a circular from the Press Section of the [Foreign] Ministry, signed by Parviz Adl, instructing all embassies, if asked about Amnesty's prize, to say that the Nobel people had made a travesty of their function by awarding the prize to an organisation whose business is to invent and spread lies. There is no reference to a Royal directive and it is not at all clear who is responsible for the circular.

I reply, saying in essence that: 1) the circular's contents are at variance with HIM's instructions giving *me carte blanche* to deal with Amnesty as I judge appropriate; 2) that, as I have been at pains to point out in previous cables, fighting Amnesty will not produce 'victories'.

Meshkinpoush remarks that, if the instructions in the circular should turn out after all to have the seal of Royal approval, the least I can expect is severe rebuke.

Monday, October 17

Kakhi [Political Counsellor at the Embassy] comes to see me on routine Embassy business. There is something he wants to tell me, he says somewhat anxiously, before leaving. While he was walking along the Portobello Road on Saturday money was being collected for Amnesty International, and he had contributed. 'I thought that if some day I was languishing in the corner of some dark and damp prison for my beliefs, I would want someone, at least, to think of me.' He pauses a moment, then asks: 'Did I do wrong?'

'One never does wrong to follow one's conscience,' I say, rather pompously, I suppose, 'but I do think you are naive.' I assure him, nevertheless, that I shall keep his secret.

Tuesday, October 18

There is a letter from Martin Ennals in the *Guardian* to the effect that Amnesty International had not claimed that the number of executions 'had risen in Iran recently', but that, according to the Iranian Government's own statistics, the number of political activists killed 'while resisting arrest' had increased.

I reflect, not without a measure of satisfaction, that the approach I had suggested to Tehran for dealing with the *Guardian*-Amnesty episode has been justified. I had resisted HIM's instructions to 'disgrace' Amnesty and, rather than having our denial of their allegations printed as an advertisement, I had sought permission to bring pressure on Ennals himself to issue a denial. Now, notwithstanding HIM's sarcastic observation about 'Radji's London point of view', the goods, as it were, have been delivered.

Wednesday, October 19

Attend a giant-size reception at the Spanish Embassy in Belgrave Square for the visiting Spanish Prime Minister. I see Callaghan, Owen, Michael Foot amongst members of the Cabinet there. Marcus Sieff[1] praises the Shah, but says, 'Your public relations are a disaster.'

Thursday, October 20

Michael Weir comes to lunch. Tony Parsons, he says, will be offered the United Nations after Tehran. I ask who will replace Tony in Tehran. That, he says, hasn't yet been decided.

'Any front runners?' I ask.

'Many.'

'Like yourself?' I persist.

'I'd be honoured if offered it,' he says.

[1] Chairman of Marks and Spencer.

Friday, October 21

A cable from Martin Ennals asking for information on an Iranian held by Savak who allegedly is being tortured. I notify Tehran immediately and await their reply.

Dr Anderson tells me the tests made in hospital show that I am a healthy man and that my affliction must be skeletal. He recommends a certain Dr Cyriax. Dr Cyriax diagnoses a broken cartilage as the probable cause of my back pain, and gives a number of quite powerful jolts to my skeletal structure. The cracks are audible.

There is a persistent rumour in Tehran that HIM now visits a crony's house three times a week in the afternoons to smoke opium. The principal reason for this new pastime is his estrangement from Farah. Princess Ashraf knows all this, apparently, but can do nothing about it. I learn also that HIM has told members of the Royal Family that they are 'on their own' and should not look to him for physical or financial security.

Good heavens! I think. This sort of activity can't be kept secret for long, and the first to learn of it would be those young and dedicated Army officers who stand guard outside while the pipe is being prepared inside. What a nefarious influence the Shah's close associates have been on him. Is this the beginning of the end, I ask myself. My mood blackens and I become depressed.

Monday, October 24

I receive a reply from Tehran confirming the arrest of the brother of the man named in Ennals's cable, accusing him of 'anti-state activities' while in the United States, emphatically denying the use of torture, and expressing regret over Amnesty's obsession with defending 'political activists' who are really terrorists. Then it adds, for my information only, that the Red Cross is investigating the conditions of political detainees in Iran for a second time. 'Would we, at the time of such a visit,' asks the telegram rhetorically, 'resort to torturing prisoners?'

My God! Maybe we are beyond redemption.

Tuesday, October 25

Lord Michael Fitzalan-Howard,[1] in morning dress, arrives in a huge car displaying the Royal Insignia to convey Her Majesty's felicitations on HIM's birthday (the next day).

Lieutenant-General Bakhshi Azar, *de passage* in London, pays me a courtesy visit. An informed and articulate man, not frightened to speak his mind, which he does intelligently. He says the gap between the intelligence of those who have to operate our military equipment, and the degree of sophistication of that equipment, is huge.

Wednesday, October 26

Today is the Shah's 57th birthday. Some two hundred and fifty people, including five Cabinet Ministers, Foreign Office seniors, Lord Mountbatten, prominent compatriots, fellow diplomats and media people come for a midday reception of champagne and caviar.

There is another interesting and disturbing article in the *Guardian* by Liz Thurgood. It speaks of yet another Letter addressed to the Prime Minister by lawyers and writers, protesting against violations of the Constitution. Things are obviously moving fast in Iran and HIM must be under tremendous pressure. At the bottom of my heart I welcome this loosening of the iron grip, but I hope that HIM's liberalisation remains controlled and controllable.

I receive a memo from Shahram Chubin[2] about the [American] Administration's mood with regard to Iran on the eve of the Shah's visit to Washington. He says that we need representation in Washington of a more serious calibre, and that we shouldn't push our request for an additional 150 F16s during this visit. I forward the memo to Tehran.

Thursday, October 27

Another article in the *Guardian* about human rights improvements in Iran, this one by Jonathan Steele in Washington. I am very

[1] Marshal of the Diplomatic Corps.
[2] A specialist in defence with the International Institute of Strategic Studies.

pleased, but I tell myself I mustn't be so impressionable as to become dejected on reading bad reports about Iran or euphoric on reading good ones.

I dine at the Spenders. Lord and Lady Longford, Al Alvarez, Cyrus Ghani and Lizzie the others. It is an enjoyable evening given mostly to literary gossip. Longford says he had once asked Evelyn Waugh to lunch with him. Lord Beveridge had been the other guest. He and Waugh never got on, and no luncheon party could have been a greater disaster. In the course of the lunch Waugh had asked Beveridge whether he had any ambitions. Beveridge, somewhat startled by the directness of the question, had replied that he hoped to leave the world a better place than he found it. Beveridge had then brought himself to ask Waugh the same question. 'My sole ambition,' Waugh had replied gleefully, 'is to spread gloom and despondency, and I shall have far greater success than you.' What a delightful creature Elizabeth Longford is!

Saturday, October 29

At Tony Palmer's insistence, I go with him to see Queen's Park Rangers play West Bromwich Albion. It's a dull, chilly day, but the fans are out in force. There is, of course, an entire ritual of movements and utterances associated with the game of football. There are, for example, ear-piercing cries of 'C'mon you R's!' which Rangers supporters, in whose ranks we are seated, frequently let out. To my uninitiated ears this sounds like 'Come on, you arse!' And the Rangers' goalkeeper must be named Phil something-or-other because, every time he makes a save, the voices of QPR rise, as in a Greek chorus, to a crescendo to announce confidently that 'Phil was there!'

On our way back, we pass a large demonstration by anti-Shah Iranians in Kensington High Street, which Tony, engrossed in explaining the intricacies of the football league system, seems, thank goodness, not to notice.

Friday, November 4

Lunch with Kenneth Rose at the Embassy. Rauh, my speech-writer-cum-Press-spokesman, describes Rose as a columnist and an historian who, since the days of Ardeshir, has been associated with the Embassy either socially or at times even as a speech-writer.

Rose is an admirer of Alec Douglas-Home, not only for his political attributes but, even more, for his human qualities of compassion and loyalty. He refers to the Queen Mother admiringly, to Princess Margaret understandingly and to the Kents as close personal friends.

He speaks at some length about the manner in which the Duke takes his responsibilities in promoting British trade and exports seriously, and of the Duchess's meticulous attention to the details of the public statements she is called upon to make from time to time. He is full of praise for Princess Alexandra.

Rose does not admire Wilson, 'who is now totally discredited by his Honours List and the Crossman Diaries'. When he says that 'Wilson used to set such great store by what the papers said, but, as you know, what the papers say today is forgotten tomorrow', I begin to see similarities to my own condition. He speaks affectionately but not uncritically of Iran, and remembers his chat with Hoveyda during which, incidentally, we first met.

Hossein Eshraghi, on his way to Tehran from Mexico and Washington, tells me that Ardeshir is busy planning and preparing for counter-demonstrations during HIM's visit to Washington. The dissident groups are already claiming that more than 2,000 Iranians have been paid $100 a head, plus hotel accommodation, to put on a pro-régime show of strength when the Royal couple arrive.

Monday, November 7

A lengthy interview with HIM by Arnaud de Borchgrave appears in the *Herald Tribune*, which quite pleases me. HIM speaks of his anxiety over the West's inactivity in the face of Communist advances in Africa. Other points he makes: 1) He will not push for a rise in the price of oil, American pressure not to do so being implicit in his remaks; and 2) there are now only 2,500 political prisoners in Iran.

Charlie Douglas-Home, who lunches with me at the Embassy, pronounces the interview first-rate and says he wishes *The Times* [of which newspaper he is the Foreign Editor] could sometimes have such interviews.

Thursday, November 10

Moinzadeh, my Savak Chief, tells me extensive preparations are underway for demonstrations at all Iranian Embassies in protest against HIM's visit to Washington on Tuesday. 'Change your daily routine,' he counsels, 'and be extra cautious.'

Saturday, November 12

A nasty article in the *Guardian* by Liz Thurgood in Tehran, which speaks of the police attacking Tehran University students and breaking many jaws and ribs. This incident, she concludes, sets back everything that had been done to promote human rights in Iran over the past year.

Sunday, November 13

HIM arrives in Paris en route to the States amid newspaper reports of 'rent-a-crowd' demonstrations arranged by the Embassy in Washington. In the early afternoon about a hundred people, wearing masks and carrying placards, march past the Embassy shouting, 'The Shah is a murderer!' There are as many policemen as there are demonstrators.

The *Sunday Telegraph* has published an Embassy letter claiming the number of political prisoners in Iran to be what the Shah says it is, i.e. 'below 2,500', and not the '20,000 to 100,000' that Amnesty thinks it could be.

Monday, November 14

The newspapers are filled with reports from Washington about the Shah's visit, where they speak of 'Vietnam-type' security operations in progress, 'rent-a-crowd', and the possibility of clashes between rival [Iranian] factions. Reports from Tehran speak of letters being circulated amongst Iranian liberals and foreign journalists, demanding 'an end to absolutism', respect for the Constitution and the abolition of Savak – measures which, the

Herald Tribune says, if implemented, 'would dismantle the Shah's régime'.

I worry about the situation in Iran. There is a sudden resurgence of political activity which surely has no parallel since 1963. The manifesto of those demonstrating outside the Embassy yesterday supports Khomeini, 'who played a role in the enlightenment of the people', while letters in the *Guardian* are from supporters of the late Dr Mossadeq and his still surviving National Front.

If liberalisation could be moderate, gradual and contained, it would be an immense blessing. Surely we have overdone the arms purchases and tolerated for too long Savak's state-within-a-state. Yet I have not the slightest doubt that the rule of the mullahs – if, God forbid, it should ever come to that – would in one year set us back fifty.

Demonstrations are expected in front of the Embassy tomorrow and the day after.

Tuesday, November 15

Sir Anthony Royle gives me lunch. Julian Amery, back from Washington, praises HIM's Borchgrave interview. He says the mistake Carter is making is to try actually to do the things he promised the electorate he would do if elected. It would have been far wiser to wait a year before doing anything, by which time the electorate would have forgotten half the promises.

Ronald[1] drives me back to the Embassy. There are no signs of any demonstrators. 'Oh, they came and went, Sir,' says Mr Strong, the Embassy's commissionaire. 'About sixty of them.'

At a reception at the Belgian Embassy, Clive Bossom comes over to 'express regret over the ugly scenes in Washington', which is the first intimation I have that something has gone wrong. The Dutch Ambassador, too, commiserates. With a *che sara, sara* sort of air he tells me: 'We all have our problems.'

I rush back to the Embassy. The nine o'clock news shows Their Majesties and the Carters wiping away tears during the White House welcoming ceremonies. In order to disperse rival groups of demonstrators the police had thrown tear-gas bombs, the fumes of

[1] Ronald Morris, the Embassy chauffeur, now in his forties, has been a faithful and trusted Embassy general factotum from his early boyhood. Until recently a member of the staff of the London Mission – now the Embassy of the Islamic Republic of Iran – he was among the group of hostages who survived the notorious six-day siege of the Embassy by Arab opponents of the Khomeini régime in March 1980.

which drifted unexpectedly in the direction of the reception platform.

Wednesday, November 16

Sympathy is not a sentiment I readily feel towards HIM, but the sight of his face buried in a handkerchief to protect his eyes against the tear-gas induces a visceral twinge. The newspapers are filled with pictures and accounts of the violence generated in Washington by the Royal visit, with the *Guardian* taking some sort of a prize for tasteless punnery with a headline that reads: 'The Shah's Welcome is a "Gas".'

On my way back from lunch at the Embassy's Cultural Section, I pass a group of Iranians demonstrating outside the American Embassy. An hour later, they reach the Embassy, shout their protests, hand in their petitions and disperse.

Friday, November 18

I lunch with Sir Michael Stewart[1] and George Jellicoe[2] at Brooks. Sir Michael and his wife, Damaris, are off to Tehran on Monday as guests of Hoveyda. I tell him he will find the political climate in Tehran now noticeably different from what it was when he was there three years ago. When I mention HIM's 'noisy but successful' visit to Washington, he says confidently, 'The noise is not important.' I say I would love to agree with him, but that it seems to me that it is the 'noise' that forms public opinion. He says that it is the height of folly to try to apply Western liberal standards to societies to which they bear not the slightest relevance.

Wednesday, November 23

Two articles – in yesterday's *Herald Tribune* and today's *Guardian* – describe [Iranian] 'workers' as having attacked groups of 'anti-state' intellectuals. Both papers speak of 'Government violence of a savage nature'.

[1] British Ambassador to Greece, 1967–71.
[2] Leader of the House of Lords, 1970–73.

124

All that painstaking effort – through our numerous contacts with the Press, with MPs and the BBC to present the Government's case as something credible if in some respects heavy-handed – must surely go down the drain in the wake of such indefensible acts of hooliganism.

Thursday, November 24

Another article in the *Guardian*, this time speaking of further attacks by 'Government-organised thugs', transported in United Bus Company vehicles to beat up 'unarmed and peaceful demonstrators' while shouting *Javid Shah*! [Long live the Shah]. Religious ceremonies for the observance of Eid-e-Ghorban have been cancelled without explanation.

Lunch with Alireza and Mina Arouzi and Haleh Bakhash. My preoccupation with the escalating violence in Tehran is total and I am in a foul temper. When someone tries to offer an explanation of what is happening I reject it out of hand: 'We are all chiefs – there are no Indians,' I tell them irritably.

I send a long and carefully documented cable in reply to an enquiry from Hoveyda, in which I say that, after a thorough examination of the BBC's coverage of HIM's visit to Washington, I do not share the opinion that the BBC has shown bias or hostility.

Friday, November 25

Yet another 'thugs attack' article, this one in the *Herald Tribune*. I cable the piece to Hoveyda in code, ending with the suggestion that if the police, rather than 'non-official groups displaying spontaneous patriotism', should intervene to disperse the demonstrators, the Western press might have less reason to comment on events in Tehran with so much hostility. Even evil must have credibility.

Meshkinpoush says he is duty-bound to tell me that my cable constitutes direct interference with the work of the security services in Iran and is clearly not a part of my function as head of the London mission. That, I tell Meshkinpoush, is exactly why I am sending the cable through Hoveyda, whom I rely on to stand up for me, should HIM decide on my immediate recall.

I learn that Dr Eghbal, the Chairman of NIOC and a former

Prime Minister, has died of a stroke in Tehran at the age of 68. It was in his government that Father was a minister, and memories of his long association with my family, particularly during my early adolescence, flood my mind.

Majid Rahnema comes an hour ahead of my other dinner guests for a chat. He says HIM is now caught in a terrible dilemma. If he wants to stamp out the present wave of dissent, even more ruthless repression would be needed than has been used so far. On the other hand, if he has genuinely decided to allow some measure of liberalisation, it is hard to see how he can keep it within bounds. Both paths, Rahnema believes, are fraught with grave dangers. HIM is now divorced from reality and surrounded by people who tell him only what he wants to hear.

Saturday, November 26

I discover to my horror that my 'thugs attack' cable has by mistake been sent to the Foreign Ministry and not to A.A.H., as I had instructed. But my anxiety quickly abates as I read the text of HIM's reply. In a tone that is unmistakably defensive and betrays injured innocence, it says: 'The National Front's rule of Iran was enforced by martial law without one single day's exception; and if a collection of known Communists seeking to bring about political disruption must now be described as human rights activists, then I have nothing more to say.'

I ponder HIM's reply the entire day, finally convincing myself that I should write a letter to the Foreign Minister, intended specifically for the Shah, in which I would reiterate my non-Communist, non-National Front, pro-Shah loyalties, but would add that criticism of the Government's manner and methods of combating dissent should not be interpreted as a defence of dissent.

Sunday, November 27

Hajebi, a courtier friend from Tehran, comes to have lunch and to bring me up-to-date on the latest gossip and scandals in the Royal Court in Tehran. In the middle of our meal, the front-doorbell rings and Abbas [the Ambassador's valet] says it's General Jam. He comes in, in a state of extreme agitation, to ask my help 'as the representative of His Imperial Majesty in England', to do some-

126

thing about the condition of his son, who, having been refused money, had begun to abuse his parents. I am grateful for the presence of Hajebi, who has known Jam for far longer than I have, which rescues me from the awkward solemnity with which I would have otherwise felt compelled to act.

I say that, unless he mends his ways, I could consult the Embassy lawyers to see if the boy could be certified in need of help and committed to a suitable institution for treatment. I suggest that the long-term solution must surely be to change the boy's environment by, for example, sending him to an army camp in Tehran where close supervision and hard discipline could perhaps help in his rehabilitation. The sight of a four-star general, his lips quivering and his eyes filled with the tears he fights to hold back, is difficult to watch. But his problem is real and he deserves sympathy and help.

Monday, November 28

The *Guardian* has an article entitled 'Shah Wins First Round Against Dissidents', which concludes that the dissident movement in Iran is a powerful force which, though cowed for the moment, cannot be ignored for the future.

Write a long letter to AAH, enclosing copies of recent exchanges with the Foreign Ministry and HIM, again protesting not so much at the principle of the thing but at the manner in which Tehran's bully-boys break up demonstrations. I say it is absolutely essential, if we are to win the sympathy of the public in our fight against terrorism, that we do not ourselves resort to terrorism.

Tuesday, November 29

At the Yugoslav National Day reception a somewhat flustered Iraqi Chargé d'Affaires tells me that a more traitorous act than Sadat's journey to Jerusalem has never been committed in the history of the Arab peoples. His heart had sunk, he says, watching Sadat lay a wreath on the tomb of the Israeli Unknown Soldier, who, in all probability, had died killing Egyptians.

Wednesday, November 30

In a front-page story the *Guardian* says the Student Section of our Embassy has paid a certain social science lecturer at Kent University by the name of Hale to compile for Savak a list of Iranian students in the UK.

I check with Dashti, the head of the Student Section; with Khonsari, who handles students' affairs in Europe, and with Savak. The Ministry of Science and Higher Education has indeed asked for such a list for the purpose of drawing up their budgetary and manpower requirements. Rauh drafts a letter which we send off to the Editor of the *Guardian*. I am convinced the Ministry's request does not have the sinister implications the paper attributes to it and to the Embassy's Student Section. But, as always with the Press, the damage has been done.

Thursday, December 1

The Begum Eskandar Mirza rings to say that Ava Gardner, her neighbour in Ennismore Gardens, who these days is rarely given to going out, will be having a drink with her on Saturday, and would I care to join them. I accept without the slightest hesitation, and get Rauh to write one of his charming letters to the people whose guest for dinner I would have been on Saturday, pleading the untimely arrival of a minister from Tehran for my inability to attend.

Friday, December 2

The *Guardian* reports that a number of MPs have asked David Owen formally to protest to the Iranian Ambassador over the activities of Savak agents in compiling lists of Iranian students in the United Kingdom 'for political purposes'. I speak to Michael Weir, assuring him of the total inaccuracy of the report and enclosing copies of our correspondence with the *Guardian* on the matter. Copies also go off to Martin Ennals.

Saturday, December 3

At six in the evening, I tart myself up and proceed forthwith to the Begum's. Ava Gardner and an English actor, Charles Gray, are already there. As soon as I discreetly can, I feast my eyes on Ava's face. She is still beautiful, with a lovely skin, dyed auburn hair and dark blue eyes. She is elegantly dressed in what I surmise is a Valentino two-piece suit, and is sipping champagne. Gray is a large man with a huge mouth and ash-blond hair, a prototype for the Nazi heavies he is frequently called upon to portray in films. After several drinks and much animated conversation the Begum suggests we go to Mr Chow's for dinner. Ava doesn't particularly want to but, after taking her dog for a walk and changing into jeans and boots, she consents to come.

She is surprised at my knowledge of her past life and says I look like James Mason. Four-letter words are introduced into the vocabulary of the evening at a fairly early stage. After dinner, of which she has very little, Ava invites us back to her flat. More drinks are served. We listen to Billie Holliday records and I eventually go home.

Sunday, December 4

Some sports commentator on the BBC World Service has apparently expressed 'surprise' that Iran has made its way to the quarter-finals of the World Football Cup, and HIM's anger knows no bounds. We are instructed to protest strongly to the BBC for the anti-Iranian bias shown by the use of the word 'surprise'.

Tuesday, December 6

Attend a loan-signing ceremony (for $680 million) at the Carlton Tower Hotel for Iran's Transport and Petrochemical Companies.

Kakhi comes by a copy of Amnesty International's annual report, due shortly for general publication. I read the chapter on Iran eagerly. No cases of torture in 1977 are given, while there are repeated references to Ennals's audience with HIM, to the release of political prisoners, and to Amnesty's contacts with our Embassy. I think that, perhaps for the first time, we come out not dishonourably. I telex to Tehran the chapter on Iran *sans* comment.

Thursday, December 8

There is a blistering attack by Parviz Adl, the Foreign Ministry's spokesman, on David Owen for remarks he made on the human rights situation in Iran in the course of a debate in the Commons. As far as I can make out, the Foreign Secretary had spoken about an *improvement* in the human rights situation, but the Adl philippic must have been ordered by HIM, who would regard *any* reference to the human rights situation in Iran by a British Foreign Secretary as an impudent intervention.

Friday, December 9

I speak to Farhad on the telephone. Tehran he says, is beginning to rumble- with a decidedly religious tone. He sounds desperately unhappy with life in Tehran, saying he gave the country his best and that it has come to nothing! 'There is no point in going on punishing myself for the rest of my life.' America, he indicates, is his only alternative. I don't discourage him.

Sunday, December 11

Wake up to see, on the front page of the *Sunday Times*, that David Holden has been murdered in Egypt. What a terrible loss.

Monday, December 12

Ruth Holden, David's widow, rings to thank me for my letter of condolence. 'I console myself because of two things,' she says. 'One, that the bullet came from behind so that he couldn't have seen it; the other, that there was only one bullet, so that he died instantly. And there is no doubt in my mind that the motives were political.'

'You are a remarkable and courageous woman,' I tell her.

Lunch with my newly-arrived colleagues from Tehran, plus Mohammad Pourdad, of Iran Radio and Television, and Kamshad. Meshkinpoush says that the reverberations in the Western press of events in Tehran are more exaggerated than the events themselves, and that everyone is far too busy making money to worry about politics.

Wednesday, December 14

Lunch with M. H. Fisher, Editor of the *Financial Times*, and one of his senior foreign correspondents, Richard Johns. David Holden, Sadat's courage, the aborted Rhodesian talks and Iran's slower rate of economic growth are the topics of discussion.

Thursday, December 15

Anthony Howard, Editor of the *New Statesman*, and Robert Stephens of the *Observer*, are my guests to lunch at Princes Gate. Stephens, who is the more knowledgeable of the two about the Middle East, is *au fond* more enamoured of Arab presidents than Persian monarchs, and his dislike of the Shah, though wrapped in courteous language, is quite obvious. Howard wants to know 'why you harass your students abroad', and I do what I can.

Friday, December 16

David Pallister, the *Guardian* reporter who 'revealed' the story about the student list being prepared, comes to lunch at the Embassy, and to counter-balance his presence I also invite Peter Gill of the *Daily Telegraph*. Gill is, to my mind, by far the more sympathetic of the two. He admits to being 'unfashionably an admirer of the Shah', and wants to know about the finances of the Royal Family. Pallister declaims, rather than asks, about Savak's activities in Britain, and compares the Shah's 'enlightened measures' in Iran to the 'enlightened measures of white South Africans'. The exchanges are long and frequently pungent, but I hold my own.

Sunday, December 18

Lunch with Parviz Mina at Princes Gate. He is on his way to Caracas for the OPEC conference. He predicts a freeze in the oil price. What does worry me, however, given his normal reticence and circumspection, is his deep gloom about the outcome of the economic recession in Iran.

Wednesday, December 21

Go to cocktails at Lord Michael Fitzalan-Howard's. Members of his family, plus a good many diplomats are there, including the Jordanian Ambassador, who says he has serious reservations about the Sadat initiative. When I say that many Egyptians believe that enough of their compatriots have been killed for a cause which isn't really even theirs, I touch a raw nerve.

'We lost the West Bank because of Nasser's empire-building dreams,' he says agitatedly. When I butt in to say that Sadat is not Nasser, he protests that, when King Hussein proposed that the West Bank should be federated with Jordan, 'even before Golda Meir had had a chance to speak Sadat shot down the plan, broke off diplomatic relations with Jordan, and called King Hussein a traitor'. Hussein was with Sadat four days before the Jerusalem journey was announced, the Ambassador goes on, and wasn't even given a hint of it. 'Now, of course, Sadat is begging my King to support his peace initiative,' he says, his voice heavy with sarcasm.

Thursday, December 22

I take Lizzie out to dinner at Odin's and tell her about a dream I have had. I have been making love to a tart whose physical appearance revolts me: short-cropped platinum hair with orange patches, pink lips, tobacco-stained teeth, heavily made-up eyes and bitten fingernails; and somehow, in the act of love-making, I have inadvertently broken her neck and killed her. I have been tried and condemned to thirty years in jail, and the sentence begins tomorrow. There is absolutely no way, I tell Farhad, who is around for some reason, that I am going to go to jail because of that whore for the next thirty years. 'I haven't even seen *South America* yet,' I tell him, as though it were the thing I should miss most in life. I have made up my mind to kill myself and everything is settled in my mind, almost. There's one question to which I demand a scientific or medical answer: which is the less painful – shooting myself through the heart or through the mouth?

Lizzie says she's surprised I don't protest or appeal against the verdict of the court. She interprets the dream as a manifestation of my dislike of certain aspects of my job, which I have to accept without protest. She equates my revulsion at the prostitute's features with my dislike of the masked demonstrators who are always haunting the Embassy.

Saturday, December 24

Lizzie, I have insisted, must go and have a proper Christmas dinner, while I stay at home and relax. My friend Mohsen Tayebi comes to dinner. We drink champagne while discussing all the juicy gossip of Tehran. The Princess's parties are no longer attended by Their Majesties because the Queen doesn't like going there any more. Competition between sister and wife is acute. Mohsen says the rumours about HIM smoking opium are untrue, and that after the Princess has spent vast sums on renovating her Sa'adabad palace, it looks perfectly ghastly.

Sunday, December 25

Wake up late and the absence of newspapers provides the first reminder that it is indeed Christmas Day.

From the radio news I learn that King Hussein will meet President Carter in Tehran, that Charlie Chaplin is dead, and that an Iranian general convicted of spying for the Soviet Union has been executed. His case attracted a lot of international attention, and it was known that his fate hung on the Shah's clemency. This was denied him. We are our own worst enemies.

Another confidential circular from the Foreign Ministry warns that 'misguided and adventurist elements' may be up to no good during the period of Carter's visit to Tehran, and advises the taking of 'all necessary precautions'.

Monday, December 26

Packing for my Paris trip with Lizzie is interrupted by a furious
cable from Tehran instructing me to 'protest to the British
Government, to the BBC, to Ennals for the damage he (Ennals) is
spreading,' – the 'damage' in question being a remark made by
Joan Baez in the course of a late-night BBC interview when she is
reported as saying: 'The Shah watches as women and children are
killed before his eyes.' I speak to Meshkinpoush, who assures me he
will do what is necessary.

We fly to Paris, which is just as cold and windy as London, and
proceed to the Plaza. After a drink at a gloomy and deserted Bar
Anglais, we feast ourselves on oysters at the Brasserie Lorraine.

Wednesday, December 28

I stay in bed to read the *Herald Tribune* – *of the same day* – until
eleven, when I hear on the radio that a bomb has caused severe
damage to the US Cultural Centre in Tehran. An apostrophe on
the coming Carter visit, obviously. Also see that Moshe Dayan has
been to Tehran.

Saturday, December 31

I see from the *Guardian* that Iran's business community is to
boycott Danish and Italian goods because the Danish and Italian
governments have been too lenient with the protesting Iranian
opposition groups which have broken into our embassies. I also
read that a group of American publishers have asked Carter, who
arrives in Tehran today, to obtain permission for Gholam Hossein
Sa'edi, a Persian writer, to leave the country.

1978

Sunday, January 1

The year begins for me rather early. At 1.40 a.m. there is a telephone call from a police officer at Scotland Yard telling me that a car bomb in the West End has just killed the Third Secretary at the Syrian Embassy and would I instruct my staff to be extra vigilant, to take all possible precautions, and to report any suspicious circumstances. I ring the Embassy and Consular officers who are meant to be on duty, and of course neither of them is at home. I go back to sleep.

The news is that Carter has agreed, subject to Congressional approval, to sell Iran six to eight nuclear reactors. I imagine HIM is highly chuffed. News films show Ardeshir sitting on HIM's right and the Foreign Minister on his left throughout the discussions – all on account of Ardeshir's Taj Class I,[1] I suppose.

Monday, January 2

Andrew Whitley reports [from Tehran] that HIM has said Iran will not stand idly by if Ethiopia attacks the recognised boundaries of Somalia. Whitley speculates that assistance by us to Somalia in the form of heavy armaments, perhaps even the despatch of an expeditionary force, may well be possible. We are spreading our tentacles far and wide, it would appear.

Tuesday, January 3

Liz Thurgood, in the *Guardian*, describes Carter's visit to Iran as 'a diplomatic coup for the Shah'. Not only have the controversial nuclear reactors been promised; not only has Iran been given a virtually free hand in the Horn of Africa; not only has America's commitment to Iran's military defence been clearly reiterated, but Carter has declared that with no other leader does he feel 'a closer personal relationship' than with the Shah. 'Human rights,' says the article, 'were not discussed.' Good for HIM!

---

[1] Iran's highest civilian decoration which accorded protocol privileges to the holder.

Thursday, January 5

I lunch with Moinzadeh at PG. My local Savak guru is pleased that 'we in London' haven't suffered the same fate as the Embassies in Rome and Copenhagen, and that 'the boys' [dissident Iranian students] have been kept quiet. He says that in July, when his London assignment ends, he wants to go back to Tehran to resume his Army career, because 'in this job, if things go well no one thanks you, but if anything goes wrong all hell breaks loose'. Some forty people wearing masks and carrying placards are demonstrating outside the Embassy as he leaves.

Friday, January 6

A long, disturbingly accurate and wounding article, by 'a special correspondent' in the *New Statesman*, depresses me. I send copies by pouch to AAH and to the Foreign Ministry, and I also decide to reply. There is a sarcastic piece in *Private Eye* about 'The Reporter[1] of the Year' and his association with HIM. Iran's international image must surely have seen brighter days.

Sunday, January 8

I had arranged for Cyrus, who was keen to meet Ava Gardner, to come and have dinner with her. Ava arrives, perhaps somewhat overdressed for the kind of informal evening I had suggested, and speaks to Cyrus about Forest Mere Health Farm where both have stayed at different times. But Ava is in a nervous and unpredictable mood. I make an innocuous observation to break the ice, which she completely misunderstands and takes umbrage at. She goes to the loo, comes back and says the Embassy plumbing is even worse than in her own house. 'I don't doubt that for a moment,' I say, agreeably. She finds that remark amusing. Hugging me impetuously, she says: 'You have a funny way of speaking that reminds me of James Mason.'

Cyrus says he has followed Ava's career with admiration from the very beginning of her childhood in Alabama and remembers an interview she once gave to the American columnist, Rex Reed. I

[1] A punning allusion to Sir Shapour Reporter, whose name had been prominent in the press in connection with the Irano–British arms deal.

138

intervene to say that I think for once Cyrus's memory has let him down, and that Ava actually comes from North Carolina.

'I bet you she's from Alabama,' insists Cyrus.

'Alabama! ALA-BAMA!' Ava fumes. Flushed with rage, she leaps up and screams at Cyrus: You don't know a bloody thing about me, you and your columnist friend. How dare you say you do? You don't know *where* the hell I come from!' With that she grabs her coat off the sofa and shouts: 'I'm not staying here a minute longer.'

By then Cyrus is on his feet too. 'Oh, no – please, Miss Gardner, I've always admired you and wanted to meet you. I'm sorry if ...' He kisses her hand, but Ava is having none of it, and runs down the stairs, still muttering and fuming.

I drive her home. 'That bastard Reed can paint a picture of you even your sister wouldn't recognise,' she says.

Outside her house, she fumbles for her key in her handbag, finds what she has been looking for, and without a word or gesture grandly sweeps through the door, slamming it shut behind her.

Cyrus is nonplussed by the drama, but I'm too bored by the whole thing to engage in a post-mortem. I try hard to keep him for dinner, but he no longer feels gregarious. Before he leaves he says he has been meaning to tell me that I ought publicly to sever all contacts with Princess Ashraf. I tell him that being publicly disloyal to her would not enhance my reputation.

Tuesday, January 10

I see by the papers that HIM has now committed himself irrevocably to Sadat's policies. We have come out explicitly against an independent Palestine state, but say that the Palestinians ought to have a homeland and the right to determine their own fate. The apparent contradiction – that self-determination should logically lead on to independence – is left unexplained. HIM is evidently following developments outside Iran more actively than before. The fate of Somalia and the future of the Palestinians now form a part of HIM's global view.

From the minutes of the Supreme Economic Council's meeting I see that, depending on the amount of money the Government is able to 'save', the deficit for this financial year will be anything between five to six billion dollars! I find it revealing that whenever in the Council's discussions HIM refers to any positive achievement he says 'we have ...', but that when he is admonishing the

Government for its failures or shortcomings he switches the pronoun: '*you* must ...' he says.

As I am about to leave the office Mrs Smith, the Embassy housekeeper – a fugitive from a Hogarth painting – runs after me shouting, 'Sir, Sir.' She wants to show me the headlines in the *Evening News*: 'Four Killed and Nine Injured in Iran.' Police had apparently opened fire on demonstrators who had attacked a police post south of Tehran. There isn't going to be any let up, I tell myself, so I'd better get used to it.

Wednesday, January 11

The story is front-page news in the *Guardian*, told with all the relish that bleeding hearts can summon up. Rioting has taken place in Qom[1] and the rioters have demanded the return of Khomeini. Five people according to the Government, twenty according to dissident sources, have been killed.

Thursday, January 12

Belinda Cadbury, Cyrus, Liz and Mr and Mrs Anthony Howard[2] come to dinner.

Without my raising the subject, Howard tells me that the Embassy's reply to a recent *NS* article was 'perfect', and that it will appear in the next issue. For him, says Howard, the most offensive thing in the world is racialism and racial prejudice; and, while he finds Uganda's Amin perfectly odious, the evil there is not based on racialism, as it is in South Africa and Rhodesia.

When I intervene to say that the problem may be more complicated in that the whites now find themselves victims of historic circumstances not of their own making, he says the whites have been warned time and time again that they should leave, and those who have stayed, particularly in Rhodesia, are 'rich capitalists who are there to suck the blood of the Africans'.

'And would you stand by and watch them being massacred?' I ask.

'Oh, listen', he replies, 'I'm not a soft-hearted liberal. The whites

[1] The religious city eighty miles south of Tehran, where Khomeini had taught until his expulsion.
[2] Anthony Howard, then Editor of the *New Statesman*.

140

know what the score is, and those who stay would deserve what they get.'

He says his favourite country could be Tanzania, 'where Western industrialism has been rejected and the Government is trying to create the perfect agrarian society'. But he admits he's never been there.

When I refer to the commendable strength with which he holds his political views, he says he would have rejected a similar dinner invitation from the Chileans, the Argentinians or the South Africans.

'And the Israelis?' I ask.

'No,' he says, he would have gone to the Israelis. He has been to Israel, 'where the Arab mayors of the West Bank remind me of the Vichy French'.

Cyrus asks Howard if his views about Iran have changed in the past year. Howard says he knows little about Iran, but he'd first have to see what organisations such as Amnesty say about it.

'Do you think,' Cyrus asks, 'that Carter compromises himself by going to a country like Iran?'

'Yes, I think he does,' says Howard, 'and that he deserves every bit of the tear-gas he got in his eyes' [during the welcoming ceremony for HIM in Washington].

Friday, January 13

Lunch with Michael Weir at Mark's. Speaking of the recent rash of letters exchanged between the Embassy and the BBC, Michael says, for the first time as far as I can remember, that the trouble arises out of our over-projection of ourselves and from attacks, presumably he means by the Shah, on the 'decadent democracies', all of which had 'spurred the BBC boys to needle you.'

M. Sauvagnargues, the new French Ambassador, pays me a courtesy call. He says he is 'not here to make better Europeans of the British because they will never become Europeans'. He speaks of an escalation of the fighting in Ethiopia, generally sharing my pessimism over Sadat's peace initiative. He leaves me with the impression of a man with a mastery of his subject – a serious and somewhat sombre intellectual.

At 9.30 the duty officer at the Embassy telephones to say that an Iranian-sounding man has called to warn that a bomb will go off at the Residence at ten, and that the police have been notified. I am mildly nervous as the clock ticks towards ten, while my guests and I

141

are assembled around the dinner table, but feel certain the threat is a hoax, as it proves to be.

I see that the Empress Farah has gone to New York to attend the Asia Society dinner, whatever that is. Some 4,000 police have been required to protect her – principally, of course, from her own disaffected compatriots – and a couple of people have heckled her as she stood up to speak.

The Empress was in Washington last summer, then again with HIM in November, and she met the Carters on New Year's Eve in Tehran. Why the hell should she want to go to New York again, when it is perfectly obvious her presence will lead to demonstrations? And, while she may deliver the most stirring speech to a few assembled dignitaries in some gilded hall, not a word of that speech will appear in any of the papers. What is absolutely certain to appear instead is massive coverage for the masked placard-bearers outside the hall. Who the hell advises her?

Sunday, January 15

Fly the Concorde to New York. Tourist-class seats with first-class service.

New York is cold but sunny. Since check-out time at the Pierre is one o'clock and I am there at eleven, my room isn't ready and I am given a temporary accommodation, where I turn on the television and watch the memorial service for Hubert Humphrey. 'More courageous than the manner he led his life,' reads Carter, 'was the way in which he left it.' I think I disagree. Towards the end of his life Humphrey never missed an opportunity to appear before the television cameras. A courageous man, certainly, but we should have been spared the agonising spectacle of a dwindling emaciated man, unable to walk, his mouth twisted into a pathetic rictus of gleaming false teeth, his throat shrivelled, trying desperately to win sympathy for his moribund condition. Surely it is more dignified to die away from the glare of publicity.

Monday, January 16

In between my rounds of appointments with doctors I lunch with Marion Javits at Orsini's. 'Carter,' she says, 'just isn't up to it,' and people are saying he's going to be a one-term President. Marion

142

had attended the dinner at which Empress Farah had spoken. 'She is a warm, lovable person and is well-liked, but it's all those jails, you know.' When I ask whether surely at least *some* people in New York believe the worst aspects of those jails have been ended, she says she doesn't think so.

I go to our UN Mission to see Fereydoun. Nympha, his doe-eyed Filipino secretary for many years, tells me, while I wait for a moment in her room, that she doesn't like to be reminded she's from the Philippines 'because it's no longer a good country to come from'. Iran used to be, I think to myself, before a disenchanted Western press ruined it all.

For once Fereydoun is calm – or is it resigned? – showing none of his habitual nervousness which had gained for him the nickname of the Cat on the Hot Tin Roof. He has, he says, given up sending cables to Tehran that 'solve none of the problems and simply create headaches'. None of his staff has the slightest faith in what Tehran says, either publicly or in coded instructions. Arthur Miller[1] had been amongst those demonstrating against the Queen's visit to New York, he says, and had been recognised by a television reporter who had asked Miller if he realised that the Shah was a friend of the United States. 'Yes,' Miller had replied, 'but he should also be a friend to his own people.'

'Did you cable that?' I ask.

'No – that's the kind of cable that would solve nothing and just create a headache.'

Saturday, January 21

I returned to the Pierre last night after two days at the New York Hospital – two days in the course of which I was put through every possible test, including the scanner and cystoscopy, to determine the nature of my back ailment. The result, as Dr Muecke, the urologist, put it, was that 'the most up-to-date equipment in the most advanced hospital in the world has found nothing wrong with you'. It may well be, he says, that the discomfort stems from a muscular spasm, but that can only be surmised, not detected. It could also be that the spasm is caused by stress, and so be psychosomatic. Rest, massage and heat therapy are recommended, and if that regimen doesn't work 'we could always block a nerve,' he says.

'Your colleague [Ardeshir Zahedi, the Iranian Ambassador] from Washington also comes to see us from time to time,' says Dr

[1] The playwright.

143

Muecke, adding after a moment's reflection, 'it can't be easy, working for the ruler of the Peacock Throne.'

I feel a sudden surge of anger at this impudent interference, this uncalled-for demonstration of sympathy and understanding from a total stranger, but hold my peace. Moreover, I have gone through all this expenditure of time and money to be told yet again that my pain is obscure in origin and, in all probability, psychosomatic.

Sunday, January 22

Speak to Meshkinpoush in London, who tells me that the clashes in Tehran, and the demonstrations in front of the Embassy, have continued, and the Foreign Ministry has issued confidential circulars asking all Embassies and Government offices to take precautions against attacks 'by Palestinian elements'. These, it seems, may be expected following an interview given by HIM to Barbara Walters in which he confessed to being 'very apprehensive' about the creation of an independent Palestinian state. Yasser Arafat had condemned the Shah's remark, saying Palestine wasn't the Shah's to give away and that he shouldn't interfere.

Monday, January 23

A last visit to Dr Forkner Jr, who merely advises a period free from excessive physical exertion, and a farewell lunch with Fereydoun, Marion and Parvine at Olivier's. When the ladies are gone, Fereydoun says he had lunch with Martin Ennals on Friday. Ennals had said that he was pleased with his relations with the London Embassy, but that pressure groups of the Left within Amnesty limited what he could do and say on the changed conditions in Iran. Fereydoun had told Ennals that in Iran things could only be done through HIM, and this is why it was necessary to show the sort of flexibility that prevented a rupture in the newly-established dialogue. Fereydoun says while it is true, as he had had occasion to witness during the Empress's visit, that she comes across a lot better with bourgeois intellectuals, Princess Ashraf is the only person with any real influence on her brother. In the course of our conversation he mentions that Ardeshir had acted as the perfect bodyguard during the Empress's visit, keeping her from contact with people he thought undesirable, telling her where

144

to sit, what to eat and who to place next to herself, etc. Ardeshir, he said, had a remarkable talent for terrorising his subordinates.

Tuesday, January 24

I fly to Barbados for four days holiday, happy to laze in the sun, read, swim, play tennis and not worry for a while about HIM's imagined reactions to my daily cables.

One of the books I read during my holiday was Isaiah Berlin's *Four Essays on Liberty* which stands, in my opinion, above any others I have read for its humanity, depth of conviction and moral courage. A quotation at the end of the chapter on 'Two Concepts of Freedom' enormously impressed me: 'To realise the relative validity of one's convictions and yet stand for them unflinchingly is what distinguishes a civilised man from a barbarian.' I determine to get it translated and circulated among my Persian colleagues.

Tuesday, January 31

Mehrdad Pahlbod, the Minister of Culture and Princess Shams's husband, stops at Heathrow for an hour to change planes on his way to the United States, and I go to the airport to see him. He says Europeans and Americans cannot adequately grasp the nature of the love and respect Iranians feel towards their monarch. 'Even someone as well-meaning as David Frost refers to the Shah as "top dog" somewhere in his script,' he tells me.

I sympathise, but observe that we must make up our minds which audience we wish to impress – the one in Iran or the one in the West. If it is the latter, then we must understand, accept and employ their own vernacular. 'Yes,' he agrees, 'but how?'

Khatib Shahidi, my Cultural Counsellor, just back from Tehran, lunches with me. He says the refusal of the university authorities, to whom he had spoken, to see what they do not wish to see provides the worst example of self-deception he has ever known. The growing volume of religious opposition can be attributed to the closure of every other avenue of expression, and 'taghieh'[1] is now popularly interpreted not as meaning compliance under duress but

[1] From the early days of their persecution Shi'a Moslems, who make up the great majority of Persians, have adopted the principle of 'taghieh' (dissimulation) which enjoins that in situations of extreme personal danger it is permissible to dissemble.

resistance under pressure.

Dinner at the Eldon Griffiths's. Kingman Brewster, the American Ambassador; a certain General Norris of the US Air Force; a Washington lawyer named Steven Martindale; Lord Aldington[1] and two or three others are there for a stag-dinner at which we are served by the Griffiths family.

Griffiths begins the after-dinner conversation by expressing 'worry' about Carter's performance in foreign policy, the economy and the Horn of Africa. General Norris expresses love and loyalty for America and is unexciting. Aldington says that one of the most disastrous aspects of Carter's foreign policy has been the introduction of the criterion of human rights as its salient principle, and that it is naive to the point of stupidity to expect the world to comply with a set of moral values that have come to prevail in certain parts of Europe and America, but only as the result of a long process of historical evolution.

Brewster intervenes briefly 'just to put the record straight'. Human rights is not the only one, but one of many principles of American foreign policy, he says.

Perhaps because of my by now fairly advanced paranoia, I feel that ever since the mention of human rights the eyes of the assembled company have been upon me. 'As the representative of a country that comes in for a fair amount of flak over the issue of human rights,' I say, 'I, too, would like to put the record straight. We in Iran have no disagreement with President Carter's ideas on human rights. On the contrary, such ideals are noble and humane, and the President's sincerity and courage in expressing them deserve admiration. Where we do differ, with regard and respect, from our American friends is in the priority we should assign to these standards in a society in the state of social development Iran is in today.' I go on to say that the alleged excesses have, in any case, been brought to an end, a state of affairs even the opponents of the régime now grudgingly recognise. I then sit back, quite pleased with myself, thinking smugly that I have sung for my supper, and wondering what HIM's reaction would be when he discovers that his man in London had actually praised President Carter's upholding of human rights.

Thursday, February 2

Parviz Khonsari, in charge of our manpower training programme

[1] Formerly Toby Low, Conservative MP for Blackpool North, 1945–62.

in Europe, telephones from Tehran to ask about the recent *Guardian* article which spoke of spying on students in the United Kingdom. I explain, and ask whether he thinks I should cable HIM requesting the withdrawal of Savak agents in the UK simply on the grounds that their nuisance value is greater than their intelligence value. He replies that if I, like him, was nearing the end of my career, he might have counselled such a move, but 'you still have a long way to go,' he says, 'and to take *them* on is dangerous.'

Buffet dinner at George Weidenfeld for the publication of Abba Eban's[1] *An Autobiography*. Eban is there himself. The sin of modesty, I remember having read in one of the morning papers, is not his. He asks me to convey his regards 'both to His Majesty and to Ardeshir', agrees Begin could be more flexible and admits that his Persian[2] 'is a bit rusty'.

Friday, February 3

Their Majesties have arrived in New Delhi and there have been the inevitable demonstrations against their visit.

Dashti, the head of the Embassy's student section, comes to see me with a gloomy account of recent Press allegations that his department is riddled with Savak agents who spy on Iranian students in the UK. 'My children at school,' he says, with a lump in his throat, 'have come under attack.' I produce a homily extolling the virtue of self-reliance until I feel the lump has disappeared. Dashti is a decent, honourable man.

Monday, February 6

There is an article by Lord Chalfont in *The Times* called 'Exporting British Insults to Iran'. He writes knowledgeably and persuasively, although I think I can see the incubus of the Shah in the article's references to the BBC and the *Guardian*.

Hushang Mahdavi, who will succeed Meshkinpoush as my Number Two, arrives and is terribly enthusiastic about his assignment to London.

Julian Ridsdale[3] is my luncheon guest. A quiet soft-spoken, mild-

[1] Foreign Minister of Israel, 1966–74.
[2] He had been a student of oriental languages at Cambridge before the war.
[3] Conservative MP for Harwich since 1954.

mannered man of tact and sensitivity, he speaks about the certainty of a Tory win in the next general election. He also dilates on the subject of Japan, which seems to be his particular field of interest. But to my surprise and annoyance – out, I feel sure, of consideration for my own sensibilities – he makes no reference to Iran. So neurotic have I become that I am actually experiencing Pavlovian withdrawal symptoms when I am not subjected to a barrage of invective over Iran's human rights record. I feel like seizing him by the collar and telling him he can't just speak to me about Japan and the Tories. 'How dare you not ask me about Savak's torture methods!' I want to shout at him.

But all this gasconnade remains unspoken as Ridsdale and I quietly munch our food in what turns out to be a pleasant, if somewhat vapid, lunch.

Tuesday, February 7

After much deliberation and honest vacillation and with Meshkinpoush's invaluable assistance I send a four-page cable to Khalatbary appraising Iran's relations with Amnesty International one year after Martin Ennals's audience with HIM. After pointing out that the tone of the organisation has not got any worse in its references to Iran during the past year, I recommend the continuation of the 'dialogue' and request that a policy of cooperation rather than confrontation be adopted towards Amnesty. 'My insistence on the establishment and the maintenance of our relations with Amnesty,' I say, 'is due to the fact that, irrespective of what Iran or any other government may feel towards the organisation, Amnesty's views and statements carry greater credibility with the media than the views and statements of any government spokesman, *whatever his rank.*'

Khosro Eghbal, a friend of the family for many years, comes to lunch. This is our first encounter since the death of his brother, Dr Manuchehr Eghbal, the former Prime Minister and Chairman of NIOC. His account of Dr Eghbal's last days portrays him as a worried and humiliated man, deeply troubled by his own diminished stature in an Iran that was going very wrong. The petrochemical and gas industries had been removed from the control of NIOC, and his own influence with the Shah, while still considerable, was less than it had been. A staunch anti-Communist all his life, Dr Eghbal was alarmed at what he saw as the penetration of the higher ranks of the Iranian bureaucracy by turncoat Reds. He had raised his fears with HIM, whose response had been that people can change their minds. 'Of course they can,' Dr Eghbal is said to have answered, but had expressed his failure to understand how former traitors could now be given the position of 'pishnamaz'[1]. Dr Eghbal had expected, even welcomed, death, says Khosro.

Wednesday, February 8

The new Bangladeshi High Commissioner, Shamso-Doha, whom I know well from Tehran, where he was ambassador, pays me a courtesy call. 'Like you,' he says, 'I am a political appointment,' given full authority by the President to deal with any situation that may arise. He also says that during his farewell audience he had said to HIM that God had given Iran a great deal by way of natural resources and human ingenuity but that what was needed at this stage was a little delegation of authority. 'Your MPs', he says he told HIM, 'should be allowed to regain their self-respect.'

I am surprised that Doha actually allowed himself to say such things to HIM. I shall be even more surprised if HIM is prepared to take such advice from – with all due respect – the Bangladeshi Ambassador. Doha is, nevertheless, an intelligent, urbane and articulate man with much personal charm.

Thursday, February 9

A telephone call from AAH in Tehran. A propos the Chalfont article he says: 'The British can go on exporting insults to Iran, but we needn't subsidise them.' One or two major projects with the British will soon be cancelled and a campaign is to be started to dissuade people from spending their holidays in the UK or sending their children to school there. Tony Parsons was given the 'message' before he left Tehran, and I should do the same in my contacts with various officials.

'The idea of faulting Iran for human rights violations was Carter's originally, but now he can and does say that things have improved. Why can't someone in the British Government do the same?' demands AAH. I ask if anything can be done to lessen

[1] Prayer leader.

Tehran's sensitivity to media criticism. AAH denies that there is any over-sensitivity.

Shams, the cipher clerk, comes in to see me. Since I first arrived he has come to my room almost daily. Always he has politely knocked, then entered, with the folder under his arm bearing Tehran's instructions all decoded and immaculately typed, but never have I been able to judge from his expression whether he is the bearer of good or bad news. Perhaps inscrutability is an indispensible element in the equipment of a cryptographer. On this occasion, too, I glance at his face, hoping through some ESP process to divine the gist of what he decoded and typed an hour ago, and have no more success than usual. But for once he does depart momentarily from his po-faced ritual to say, as he approaches my desk and hands me the folder, 'Congratulations, sir.'

My jittery nerves are put to rest by HIM's reply to my Amnesty cable of February 7:

'L-2279 received the high consideration of His Imperial Majesty.

'His Majesty was graciously pleased to observe: "Your proposals are correct and must be implemented in the manner you recommend." In compliance with His Imperial Majesty's command, the necessary instructions will be issued to the relevant authorities. It would not be unhelpful, however, if strongly-worded rejoinders were sent to Amnesty whenever appropriate occasions should arise. [Signed] Khalatbary.'

Meshkinpoush and Mahdavi, who have seen the cable, come in to share my relief and elation.

Monday, February 13

Julian Amery[1] comes to see me. He is alarmed at the turn of events in the Horn of Africa and plans a fact-finding mission to Mogadishu, following the completion of which he would go on to America 'to alert that influential political sector in America with whom the Conservative Party still carries some weight'. I say he is certainly welcome to kick up as much dust as he wants to, but inwardly I don't share his alarm. What I would find infinitely more alarming would be for HIM to send some 3,000 Iranian soldiers to some God-forsaken corner of Africa in an open-ended military and financial commitment that could only prove disastrous.

A farewell reception in the evening for Meshkinpoush and an

[1] Conservative MP for Brighton Pavilion since 1969.

opportunity at the same time to introduce his successor, Hushang Mahdavi. I am sorry to lose Meshkinpoush. I have come to trust him and to rely on his judgment and ability completely, and his gift for lucid writing and rational thought will not be easy to replace. Above all, Meshkinpoush is a good man.

Tuesday, February 14

At a luncheon given by the NIOC man in London, I speak privately to Dr Fallah, one of the Company's most senior executives, who predicts that, if our current production and expenditure levels are maintained, 'we'll be in the red in five years'. Our overseas investments, he says, are minimal and, in any case, have not been profitable yet. As for our domestic investments, our Paykans ['Arrows', Chrysler-built cars largely kit-assembled in Iran] will never be able to compete with Japanese cars; nor, he adds, our petrochemicals with ICI. The only hope lies in reducing expenditure. He has written all this down and sent it to HIM via Hushang Ansari.

Dr Fallah corroborates Khosro's account of the petty humiliations that a proud and once powerful Dr Eghbal suffered before he died, but adds that, while he was saddened by Eghbal's death, his disappearance could only be a boon for NIOC which under him had become a dusty, ossified bureaucracy.

I am a guest of Jack and Frankie Donaldson's, along with George Jellicoe, Diane Summers and Susan Crosland at a performance of Verdi's *Requiem* at the Albert Hall. Though it's not really my scene, I enjoy the occasion. We go to the Donaldsons for dinner.

Thursday, February 16

I receive the following post-Valentine's Day *billet-doux* from Philip Roth[1] whom, along with Claire Bloom, I had asked to a dinner I plan to give for Ted Heath.

Dear Parviz:

Inasmuch as you are the official representative of a régime whose methods of putting down political opposition and suppressing freedom of expression I find wholly repugnant, I am unable to

[1] The American novelist.

accept your invitation for dinner at the Iranian Embassy on March 14 in honor of Edward Heath.

> Sincerely,
> Philip Roth

Sanctimonious little shit. I wonder if he has ever protested over Israel's treatment of the Palestinians.

In the afternoon there is another telephone call from AAH who had just had a meeting with the British Ambassador: 1) Tony Parsons had had a high-level meeting in London with Foreign Office officials, at which the BBC was represented, and 'they've got the message'. 2) The Defence Secretary, Roy Mason, is going to Iran in March to patch things up with HIM. 3) 'The Brits are going to see if they can invoke the clause of "national interest" to protect their military and commercial sales to Iran in toning down BBC's Persian Service.' AAH does say, however, that a similar attempt at the time of Suez did not succeed. 4) The Prime Minister is going to speak in support of Iran in the Commons soon.

All very interesting.

Friday, February 17

Lady Falkender[1] is my sole guest to dinner. She wears a long skirt, has been to the hairdresser and is quite obviously nervous. She 'hates caviar', so the first course has to be changed. The dining-room she finds ugly, the Embassy gloomy and the atmosphere oppressive. We hurry through the dinner and rush back upstairs to the more agreeable surroundings of the drawing-room.

Wilson has great admiration for HIM, says Lady Falkender. She refers to Callaghan as a 'bent copper', whatever that means when applied to a Prime Minister, whom 'we put there'. She professes to be an avid admirer of Jews and Zionists, and says both George Weidenfeld and Chapman Pincher have spoken highly of me to her. The Ennalses – and Martin in particular – are Trotskyites and 'you shouldn't have anything to do with them'. Isaiah Berlin, whose book she sees on my desk, 'is brilliant but a phoney'.

She says she knows all about me, my relationship with Lizzie, my jogging habit, and my closeness to the Imperial Court. And she disarmingly admits she was so nervous 'I nearly didn't come tonight'.

[1] The former Personal and Political Secretary to Sir Harold Wilson.

152

Sunday, February 19

There have been disturbances in Tehran, I learn from the BBC World Service, in which six people have been killed and 125 injured. I also hear that Dr Owen is shortly to visit Tehran and wonder whether AAH's reference to Roy Mason was inaccurate or I misheard him.

Monday, February 20

I ask my secretary, Nadereh, to send the following reply to Philip Roth:

'Dear Mr Roth,
   The Ambassador wishes me to inform you of his regret that he is unable to accept your letter of February 15, 1978. Accordingly, I return it to you herewith.

> Yours sincerely,
> N. Richard
> Private Secretary to
> the Ambassador.'

   Lunch at PG with Julian Amery, Billy McLean[1], Peter Temple-Morris[2] and Dennis Walters[3]. The Horn of Africa and the Middle East are, not unnaturally, the principal topics of conversation. Julian, Billy and Winston Churchill[4] are off to Mogadishu on Thursday to see for themselves 'the Soviet penetration of Africa' and are to come back and make enough fuss to oblige the irresolute Western world to make up its mind.
   On his way out Billy says I have gained a reputation as 'an idealist', by which I suppose he means I am dripping, soaking wet.

Tuesday, February 21

Lady Falkender comes for a drink and brings me this time an

[1] Conservative MP for Inverness, 1954–64.
[2] Conservative MP for Leominster since 1974.
[3] Conservative MP for Westbury since 1964.
[4] Conservative MP for Stretford since 1970.

153

inscribed copy of Harold Wilson's *A Prime Minister on Prime Ministers*.

When I remind her of the colourful language she had used to describe some of her former colleagues she regrets her indiscretion. But in almost the next breath proceeds to describe Denis Healey [Chancellor of the Exchequer], who is having lunch with me tomorrow, as a man with a 'first-rate mind, a brilliant sense of humour – but a political thug.'

And Isaiah Berlin's 'phoniness'? 'The phoniness,' says Lady Falkender, 'lies only in his lack of original thinking.'

Wednesday, February 22

Denis Healey and two of his colleagues come to lunch. The future of oil, the Middle East, the BBC's Persian language broadcasts, Irano-British trade and the relative merits of different types of nuclear reactors, AGRs and PWRs, are amicably discussed.

The Chancellor, whom I had met in Tehran during his last visit there to attend an Irano-British conference on banking cooperation, is indeed gifted with a quick analytical mind as well as with a withering sense of humour.

Thursday, February 23

Frank Judd, a Minister of State at the Foreign Office; the Jordanian Ambassador, and Frank Giles of the *Sunday Times*, come to lunch at the Embassy. When the Jordanian Ambassador raises the possibility of a British or Common Market initiative in the Middle East, Judd says that 'because of internal political considerations' and the imminence of a general election the Government is unlikely to do anything that would alienate an influential sector of the voting public. The truly Conservative Party in Britain, says Judd, is the Labour Party – 'the guardian of all that is noble and worth preserving in British society, including its tradition of racial tolerance'. And, on the same theme, he adds that Mrs Thatcher's 'playing politics with the problem of immigration is insensitive and irresponsible'.

'Is there then no problem of immigrants in this country?' I ask.

'Of course there is,' Judd concedes, 'but the existing regulations governing their inflow are perfectly adequate. Heath was right

154

when he said the current regulations can cope with the situation, but if we are going to adopt policies that are racialist, how are we going to answer for them at Helsinki?'

Frank Giles wants to go to Tehran to interview the Shah.

Saturday, February 25

Drive with Nadereh to Bushey and visit a dog-training centre to see an Alsatian I want to buy. There is an eighteen month-old, house-trained, lovely black-and-white creature that I like immediately. His name is Pride.

Monday, February 27

Fleur Cowles[1] comes to lunch. I had not known her previously, but she had telephoned the Embassy to introduce herself as 'a friend of the Shah's, of Iran and of one of the Ambassador's predecessors [Ardeshir Zahedi]'. A gentle, kindly woman in poor health, she says she knows HIM from the time of a visit she made to Iran in 1952 as a roving ambassador for President Eisenhower, and from having played host to him and Queen Soraya during their subsequent visit to America. She speaks about the vocal opposition to the Shah abroad, giving off faint hints of sympathy for their cause. She says she has 'three very beautiful houses' which I must see. Later, she sends a copy of her book, *Friends and Memories*, inscribed 'To a new friend'.

Pride, that behemoth of an Alsatian, becomes my latest toy.

Wednesday, March 1

Martin Ennals and David Simpson, head of the British Section of Amnesty, come to lunch at the Embassy. Martin says: 'There are two things you can do to disarm your critics – open up the system to foreign journalists and let them see things for themselves, including your faults, as the Egyptians have done, and publish the Red Cross report on your prisons.' Both recommendations I

[1] American artist and writer and prominent London hostess.

forward to Tehran, adding a considerable sprinkling of salt and pepper of my own.

Thursday, March 2

I see in *Kayhan International* that HIM has said Iran's policy of liberalisation will continue, in spite of the abuse of the greater freedom by the political opposition. The revolutionary changes he has introduced, says HIM, have so strengthened the pillars of Iranian society that more freedom and flexibility can now not only be allowed, but have become essential. Lovely.

Friday, March 3

Moinzadeh comes to tell me that dissident elements from Germany have arrived in England and that on Monday morning they plan to break into either the Consulate in Manchester or the Student Section in Kensington. He says if we notify the police his informer will 'burn'. I tell him that he himself should keep well away from the Student Section, since it would be difficult to explain his particular functions to the Press if he should be recognised. I tell him to hire more private security people for all Iranian Government buildings in London. I then ring Dashti, head of the Student Section, to tell him to keep his cool.

An article in the *Guardian* by Liz Thurgood from Tehran expresses surprise at the leniency with which anti-Government demonstrators in Tabriz are being treated. The first public statement by the new Governor-General of Azerbaijan says that granting the maximum freedom will continue to be his administration's policy.

Pamela Egremont and the Peter Walkers come to lunch while a few dissidents demonstrate outside the Chancery ten doors away. Peter Walker[1] says that, no matter what different individuals may say about the actual contents of her speeches on race, Margaret Thatcher will be seen by the voting public to be against a greater number of immigrants in this country – 'and that is an election plus.'

My attention is diverted throughout the lunch by the chanting outside and I feel quite frankly somewhat embarrassed.

[1] Conservative MP for Worcester since 1961; Minister of Agriculture, Fisheries and Food since 1979.

Pride, the Alsatian, leaves my life. I send him back with a heavy heart. In the mornings I would walk him with me to the office, where from a corner he would watch my every move. Occasionally, when I was alone and glanced in his direction, he would rise and meekly walk towards me, ears flattened, head lowered, seeking a sign of recognition, a gesture of affection. At night he would wait for me behind the front door, erupting into a paroxysm of joyful movement at the sound of my key turning.

I had grown immensely fond of him, but the truth is I didn't have the time to look after him properly. He would refuse to go for walks with any of the staff, and on one occasion when he'd been forced to by Rosa, the Embassy housekeeper, had bitten her hand. At other times he had peed all over the most precious of the Embassy carpets. And so he went back – a noble creature, genuine in his affection and loyalty, qualities all too rare amongst his human 'superiors'.

Sunday, March 5

Tennis with Richard Kershaw, who has just come back from Tehran where he interviewed HIM for the BBC. Dissident voices are becoming increasingly audible in Tehran, he says, and 'people like Tony Parsons' believe that to label any and all opposition either 'Red' or 'Black' is to oversimplify and to exaggerate their importance. Tony thinks that there now exists in Iran a body of middle-class liberals who could be trusted to behave responsibly. Richard says HIM had been 'totally trustful and exceptionally nice' during and even before the interview. Had Richard been to ski at Dizin? HIM had asked while the television cameras were being set up. No, he hadn't, Richard replied, but he had been playing tennis. Who with? HIM had wanted to know: and, when Richard had mentioned Cyrus Ghani's name, HIM had confessed to being 'amazed at how that elephant could move so fast on the court'. Then HIM had agreed with Richard that the British Ambassador to Tehran was as 'cute' as his own Ambassador to London. All terribly chummy and crony-like. Richard does say, however, that the content of the interview is 'unexciting'.

Monday, March 6

Lunch with Major Bahrami, a police officer and friend of long standing ever since he was assigned as security officer to Hoveyda

157

in 1968. He is in London to accompany Mrs Amouzegar. Compared with Hoveyda, Amouzegar is remarkably relaxed, Bahrami tells me. He arrives at the office each morning at about 9, works till about 1.30, has lunch – more often than not alone – siestas until about 5 and stays in most nights, avoiding the social whirl of the Court. Either from lack of interest or as a matter of policy, he leaves a great deal of initiative to his ministers and appears not to want to know about their problems.

Bahrami also says that much of the general scepticism and disillusion in Tehran could easily be avoided and is completely unnecessary. He gives as an example the recent Congress of the Rastakhiz Party, when delegates from all over Iran had assembled to elect 'in complete freedom', everyone had been assured, a new Secretary-General to replace Amouzegar. Then, three days before the Congress was due to announce its decision, HIM stated publicly that the posts of Secretary-General and Prime Minister were inseparable. 'The spectacle of 15,000 delegates furiously debating for three days only to arrive at a decision which had already been announced was quite pathetic,' he says.

Tuesday, March 7

Farhad arrives in a good mood, thank goodness.

Four members of the House of Commons, part of a bipartisan group of ten MPs who will be going out to Tehran later in the year, come to lunch. Peter Temple-Morris comes along to help me with their programme. The four are Colin Phipps and William Garrett (Labour) and Peter Viggers and Geoffrey Finsberg (Conservative). The conversation consists mostly of my painting a rosy picture of Iran. Phipps states his preference succinctly: 'Let us discover on our visit that, despite what the Left wing of the Labour Party says, Iran pays greater respect to individual liberty and personal freedom than, say, East Germany.' I quote his phrase verbatim in my subsequent cable to Tehran.

Later in the day, with Farhad and Kiu[1], I watch Richard's interview with HIM on BBC. The Shah reaffirms his commitment to liberalise and to release political prisoners, though when Richard mentions the abandonment of torture, he spoils that by saying: 'What is the meaning of torture? It's a big word;' and later, when he says, 'If Iran should disappear, you in Europe would just die.' Par for the course, I suppose.

[1] Kiumars Bozorgmehr, formerly editor of the English language daily, *Tehran Journal*, and a personal friend.

158

Wednesday, March 8

David Watkins, Marcus Fox and Bryan Magee, part of the team of MPs to visit Iran, come for a drink and a chat. Magee spells out the position. Iran's image is bad, he says; there are accusations of torture and oppression. Will the Iranian Government see it as ingratitude if, on their return, members of the delegation, 'who are bound to be quizzed on such topics by their constituents, openly speak their mind'?

I reply that the inclusion of people like Mr Magee in the delegation, rather than packing the visit with right-wingers, surely answers his question. I speak about HIM's commitment to liberalisation, to the ending of the practice of torture, assuring him a little irresponsibly that neither in Iran nor on his return should he feel in any way muzzled.

Friday, March 10

Lunch with Julian Amery and Billy McLean, back from their East African expedition. Julian says that, after the Ogaden and Eritrea, the Soviets and their Cuban allies will turn their attention to North Yemen. Julian says HIM has many qualities which he admires. He recalls that the very first time he had met HIM was at a reception at the Embassy during the Fifties. The then Ambassador had presented Julian, who was then 'only a backbencher', to HIM. His second sentence to Julian had been: 'We must get rid of that man Nasser.' Seeing from my puzzled expression that I had missed the point, Julian says what he had admired on that occasion was HIM's power of 'total indiscretion'.

Sunday, March 12

Dinner at George Weidenfeld's for Harold Wilson's sixty-second birthday. Lady Falkender sits at the head of one of the tables; I am placed on her right and Sir Harold on her left so that Sir Harold and I face one another. 'I once described the Shah as "one of the world's great re-distributive leaders", and he liked that,' says Sir Harold. For the most part, his conversation begins with 'When I was at the Board of Trade ... when I was ...'

Monday, March 13

A report on the BBC says HIM's much ballyhooed amnesty for
political prisoners now seems to involve far fewer numbers than
had been previously supposed would be the case.

John Davies, the Shadow Foreign Secretary, is my luncheon
guest. He is familiar with Iran, which he has visited several times
as an oil company executive. He is not too worried about the
outcome of the French elections, he says, as he believes the French
people's attachment to property runs deep, and even if the Left
should win a majority it would be short-lived. What he does find
worrying is that the West extracted no promise from the Russians
and the Cubans that they would move out of the Horn of Africa
once they had reached the borders of Somalia. But he believes it
would be wrong to arm the Somalis now, as they are not
dependable, and the only reason why they have turned to the West
is that their interests are in danger. He says the existing world
crisis, while it takes the form of an economic recession, is in fact an
energy crisis, and that until alternate sources of energy are
discovered the global dimensions of the problem will persist, even
though the American aspect of it may be solved before then. He
does not agree that the age factor in Soviet leadership acts as a
moderating influence on Soviet policies; it only ossifies their
attitude on such issues as human rights. Otherwise, their plans for
expansion are already drawn up in detail, and in the second half of
the Eighties, when their shortage of oil becomes serious, they will
start looking for new sources.

John Davies strikes me as a gentle, civilised and highly cultivated
man with a first-rate mind. His views I put down in a long cable to
Khalatbary.

Thursday, March 16

In reply to my cable on the John Davies lunch, HIM observes:
'Davies's views bear close similarity to our own.'

Lesley Blanch comes to see me at the office. Because of bureaucratic
wrangles her book on the Empress has taken longer to appear than she
expected. 'Afshar,' she says, 'is simply the wrong man to be dealing
with books.' She has not been able to include my name in the
acknowledgements because 'Mr Afshar said it was not necessary'.

'For once I find myself in agreement with Mr Afshar,' I say, and
tell her not to worry.

Monday, March 20

Lunch with Lord and Lady Home at the House of Lords. Mrs David Douglas-Home and Selwyn Lloyd are amongst their eight or so guests. Lord Home has just published the recommendations of a Conservative Party committee he chaired on the reform of the House of Lords. He says he has given Mrs Thatcher four options from which to choose, and 'knowing her, she'll probably choose none of them'.

Selwyn Lloyd says he has just finished a hundred-page book on the Suez crisis, and when I ask if it contains any startling revelations, he says: 'I have told the absolute truth. If people conclude there was collusion, they are free to do so. I certainly don't believe there was.'

Off to Claridge's to be received by His Majesty Mohammad Zahir Shah, the ex-King of Afghanistan, who asks me to convey his gratitude to HIM, 'our dear brother, for his habitual affection and generosity'.

Tuesday, March 21

Hossein Eshraghi and Patricia, his Mexican girl-friend, in London for the Now Ruz holidays, come to lunch with Farhad and me. There very definitely has been a loosening of the reins in Tehran, says Hossein, but no one believes the change came about voluntarily, with the finger pointing obviously at Carter. Amouzegar, it is generally felt, has not performed well as Prime Minister. He is considered mean for the way in which he has cut many people's salaries, and to have gone too fast and too far in his attempts to bring down inflation. 'Everyone at the Ministry seems to agree that your cables are the most interesting, especially when you read the sort of nonsense some of our other ambassadors cable.' He encourages me to continue, but cautions me not to become big-headed.

Friday, March 31

Shiva Naipaul, the award-winning novelist, who occasionally publishes articles in the *Spectator* and who has been invited by the Ministry of Information to spend three weeks in Iran through no initiative of mine, is my guest to lunch, as are David Housego of the *Economist* and my Embassy colleague, Kakhi. I am not at all sure whether I can fit Naipaul, *qua* journalist, into any of the categories I already know. With his Indian-West Indian background and thorough British upbringing he strikes me as a rootless individual who ought to find it easier to write for the *New Statesman* than the *Spectator*.

David, on the other hand, is a friend from his working days in Iran[1] whose judgement and analysis I have always respected. His concern is over the rise of Islamic fundamentalism, not only in Iran but in Pakistan, Turkey and Egypt as well.

Saturday, April 1

Hassanali Mehran, now a deputy to Ansari at NIOC, comes to see me at the Residence. He too calls Amouzegar's performance 'very disappointing'. Pressed by an increasingly vocal opposition during a debate at the Budget Commission of the Majlis, Amouzegar retorted that he 'couldn't put right in four months the damage inflicted during the last fourteen years'. He had been immediately hauled over the coals by HIM, and had subsequently apologised, claiming, not very convincingly, that what he actually said was that he 'could not rectify in four months a situation that required fourteen years to put right', and that he had been misquoted. AAH had not, however, been unduly disturbed by this unflattering comment on his years of office. Mehran believes that, if and when Amouzegar should go, Ansari would not be the best man to succeed him, and that someone more acceptable to the Left would be more appropriate.

There have been further disturbances in Tehran and some other cities. What the Government calls 'benighted, reactionary elements' have attacked, with clubs and knives, such symbols of Western culture as libraries, cinemas and women's hairdressing saloons.

Wednesday, April 5

Mostafa Elm, our Ambassador in the Sudan and Hossein Eshraghi's first cousin, has been summoned to Tehran and detained

[1] He was the *Financial Times*'s resident correspondent in Tehran in the early 1970s.

162

on charges of embezzlement. His photograph and the accusations made against him, printed in large type, cover nearly the entire front page of the *Kayhan International*.

Ali and Mehri Nouri Esfandiari, a colleague from the Foreign Ministry and his wife, come to lunch. Ali is a quiet, gentle person whom I first met in the early sixties in Madrid, where he was on assignment. Mehri is more articulate and rather out-spoken on the subject of her own compatriots. 'We are,' she says, 'culturally and intellectually the displaced pesons of the Iranian society of today'. Those of our fellow countrymen who, for whatever reason, have not shared our experience of a western life, leave much to be desired in their general behaviour. Of London's sizeable community of Iranians she sees only Homayoun Mazandi. She had been thoroughly and genuinely apalled by the table manners of a group of Iranians the other day at London Airport who apparently had been eating melons while waiting for their suitcases, and others whom she had encountered at the Kensington branch of Bank Melli 'with filthy long hair and unshaven faces'. Ali says very little throughout.

In the evening I attend the Lord Mayor's Easter banquet at Mansion House. White tie and decorations are indicated on the invitation. No one sits on my left, and on my right I have Señora Pineda-Milla, wife of the Honduran Ambassador, and the Ambassador himself, neither of whom, I very soon discover, seems to speak a word of English. The Lord Mayor makes a speech notable for its lack of content. He then sits down, sniffing snuff, while his wife, Lady Vanneck, scrutinises her guests from the top table through a lorgnette. All quite silly, really. The Foreign Secretary makes fairly mild references to the Russian and Cuban presence in Ethiopia, but the Ethiopian Ambassador doesn't find the comments mild enough and leaves the room in protest, making as much noise as he can in the process.

Saturday, April 8

The CENTO meeting, due to have taken place in Washington, will now be held in London. I invite Khalatbary to stay at the Embassy for it.

Reports have appeared in recent days of a hunger strike by political prisoners at Qasr Prison in protest against their maltreatment by the authorities, and Amnesty has now asked permission to be allowed to investigate their conditions. I send a three-page cable, drafted with Kakhi's nervous assistance, to the Foreign Minister, asking Tehran to grant Amnesty's request and arguing that now that we have a solid case, as I believe we have, for telling the world that no torture has been used, and since the 'maltreatment' alleged refers to complaints about the quality of prison food, etc., it would be a pity not to allow Amnesty to investigate. 'For Amnesty to say in its findings, as it would have to do, that no evidence of torture had been discovered during an investigation of conditions at Qasr Prison, would have immeasurable propaganda value,' I say in my cable; and add that it would supply us with the moral justification, should Amnesty wish to investigate any future complaints, to tell the organisation to 'shut up' for months to come.

Sunday, April 9

Khalatbary thanks me for my invitation to stay at the Embassy but declines. There is no reply yet to my Amnesty visit cable, which is somewhat nervous-making.

Monday, April 10

As I am bidding Farhad farewell before his departure for Tehran, there is a telephone call from Tehran. It's the Foreign Minister who, after a cordial exchange of formalities, refers to my cable about 'that organisation,' and adds: 'There is no objection to implementing your proposal, but do *you* think the organisation will agree to act in complete secrecy and with complete impartiality?'

'We can certainly insist on these conditions', I say, attempting to hide my surprise, 'but if we want secrecy, to avoid leaks, I think I should tell the organisation to send its representatives within the next twenty-four hours.' The Foreign Minister says he would like to check to see if it would be possible to receive the representatives so soon, and will let me know his answer later today or tomorrow.

Amir Khosro Afshar comes to say good-bye. Alam, he says, is dying, and the only thing to do is to hope for a quick end. HIM would be unable to replace Alam's love, loyalty and counsel, and AAH could never command an equal position of power and importance as Court Minister. He himself has no personal ambitions, and would prefer to retire to a life of peace and quiet somewhere in the South of France.

Tuesday, April 11

Marion Javits, on her way back to New York after a holiday in Senegal, comes to lunch. Jack, she says, hasn't made up his mind to run for the Senate again or not, but either way Kissinger, who is flirting with the idea of running himself, 'will have a difficult time getting himself accepted as the Republican candidate because the Jews don't trust him and because he is too much under the influence of the Rockefellers'. She speaks of 'Savak and torture', and adds that America, by backing Iran militarily, 'is a part of it'. 'So are you, my dear', I remind her. But Marion, as always is devoid of malice.

There is a cable from the Foreign Minister agreeing to a visit by Amnesty representatives 'in their private capacity'.

Thursday, April 13

I have lunch with Michael Weir at the Embassy. With the CENTO conference about to start next Wednesday, I expect he wants to clear the slate of any outstanding issues. From him I learn: 1)of HIM's displeasure at the manner in which the recent disturbances have been reported by the BBC, casting the dissidents in the role of heroes; 2)of Zia ul-Haq's[1] private assurance to the Saudi Arabians that he will reprieve Bhutto; 3) that we have brought pressure on the South Africans, who depend heavily on us for oil, to agree to some sort of formula for the independence of Namibia. What Michael wants to know is why, all of a sudden, we are giving such massive coverage in our press and radio to reports of disturbances throughout Iran.

Mr Oosting of Amnesty rings in the afternoon to say that they have received reports that, since the authorities at Qasr prison have granted the demands of the prisoners, the hunger strike has been ended. He wishes to thank the Iranian authorities for their cooperative attitude, but since there are no longer any pressing humanitarian issues sufficient to justify an investigation the visit will not now take place. Bloody hell, I think to myself.

[1] The President of Pakistan.

Nor am I consoled when I am shown the following item in *Private Eye*:

At the Shit of Persia's embassy in London there is employed a very skilled man. His work takes place night or day at any far-flung outpost of the capital city. His tool: an aerosol spray.
He is By Appointment 'slogan remover' to the Shit, who has seizures when dissident elements spray slogans such as 'Shah's Fascist State'.
If you are bothered when any of these most offensive legends appear in your area, ring the Shah's man. ... (01-584-8101).
'Several people have actually rung to speak to the aerosol man, Sir,' Mrs Smith, the caretaker, tells me, with a tee hee.

Friday April 14

Amir Assadollah Alam has died.

Sunday, April 16

Patrick Seale, in an article in the *Observer*, writes of the power of the mullahs and the stupidity of the security forces; and Frank Giles's interview with HIM appears in the *Sunday Times*, photo and all, in which HIM comes across well, on the whole, if a little aggressively.

Monday, April 17

Drive to the airport to welcome Khalatbary. After a lukewarm cup of coffee at the Alcock and Brown suite, we drive to Claridge's, with Inspector Parsons of Scotland Yard sitting beside Manuel, the driver. The Minister says he may want to complain to David Owen about the tone of the BBC Persian language broadcasts and asks my opinion. It is, of course, entirely as he wishes, I reply, but point out that HIM, in the Giles interview, has left little doubt about his opinion of the BBC, and see no reason why we should show ourselves more sensitive.

166

Tuesday, April 18

The *Daily Telegraph* and *The Times* both carry the adjudication of the Press Council[1] and a cable from AAH informs me that my own despatch on the subject 'was seen by His Imperial Majesty'. The only vague note of approbation of the outcome I can decipher comes, not from HIM but from AAH, who starts his cable with 'My dear Parviz'.

Lunch alone and work on a paper for AAH which points out some very obvious flaws in the way in which the policy of liberalisation is being implemented. As always when speaking indirectly to HIM much semantic acrobatics are required.

Wednesday, April 19

I learn that Amouzegar, who has accompanied his spine-troubled wife to Washington for treatment, will stop briefly at the airport tomorrow to change planes for Tehran.

I go to Lancaster House for the Foreign Secretary's lunch for CENTO Ministers, passing en route some sixty hooded demonstrators shouting anti-Shah slogans. As always, nothing terribly important is expected to emerge from the CENTO conference, but the maintenance of contacts is considered valuable.

While we wait for the meeting of the Foreign Ministers to break up, I speak to John Graham. He has just returned from Africa where he had represented the Foreign Secretary in talks on Namibia and Rhodesia. He is more hopeful about the outcome in Namibia than he seems to be over Rhodesia. He describes HIM's démarche with the South Africans as helpful.

John Leahy joins us and refers to the Giles interview with HIM. Gerry Mansell, he tells me, will soon invite me to the BBC to show how news is selected, translated and broadcast in the Persian service, in an effort to demonstrate the absence of any bias.

The session breaks up and David Owen walks up to me, followed by Khalatbary, who raises the vexed subject of the BBC. He confesses to be 'puzzled why the BBC is more anxious to broadcast the views of the opponents of your friends than the views of your friends'.

The Foreign Secretary laughingly says, 'I agree with everything you say, but there isn't a thing I can do about it,' again insisting on the BBC's independence of the Foreign Office.

[1] Upholding the Embassy's complaint over John Bulloch's article in the *Daily Telegraph*.

After lunch I return to the Embassy, angry and humiliated by what had been said about the BBC. I draft another long cable to Tehran, enumerating the points raised by Graham and Leahy, and quoting as accurately as I can remember the exchange between Khalatbary and Owen. I end my cable:

'At the risk of appearing insolent, I must add in parenthesis that witnessing this exchange left me with a distinctly unpleasant sensation, and with my sense of national pride somewhat offended. Because whether the BBC is fair or biased, whether it is friend or foe, liberal-minded or imperialistic in its attitude, it is, after all, no more than a foreign broadcasting station. The spectacle of the Iranian Foreign Minister showing such sensitivity and vulner-ability to its 15-minute daily analysis of political events in Iran I found painful to watch.'

When Khalatbary comes to dinner later in the evening, I ask him to come upstairs for a minute to read the cable, adding that I shall send the cable anyway, but want him to see the references to himself. He reads it with an impassive, inscrutable expression and says he has no objections, but adds that he doesn't feel particularly sensitive or vulnerable to what the BBC says.

'I know,' I find myself saying, 'but it's not you I have in mind, Sir.'

Thursday, April 20

Wake up early to welcome Amouzegar and to see Khalatbary off. The only opportunity for a meaningful exchange with the Prime Minister is provided on the two-minute drive to the aeroplane. I say I welcome the policy of liberalisation but realise the enormous difficulties. The initial steam will blow off, and things will quieten down after a while, I say, 'if we keep our courage'. He concurs fully, and says those showing the greatest panic are 'the people who robbed the country blind', and who are now desperately urging extreme hardline measures.

Back at the office, I am shown an interview in *The Times* in which an Iranian National Front representative claims that Savak has bombed his house in Tehran. In the interview the victim says that 'the homes of two other Front leaders were bombed on the same night, and a car belonging to another had been blown up. A fifth was kidnapped and beaten. Responsibility for the attacks was claimed by a previously unknown underground organisation, which said it was taking vengeance on opposition leaders who were in the pay of foreigners'. The perpetrators, the article goes on to say, 'wore armbands of the Rastakhiz, the only political organisation permitted by the régime'.

Friday, April 21

A letter from Cyrus Ghani, now back in Tehran; 'Saw the former PM last night who was singing your praises. He was especially laudatory re the *Daily Telegraph* affair. I asked him whether HIM is fully aware of its significance and the delicate way you handled the matter. The answer was a resounding "Yes". See you soon.'

The good mood induced by reading Cyrus's letter evaporates the minute I see a longish piece in the *Guardian* in which Liz Thurgood describes how 'The Underground Organisation for Revenge' is intimidating opponents of the régime.

I spend the day agonising over the drafting of a paper for AAH, asking some of my colleagues to suggest moderations in its phraseology, and preparing a reply to *The Times* interview, which I consider too damaging to be left unchallenged. By 7 in the evening the paper and its enclosures are sealed into the pouch.

After praising the effective steps taken since the introduction of liberalisation 'to discard the rigid discipline that, thanks to HIM's revolutionary changes, a society of Iran's present social and intellectual maturity no longer requires', my paper goes on to regret that, simultaneously with each relative improvement in the régime's image abroad, a series of 'excessive measures' have been perpetrated of such a nature 'that even our most ardent supporters would find difficult, if not impossible, to defend'.

The *Times* story on the bombings, kidnappings and attacks by thugs is juxtaposed with HIM's assertion in the Frank Giles interview, that the newspaper was 'spreading falsehoods' about Iran, and points to the obvious damage to credibility that would result from any Embassy denial of the *Times* allegations.

The paper concludes: 'The creation of such groups as the Committee for Revenge, and countering club-wielders with club-wielders of our own, will be seen outside Iran as extreme over-reactions which, in effect, transfer to irresponsible elements the legal powers of the forces of law and order. It thereby robs a government, which professes faith in, and is responsible for, upholding the rule of law, of any semblance of moral authority.

'In order to reap positive rewards from the policies of liberalisation and the granting of greater freedoms that have been embarked upon, it is imperative that we remain, with cool-headedness and patience, but also with firmness, ever watchful over the safety-valves that have been opened. We should wait for the intense intitial head of steam, even if it should not completely disappear, to subside after a while.

'But if it is intended that, parallel with liberalisation, the Committees of Revenge or National Resistance are to resort to practices that world public opinion must regard as totally unacceptable, we shall find, as is already apparent, that it is not possible to conceal the true identity of those responsible, and Iran's image will suffer such enormous damage that it would be a thousand times preferable to return to our former ways.'

Sunday, April 23

Frank Giles's article in the *Sunday Times*, or rather its two final paragraphs, I judge to be quite positive. However, no one seems any longer to be defending the Shah; the best that can be done, it seems, is to predict that what might succeed him will be worse!

Monday, April 24

Lunch at PG with Richard Luce, Marcus Fox, John Wakeham and Bryan Magee, the other members of the British Parliamentary delegation to visit Tehran. Magee is the most articulate and the only Socialist amongst them, although he does say jokingly that someone who knew of his prospective visit had asked him whether he was part of the Conservative or the Socialist quota. The conversation and the questions are friendly and subdued. Everyone had apparently read the Giles article, which lessened my load.

Fereydoun Hoveyda, in London en route to New York after a brief visit to Tehran, comes to see me in the evening. He had gone to Tehran for work on the French translation of HIM's latest book, *Towards the Great Civilisation*. The book, he says, is badly written, repetitive, muddled and, at times, extremely pompous. Fuad Rouhani, who had been asked to do the English translation, made several suggestions for improving the original text, but eventually gave up all attempts to tone down the more jarring passages and settled for a straight translation. The typist who pointed out the apparent confusion arising from the alternate employment of the terms 'economic democracy' and 'democratic economy' was told to shut up. In the book Iran's democracy is at times described as 'the most perfect in the world'.

Much is also revealed in the book, says Fereydoun, about HIM's feelings for his father. For instance, Reza Khan is said to have established a judicial system in Iran where none previously existed – but not completely. He is said to have freed women from their traditional disabilities – but not entirely; to have restored to the Iranian people a sense of national dignity – but not fully. The full realisation of all these goals, it is implied, had to await the reign of his son.

'The opposition,' says Fereydoun, 'be it bourgeois, the Left, or the clergy, have made Saipa[1] and her life style the main target of their criticism. Many people's susceptibilities have been quite genuinely and deeply offended by her alternate visits to Mecca and Monte Carlo.' HIM, he says, is determined to continue with his policy of liberalisation, despite the many who advise him against it. Amouzegar is in trouble, and his opponents and prospective candidates for his job, are doing their best to add to his problems. Rumours are rife in Tehran, and one has it that Reza Ghotbi, the Queen's cousin, has thrown his weight behind Jafarian of Iranian Television for the premiership, a move he was assured had the full backing of Her Majesty. We both agree that HIM's decision to liberalise is both correct and courageous, and that morally and intellectually we are in duty bound to support it.

Wednesday, April 26

Lunch with Hassan Kamshad, just back from a month's visit to Tehran.

Hassan says he does not want to live in Iran again under the present circumstances and describes some of the early experiences which robbed him of any desire for political office. As an ardent young Leftist in the oil industry, he had been instructed by his party superiors, when Stalin died, to go round the party cells in Ahvaz, gather the workers together, sing the Internationale with them, and eulogise over Stalin's stupendous contributions to the

[1] Son Altesse Impériale la Princesse Achraf (Princess Ashraf).

171

liberation of the world proletariat. In the afternoon heat of a Khuzestan summer, with temperatures well into the forties, he would set out with his badly scratched record of the Internationale and obediently carry out his instructions. He managed always to keep a step ahead of the security forces, who would certainly not have hesitated to shoot him if they had caught him. Then in 1956 had come Khruschev's denunciation of Stalin, and with it, his own complete political disorientation and loss of identity. For days he shed bitter tears over his gigantic disillusionment and the utter worthlessness of everything that he had so absolutely believed in and had done in the name of, and for, his beliefs.

Mrs Thatcher, who is shortly to visit Tehran, and Denis Thatcher, the John Davies's, Michael and Hilary Weir and Adam Butler,[1] Mrs Thatcher's PPS, are my guests to dinner.

I try to impress Mrs Thatcher with my analysis of the Iranian/ Middle Eastern situation but suspect that I somehow fail. There is, to be sure, 'perfect understanding', to use the hackneyed diplomatic phrase, on such subjects as the dangers of world communist expansionism, the need for strong defences, and a firm hand in dealing with terrorism. But on less clear-cut issues, such as the rise of Islamic fundamentalism and its anti-Western bias, I don't believe I retain her interest. And – I am not sure whether it is done deliberately – she does jolt me when, speaking admittedly in the context of British trade unions and the hostility of some of their leaders to secret ballots and the 'one-man, one-vote' principle, she accuses them of being 'despots', and adds: 'And the worst kind of despot, in my opinion, is the benevolent one.'

I fare better with both Davies's, but don't really get a chance to speak to Mr Thatcher or Adam Butler, although Butler, for some reason, strikes me as someone who is content merely to count himself amongst those to have won first prize in the lottery of life.

Michael and Hilary stay on for a while after the others have gone. Michael, feeling I suspect that the Shah's liberalisation hasn't gone far enough, wonders whether the next step should not be the reactivation of the Majlis, while I openly wonder about the dangers of proceeding too fast.

Thursday, April 27

AAH telephones in the evening to reply to my cable enquiring about the ownership of a farm, Stilemans, which the papers say has

[1] Son of 'Rab' Butler and Conservative MP for Bosworth since 1970.

been purchased by the Iranian Horse Society, but which in reality belongs to the Crown Prince. He tells me that, if the Press makes enquiries during the Crown Prince's forthcoming visit to England, the Embassy may say that the property belongs to the Prince.

'Is that all, Sir?' I ask, feeling the conversation is drifting towards a friendly personal chat. 'Was there anything else?' he enquires. 'What about the paper I sent you, Sir, on the activities of the Revenge or Vengeance Committees?'

'Oh,' he says, with no trace of emotion in his voice, 'new situations lead to new reactions to those situations, and we must wait and see and hope that pressure, on both sides, will subside.'

'Yes, Sir.'

Friday, April 28

The Embassy's reply to the *Times* interview appears in the paper. It is over my signature and begins:

'May I say at the outset that while it is a source of deep regret to my government that the home of Mr Mahmoud Manian, whom your article describes as one of the leaders of the Iranian National Front, was made the subject of a recent bomb attack in Tehran, my government, in like manner, deplores the fact that many of Mr Manian's co-ideologues have been responsible in recent weeks for acts which can only be described as the lowest form of hooliganism.'

Lunch at the BBC for a two-hour sparring session with Gerald Mansell and his colleagues.

I say that what comes out from the BBC, or for that matter from other foreign Persian language broadcasts, such as those from Radio Moscow, Radio South Yemen or Radio Iran Courier (which operates from East Germany), is not going to decide the destiny of Iran, and is not particularly important either. 'There is, however, one distinguishing factor about the BBC. While the other Persian language transmissions are honest in their desire to see the overthrow of the régime in Iran, the BBC, which is quick to boast its independence and impartiality, remains the broadcasting agency of a country that is a military ally of Iran. It is an agency which is directly financed by the British Government, with the length of each foreign language broadcast determined in consultation with the Foreign and Commonwealth Office.'

'We don't even mind,' I go on, 'that the Corporation should have turned itself into an instrument for the dissemination of the views of the opponents of the Iranian régime; but is it fair that we should be expected, through our massive military and commercial purchases, to pay for that abuse?'

Mansell reiterates the BBC's impartiality and says there has never been any occasion when only the views of the régime's opponents have been given. Statistics are produced to support their claims to impartiality and their care not to give exaggerated reports about the current disturbances. Of course, they admit, mistakes may have been committed, but the BBC cannot engage in the sort of 'positive reporting' favoured by Eastern bloc countries.

Could it be, Mansell wants to know, that the BBC is distrusted and disliked in Tehran 'for historic reasons that go back to the last days of Reza Shah's reign'?[1] He wonders whether there would be any point for him in stopping off in Tehran on his forthcoming trip to India for a 'meaningful exchange of views, but not simply to be lectured to'. I deny the existence of the historic suspicion, and say that, while I personally believe his visit would be useful, I can't commit Tehran without asking.

Dinner with Liz at David Frost's.

Jimmy Goldsmith says he has just concluded a deal 'in the lower millions', to launch seven provincial newspapers in an attempt to get his own back on the Press. No sensation is more pleasing to him, he says, than the taste of revenge.

Elton John, shy to begin with, emerges as the evening proceeds as an articulate and shrewd businessman. He has just bought the Watford Football Club and speaks knowingly about the finances of the football world. At some stage, he removes his cap to show us the still raw scars on his scalp from a recent hair transplant operation.

David speaks more hopefully than optimistically about the prospects of selling his film on Iran to the networks.

Sunday, April 30

I see that the Secretary General of the Communist Party has formed the new Government in Afghanistan, and wonder whether this would mean a shift of military emphasis for us from the Gulf to our eastern borders.

---

[1] Shortly before the Allied invasion of Iran in 1941, the BBC, in its Persian language broadcasts in particular, abandoned its previous impartiality and attacked Reza Shah for his dictatorial rule and pro-German sympathies.

Monday, May 1

Farhad telephones from Tehran with the amazing news that my letter to *The Times* has been published in the Persian papers, but that 'it doesn't sound quite right in translation'.

Why hadn't a government spokesman denied the allegations in Tehran, I wonder. Being cast in the role of defender of Savak's actions I find none too edifying.

Wednesday, May 3

Lord and Lady Home come to dinner. Lord Home asks if the Shah is concerned about events in Afghanistan. 'Alarmed,' I reply. He has just come back from the States and is critical of Carter's leadership, but does say that Dean Rusk,[1] whom he greatly respects, had told him one must not underestimate Carter's mind or intellectual capacity.

In a lighter mood he tells a story about George Brown's drinking days. After his invitation to dance at some diplomatic function had twice been refused by the object of his affections, George gulps down a few more and tries a third time. When the answer is 'no' again, he demands to know 'why the bloody hell not?'

'Firstly, because you're drunk,' is the reply, 'and secondly, because I'm the Apostolic Delegate.'

Friday, May 5

My cold warrior friends, Julian Amery and Billy McLean, come to lunch. They want to know whether there had been 'a failure of intelligence' with regard to the coup in Kabul, whether the Americans knew and, if they did, had they warned us. Is there a plan to de-stabilise the communist régime now in power and, if so, who should the West back in Afghanistan? Are any plans being formulated and, if they are, should they not be formulated in Tehran?

[1] US Secretary of State, 1961–69.

Saturday, May 6

The events in Tehran now completely dominate my mind, and I find myself locked in a crisis of thoughts and emotions in which duty, conscience, loyalty, good sense, wishful-thinking, self-delusion and fear all play a part, and in turn shape my behaviour, mood or actions for the day.

The loosening of the grip in Tehran has been genuine and is now perfectly obvious, and there has been a revival of political activity throughout the country. The universities are witnessing their share of the agitation. People are being arrested, released and re-arrested for distributing pamphlets, etc. In the Majlis the debates are becoming heated and at times deal with highly sensitive matters. One deputy has openly attacked the role of the 'Revenge' and 'Resistance' committees and demanded a full explanation of the bombings.

There are many who fear this sudden release of political emotions, but I don't. This is perhaps partly because I feel the disturbances, the chaos and the criticisms all give a more authentic picture of the political scene than did the frightened silence of pre-liberalisation days; partly too because the very existence of the disorders confirms the sincerity of liberalisation, thus making my job in London easier.

But I am also anxious about the uncanny parallel between current events and those which preceded the Shah's forced departure from Iran in 1953. I fear that sooner or later someone in the Majlis is going to talk about the Constitution, about the Shah reigning and not ruling, and – heaven forbid – about corruption. What will the government do then? Ought we not to have rid ourselves of at least our more glaringly obvious faults before exposing ourselves to the full force of national and international criticism? But perhaps we shall just stumble along with no clear objective in sight, and nothing will happen.

From Tehran I receive the English translation of HIM's book, *Towards the Great Civilisation*, to forward to the publishers. But I decide to ask Donald Rauh, the Embassy's speech writer, who knows enough about us anyway, to read the script critically and to tell me whether he thinks cosmetic changes would be enough, or whether radical surgery is required, and to dilute some of the more bombastic passages. I shall have to think later what to do with Rauh's suggestions.

Monday, May 8

Le Monde has an interview with Khomeini, in which he castigates HIM's obsession with military gadgets on which billions of Iran's unreplenishable oil resources have been wasted. The disastrous state of agriculture, as well as Iran's links with the US and Israel, also come in for harsh criticism.

His animosity to the Shah's father, to the Shah and to his son, are unconcealed, and he calls for the violent overthrow not only of the Pahlavis but of Iran's Constitution as well. In his view the only perfect society was that which existed at the time of Mohammed and Ali. He repeatedly says: 'When we assume power ...'

Tuesday, May 9

William Deedes, Editor, and David Adamson, Diplomatic Correspondent, of the *Daily Telegraph* come to lunch. Deedes refers to the Embassy's action against the *Telegraph* and says: 'You were quite right to do it and I'm glad the outcome was in your favour.' I say it gave us no joy to bring the action, but the accusation couldn't be allowed to stand. He had had many secret laughs, says Deedes, because the Press Council, 'which is riddled with left-leaning NUJ reporters', had to find in favour of the Shah of Iran.

As we move to other topics, he says he is writing a letter to the editor of *Pravda* to protest against their allegation that the *Daily Telegraph* is collaborating with the Conservative Party in attacking the Soviet Union. 'Our anti-communism is our own, and has nothing to do with the Conservative Party,' he will write, explaining that the *Telegraph* has no affiliation with political parties and acts independently. 'The Russians lack the subtlety to understand that a newspaper can be independent,' he says. 'The exercise will come to nothing, but we should do it all the same.'

I feel a twinge of envy, after my guests have gone, at Deedes's sense of fair-mindedness and commitment.

Wednesday, May 10

At least eight people have been killed in rioting in Iran, and the authorities have acted, according to one paper, 'with unaccustomed nervousness'.

Thursday, May 11

Two thousand soldiers have surrounded the bazaar in Tehran and fired shots into the air to disperse the demonstrators. All the leading dailies carry front page news of the disturbances and speak of the government's determination to stamp out unrest. HIM has postponed an official visit to Bulgaria because of a cold, but everyone suspects the bug is of the Qom variety.

I do a radio interview with the BBC World Service and speak to Farhad again in the evening. No one, he says, seems to know what's going on. A clamp-down is not only needed, he thinks, but is overdue.

I hear on the BBC news driving home someone called David Watts from *The Times* actually say 'reliable sources in Tehran say one in every three Iranians is a member of Savak'.

Friday, May 12

The AFP man rings to say they have a report from Ankara that a coup d'état has taken place in Tehran, and would I comment. 'Yes. Nonsense,' I say.

Saturday, May 13

David Adamson of the *Daily Telegraph*, writing from Tehran, says: 'Faced with Persia's worst internal unrest in almost two decades, the Shah has been forced to end his 'New Freedom' policy, introduced only two months ago at the urging of President Carter.' There is a reference to the return of censorship. The despatch then goes on to say: 'Ranged against the Shah are the religious hierarchy of the Moslem Shia sect and a significant proportion of the university students.' It concludes: 'These developments leave the Shah's throne shaken but by no means near collapse. The army and the police show no sign of disaffection, and the middle classes are not siding with the ayatollahs and the mullahs, whom they regard as primitive.'

In the afternoon I hear that the expected clamp-down has come at last. HIM has declared he will not tolerate Iran's being turned into a Soviet republic. A number of religious leaders are 'to go abroad for medical treatment'.

178

That the mullahs should have seized on the new freedoms to air their views is hardly surprising. For a while we began believing our own propaganda, thinking, or perhaps wishing, that ingrained attitudes could be changed overnight. All that nonsense about 'the fifth most industrialised nation in the world'! We are in fact a primitive, under-developed country, in which the influence of religion, as interpreted by a bigoted, ignorant clergy, reigns supreme. This we were too proud to accept, far less to admit.

But I wonder whether the events of the past few weeks will ultimately prove to be a healthy lesson for HIM; whether he will now see fit to limit the activities of members of his own circle; whether some of his more objectionable associates will be, if not dismissed in disgrace, at least placed at some distance from him; whether the casinos and the Madame Claude girls[1] can now be regarded as not essential to Iran's forward march; whether less money will be spent on arms and more on such neglected sectors as agriculture; and whether the Rastakhiz Party will be allowed to disappear.

More selfishly, I think of the Embassy's work in London. The exile of the religious leaders will mean continued and intensified student agitation. Moreover, the clamp-down must mean the reactivation of Savak and along with that a resurgence of charges of torture and ill-treatment. The dreaded correspondence with Amnesty will then be resumed.

But I also have a visceral feeling that the entire episode – the initial relaxation, the subsequent riots, the ultimate clampdown – have somehow strengthened, rather than weakened, the Shah's position. It can now at least be argued that the removal of all constraints on personal freedom must be seen as a perilous experiment that only favours the clergy at the expense of the Shah. The pressure on HIM to mend his ways will abate somewhat, and with the armed forces unswervingly loyal he would be okay.

I do wish, however, he would make at least nominal concessions, such as dissolving the Rastakhiz, which really was an appalling mistake right from the start; and that, instead of making the National Front and the Communists bear the brunt of his attacks, he would also pillory those who wish to take the country back to seventh-century Arabia.

Random thoughts, futile and ineffectual, and certainly of no consequence.

---

[1] An allusion to a notorious call-girl network in Paris.

Monday, May 15

HIM has given a press interview in which he has said, in essence, that '*l'état, c'est moi*'. The Rastakhiz is to stay ('what bed of roses has multi-party democracy brought the West?'). Both the *Telegraph* and the *Financial Times* report that the middle classes are disappointed by the continued existence of the single political party.

Tuesday, May 16

A leader in *The Times*, to my surprise and relief, is not scathing or damaging, but perceptive and fair. I ask Adam Fergusson,[1] now working part-time for the Embassy, to draft a reply, supporting the leader's point of view.

I attend a luncheon in honour of Judith Hart, Minister for Overseas Development, at the Hampstead home of the Bangladeshi High Commissioner, Shamso-Doha. My motives for doing so are not completely innocent. Miss Hart[2] is one of the sponsors of CARI, the Committee Against Repression in Iran, and her name appears on the Committee's letterhead.

Perhaps not surprisingly, I find myself seated next to her at lunch. Do her extra-curricular activities, I ask, extend to countries other than Iran, and when she looks puzzled I mention CARI. To my delight, she blushes visibly, and asks whether her name *still* appears on the letterhead. When I confirm that it does she says, 'It is wrong for a Government Minister's name to be there, and it must be removed.'

Does she sponsor similar committees against repression in other countries, I persist – countries like Ethiopia, Cambodia, Eastern Europe, the Soviet Union itself, or indeed Mozambique, about which she has been speaking.

She sits upright in her chair, turns to me as much as the table allows and says, in forceful, measured tones: 'I am a human rightist, and would defend those rights wherever they are violated.' She adds that the Western press has painted an incorrect picture of Mozambique: 'They have a way of twisting facts around.' I stare at her. 'But of course you'd say the same thing from the other angle,' she adds.

Her assistant, Tony, knows Fereydoun Hoveyda from his

[1] Conservative MEP for West Strathclyde since 1979; formerly feature-writer for *The Times*, 1967–77.

[2] Subsequently Dame Judith Hart.

180

UNESCO days. 'The British', he says, 'shouldn't talk about human rights to others as long as Northern Ireland goes on'. As we rise to leave the Minister turns to Tony and says, 'Remind me to remove my name from that letterhead.'

I hope I have succeeded in spoiling her day a little, I say to myself, as Ronald drives me back to the Chancery.

Dinner at the Mexican Ambassador's. Lord Barnetson[1] says he will soon be off again to the Aspen Institute in Colorado to hear Empress Farah. At the last session, he says, Ardeshir, in the course of his remarks, had described himself as a devoted and faithful servant of His Majesty's, and had ended his remarks by saying, 'And to hell with the Iranian Government.' The Empress, perhaps somewhat embarrassed by so complete and public a damnation, had intervened to ask whether Ardeshir's views were not influenced by the fact that he himself wanted to become Prime Minister. Whereupon Ardeshir had risen from his seat, walked over to the Empress, lifted the pony tail of her hair, and planted a kiss on the nape of her neck. Barnetson and Kissinger, also present at the occasion, had exchanged astonished glances.

Wednesday, May 17

Dr Fallah, back in London, comes to lunch. Qom, he says, is under 'military occupation', an operation in the course of which Ayatollah Shariatmadari's son-in-law has been shot dead by the troops. In protest, Mehdi Bazargan had led a crowd of Koran-carrying demonstrators up Nasser Khosro Avenue under the nervous eyes of the police. The inclusion of the religious element, he says, makes the absolute reliability of the security forces less certain.

Dr Fallah also says: 1) AAH is not winning the fight to rid the Court Ministry of elements he considers undesirable, and has not been allowed to make a single dismissal or appointment of his own; 2) Ardeshir is at last to be recalled from Washington and replaced by Khalatbary, according to the latest rumours; 3) HIM had not agreed to a request to disband Rastakhiz; 4) He had not the slightest doubt that the two hundred people who paraded in central Tehran the other day carrying 'hammer and sickle' placards were all members of Savak.

In the evening I hear an interview on BBC Radio 4 with an

[1] Chairman of the *Observer*, 1976–80.

Iranian ex-army officer who describes in gruesome detail the tortures he has been subjected to. My mood blackens as I realise that months of endeavour to achieve – if we ever did achieve – a snail's pace improvement in our image abroad is yet again being washed away, and our much vaunted protestations of liberalisation turned into a sham.

Thursday, May 18

Sure enough, there is wide coverage of yesterday's radio interview in the papers, with elaborate details of the torture methods employed, the instruments used, etc.

I chide myself for being so naive as to think that the more distasteful aspects of Savak's activities had been terminated and its over-zealous goons brought under control. I call in Kakhi to draft a cable to Tehran, suggesting: 1) that we publicly express regret over the excesses committed, but stress that the events relate to the period before the introduction of liberalisation; and 2) that we provide as much detailed information as possible on the accused persons' alleged involvement with communist organisations. I know this won't please HIM and prepare myself for his wrath.

The Enoch Powells and the Woodrow Wyatts come to lunch. Lively debate soon rages between Enoch and Verushka, Woodrow's Hungarian wife, about whether the Russians have expansionist designs throughout the world, with Enoch denying, and Verushka insisting, that they do.

A man obviously of vast erudition, with an elephantine memory, Powell seems to enjoy espousing controversial opinions. 'After the first year of our marriage', says Mrs Powell, 'I felt as if I had received a university education.'

Friday, May 19

An unfavourable article by David Watts in *The Times* on the plight of political prisoners and the continued practice of torture in Iran.

I am reminded of the thinness of the ice on which I tread when I learn that our man in Bonn, Amir Mokri, has been recalled after only six months, because he had incurred HIM's displeasure.

Monday, May 22

Hossein Eshraghi has called twice from Budapest yesterday and I have foolishly not connected Budapest with the fact that HIM is on an official visit to Hungary and that Hossein and Khalatbary are in his entourage. He finds me at 7.30 in the morning and in a rather serious tone conveys to me H.I.M's comments on my *Times*-torture-interview cable. This is that the allegations are complete fabrications and Radji should give a press conference and say so. I protest that I know nothing about the alleged guilt of the individuals involved, and to speak to the press and deny allegations of mistreatment when the victims still bear the scars of their physical tortures would be to invite ridicule.

'Sorry,' he says, 'these are HIM's instructions.'

'Then tell the Foreign Minister that I respectfully request the instructions be revised.'

He will, he says, but the Foreign Minister isn't available, and they are returning to Tehran in a few hours.

I sit behind my desk at the office and simply fume for a while. I then send another cable to Tehran, repeating what I said to Hossein, and arguing that for me to give a press conference now would be to refocus public attention on an ugly episode that is best forgotten.

Sir Harold Wilson, shortly to visit Iran at the invitation of some obscure international academic association, comes to lunch. He is going to Tehran, he says, really only because HIM will see him while he is there. I do my stint on Iran, but get the feeling that he is neither very up to date on Iran nor madly interested in it.

In the evening Edward Heath, Stephen Spender, Cyrus Ghani, Graham Storey, my tutor at Trinity Hall, and Charlie Douglas-Home come to my first ever stag dinner. Heath has just come back from Mali, which he visited under the auspices of the Brandt Commission, to make recommendations for bridging the gap between the rich and poor nations. It is in that capacity that he will soon be visiting Iran.

When he absents himself briefly to go and vote in a division, the conversation switches entirely on to him, and the view is again expressed that his inability to make contact with people robs him of a human vision when he is dealing with political or social situations.

After dinner we resume the conversation in the more relaxed atmosphere of the drawing-room. All agree that the qualities that make for a successful one-term Governor of Georgia are not those that are needed for the leadership of the non-communist world. The Chinese, says Heath, were angry that Cyrus Vance had gone to Peking with nothing new to offer on Taiwan. He believes that a combination of Japanese technology and Chinese manpower could potentially pose the greatest threat to the economic well-being of the West.

Cyrus seems quite fascinated by Heath and the political chatter, and so I think is Stephen.

Tuesday, May 23

I learn, with massive relief, that HIM has accepted my reasons for not holding a press conference, but has reiterated his view that I 'must not dismiss the possibility that the alleged ill-treatment was pure fabrication'. HIM, I tell myself, is speaking for the record. I am so grateful to be off the hook.

Wednesday, May 24

I see off Prince Gholam Reza at the airport and get back in time for lunch with Peter Avery and Nicholas Bethell. Afghanistan as well as the Iranian political scene are discussed, and from them I learn that during Mrs Thatcher's recent visit to Tehran and audience with HIM, he had raised the vexed subject of the BBC's Persian language broadcasts. Naturally, I was told nothing.

In the evening I am Mrs Thatcher's guest at the Carlton Club. William Whitelaw and his wife, Adam Butler and wife, Eldon Griffiths, Richard Luce and several bank and business chairmen are there assembled in the Disraeli Room. The conversation is friendly rather than serious and I tell my host that HIM had been most impressed by her courage and strength of personality. The evening ends at 10.

Wednesday, May 31

I spend the afternoon speaking to people in Tehran on the telephone. Hossein Eshraghi says that, in spite of all the care taken

184

over arrangements for it, he fears that the visit of the British MPs may not be immune from its share of Iranian bureaucratic bungling. My position in London, he says, is 'very strong', but 'there is a campaign against you, along the lines that Radji's policy of combatting the mullahs is wrong, and that such a policy will never succeed'. Adl, however, he assures me, is not to be taken too seriously.

I then speak to Farhad. They had all been at Cyrus Ghani's last night and some had been quite panicky 'not about the stability of Iran, but about the survival of the régime'. The constant machinations of the mullahs have given much cause for apprehension.

Friday, June 2

Roberto Campos, the Brazilian Ambassador, comes to lunch. He too is off to Iran for a meeting of the so-called Aspen-Kissinger Committee which will meet in Ramsar. Roberto, as always, is in excellent form. He says Pinochet in Chile has done wonders for the economy, brought down inflation from 1,400 per cent during Allende's last days to an acceptable figure, and raised real living standards, although his public relations are bad and there is brutality. But that is not exceptional in Latin America. 'The Spaniards and their South American descendants have a feel for blood which the Portuguese and, consequently, the Brazilians, have never shared,' he says, 'and this partly explains the employment of cruel methods.' He is sensibly and moderately hawkish on Africa and the Middle East and believes the Western objective ought to be the eviction of the Russians from Afghanistan and curtailment of their influence in Iraq.

One reason why the West has not been able to produce an effective strategy for the Middle East, he says, is Begin's religious and ethnic fanaticism. Begin shares with the Ayatollah the characteristic of being a theologian who wants to rewrite geography in the light of the Holy Scriptures. The need not to antagonise Begin prevented the Americans from directing their attention to the bigger issue of the Soviet penetration of the area, which is facilitated by the continuing 'Palestinian diaspora'. It was no solution, he believed, to end the Jewish diaspora by creating a Palestinian diaspora.

The most dangerous creatures of our day and age, he thinks, are not the revolutionary Marxists but the romantic socialists: 'The sons of bitches are utterly respectable in intention and utterly

185

ineffectual in practice.' Of the others on the committee who are going to Iran, he describes Heath as 'articulate though not always profound'; Charles Schultze as 'a marvellous thinker though not always articulate', and Raymond Aron as 'physically enfeebled but still one of the great minds of our time'.

I cable the gist of Roberto's remarks to HIM, making sure the 'sons of bitches' reference is included.

Saturday, June 3

I read in the *Guardian* that Mehdi Bazargan, a National Front activist, has invited HIM to a live TV debate, American-style, and that big demonstrations are expected in Tehran tomorrow, as they are in London.

Sunday, June 4

AAH telephones to say that William Butler, an American human rights lawyer, has made a number of suggestions for improving the procedure of our military tribunals, a copy of which he wants me to pass on to Amnesty. I ask about the demonstrations. 'They won't be serious, as the religious leaders are against them,' he says.

I have a tendency to accept everything AAH says unquestioningly, even though I feel in my heart of hearts that what he says can't be right.

Monday, June 5

General Nassiri, head of Savak, has been removed. A wise and expedient move, even if it is, as I suspect, a change in appearance rather than substance.

Tuesday, June 6

Mohsen Goudarzi, head of the Foreign Minister's Private Secretariat, who is passing through London, stops by to see me. He says that, while my cables are the most interesting ones to read and he respects me for saying the things I do, I should exercise greater caution. He singles out three cables in particular – my comments on the Owen–Khalatbary exchange over the BBC Persian Services, the recommendation that Amnesty be allowed to visit the Qasr Prison food strikers, and the 'no' to HIM's specific instructions to hold a press conference. He adds: 'As a friend, I tell you, be careful.'

I see, to my delight, that General Nasser Moghaddam, and not Nassiri's number two at Savak, has been appointed in his place. I know Moghaddam from my days at the PM's office, and feel he will be a humanising influence at Savak.

As guest of John Dickie of the *Daily Mail* I attend a press luncheon for Moraji Desai, the visiting Indian Prime Minister. His lunch, I notice, consists of dried almonds which he dips in honey, apples and pears, and orange juice. He is a smelly sort of person, I suspect. However, one phrase from his well-written but not well-delivered after-lunch speech I include in my cable to Tehran, just to keep up the pressure: 'India does not believe that bread and liberty are incompatible.'

Drinks with Edward Heath, who has asked to see me, in the course of which I do all the talking, and walk back to the Embassy with the confusion of all sorts of thoughts raging fiercely in my head. Some relief is supplied by watching the World Cup match between France and Argentina, and the pleasure of seeing the Frogs lose.

Thursday, June 8

There are two fairly positive references to the Moghaddam appointment, one oddly in the *Guardian* describing him as 'a legal reformer and an opponent of torture'.

In my note of congratulations to Moghaddam, which I mark 'Personal', I include the two clippings. I also write a letter to AAH, 'congratulating myself' over the Moghaddam appointment, and suggesting, should HIM deem it appropriate, that the General holds a press conference in the next few weeks, in the course of which he declares the Government's firm determination to combat lawlessness, asserts that the practice of torture has been strictly forbidden, and declares himself personally available to look into any violations of this ruling that are brought to his attention.

Sunday, June 11

There is a cable signed by Amir Aslan Afshar, Chief of Court Protocol, asking me to intervene with the FCO to have Behbahanian, Under-Secretary at the Court Ministry, included in the dinner being given at Windsor for the Crown Prince. I decide to do nothing, but smoulder for a while.

Monday, June 12

My dinner guests, ten in all, include the Earl of Dudley and his attractive wife, Maureen. As we assemble in the drawing-room upstairs Lord Dudley observes that 'this is not the first time Maureen finds herself in the more private apartments of your Embassy'. Maureen then tells how in 1959 or 1960, she can't remember which, before she had married her present husband and was still his girl-friend, and on a night when they had had an argument, Geoffrey Keating had telephoned to ask whether she wanted to dine with the Shah of Persia. The Earl had returned later to make up the quarrel, only to find that his girl-friend was about to step into the limousine waiting to take her to dinner at the Iranian Embassy.

On arrival at the Embassy she had discovered that the other guests of the evening, some twenty in all, were men. The Shah shortly thereafter had arrived – 'he wasn't good-looking' – had given her the once, or twice, over, after which dinner had been served, 'in the same room, can you imagine?' After dinner, the game of Cardinal something or other had been played, where everyone was required to down a glassful of whisky or some such, and perform complicated acts of bodily contortions in turn. Gradually the others had disappeared discreetly and left the Shah and her alone. It was only then, free from the presence of the others, that she found him to be a shy, warm and gentle man. But he would repeatedly revert to his role-playing, and had put on a tango record and asked her to dance. 'I refused,' she says, 'and despite anything Geoffrey may have told you, my evening with the Shah, and my relationship with King Hussein, were both perfectly innocent.' With an air of resigned contentment she adds: 'I ended up marrying an English earl. At least this way there won't by any bullets flying around.'

188

Tuesday, June 13

Dinner at the Hampstead home of the Andrew Knights.[1] Christopher Soames is the least inhibited in voicing his opinions of others, and wastes no time in ridiculing Thatcher ('was His Majesty impressed with her immense knowledge of the international scene?'); castigating Heath ('incapable of flexibility ... should either accept the new leadership, as Alec did, or get out'); and deriding Owen ('sad that the British Foreign Secretary should put his faith, and fate, in the hands of someone like Andrew Young'). He also laughs at some of Ansari's boastful exaggerations about Iran's industrial capacity during the negotiations for EEC concessions. But although I consider Christopher an incorrigible bully, I quite enjoy his company.

As the name of Allah, inscribed in graceful Arabic calligraphy, peers down upon us from the wall of Mrs Knight's elegant dining-room, and we sip her delicious wine, I reflect that she has reconciled, with gentleness and serenity, the contradictions between her Moslem upbringing and her adopted life style.

Thursday, June 15

I receive a letter from Bryan Magee in which he says:

'If your and their chief aim was to convince us that the present régime deserves more sympathy and understanding than it commonly receives here, you succeeded, at least as far as I am concerned (and I think as far as my colleagues are concerned also). This is not to say that I have suddenly become an uncritical admirer: you would not expect that. But I have reached the view that the present régime, for all its shortcomings, is preferable to any alternative which is actually available, and is therefore to be defended against them; so I would now, as I would not have done before, oppose those who call for its overthrow. This shift of opinion is as much the result of the reading I did in preparation for my visit as the visit itself – but of course without the visit I would not have done the reading.

'Having been through this experience, may I make bold to say to you that I do not think the régime you serve has conducted its public relations well? If one lives here in England one has only the choice between your government's propaganda – which one actually ignores or disbelieves because it is so obviously propa-
[1] Editor of the *Economist*.

189

ganda (and which in the recent past has been so excessively boastful) – and the extremist attacks of its opponents. Straightforward, unadorned, objective information is so hard to come by that most people here never see any. Yet it is this more than anything which would influence their opinion in your favour ... In other words, what it would be more in your interests to provide than anything else is a flow of accurate and reliable information, including information unfavourable to yourselves.'

To ensure that it receives as wide a circulation as possible, I send copies of the letter separately to the Court and Foreign Ministers.

Ali Ghaffari, one of AAH's aides at the Court Ministry, telephones to say he has just sent me a cable transmitting the Court Minister's instructions that I indicate to the FCO that Behbahanian should be included in the Windsor dinner.

I explode. 'There is nothing I consider more deeply offensive to my dignity,' I tell Ali, 'than to beg for an invitation – for myself, for Behbahanian or for anyone else no matter how attractive the Windsor dinner may be.' If they are serious about the request, I suggest they convey it through the British Embassy in Tehran.

'You don't seem to understand,' Ali protests, 'these are HIM's instructions.'

I reply that had HIM been properly apprised of the circumstances he would certainly not have issued such instructions, if indeed he has issued them at all.

The minute I hang up I get an attack of cold feet. Am I not, I ask myself, over-reacting to what, after all, is only a dinner invitation? Should I not display less temerity in dismissing what are, or are purported to be, my sovereign's specific instructions?

I ask a colleague to inquire from the FCO whether there would be any chance of raising the quota of Iranians at the dinner by one. They ring back an hour later to say that 'it is embarrassing, but the reply from the Palace is "no".' I cable the Palace's 'no' to Tehran, but my mind is only set at rest after I have rung Tehran and spoken to AAH. I explain the circumstances to him and say that I would find it infinitely easier to challenge Martin Ennals to a duel than to appear to attach so much importance to attending a dinner. His prolonged guffaw is sufficient to dispel any remaining anxiety. He fully understands, he says, and mocks Behbahanian's insistence on being included at the dinner. He suspects that Behbahanian himself initially put the wheels in motion. Laughingly, he refers to the Court Ministry as 'a nest of vipers', and bemoans the fact that he has jumped out of the frying-pan into the fire. I am to do nothing more on the matter of the invitation unless I hear from him.

Monday, June 19

BBC's Radio 4 had a programme on Iran yesterday, the tape of which I listen to at the office. Unidentified dissident voices, recorded in Tehran, speak of constant harassment by Savak, of intimidation, of threats of kidnapping, of beatings. One voice, describing HIM's claims of liberalisation as bogus, believes 'one cannot hope for Stalin to change into Bertrand Russell overnight'. Another, speaking even better English than the first, complains that 'at least with the Mafia one has a choice of families. Here, there's only one'.

Amouzegar has been interviewed for the programme, and to my surprise he sounds nervous, unconvincing and at times unnaturally jolly.

I cable the gist of the programme to Tehran, knowing full well that their only reaction will be to castigate me for not doing enough to silence the BBC.

Tuesday, June 20

I read an interview by HIM in the *International Herald Tribune* which makes my flesh curl. 'No one can overthrow me', he says, 'because I have the support of 700,000 troops, most of the workers and the majority of the people.'

At 5.30 the Crown Prince arrives. His Boeing 707 taxis to a remote corner of Heathrow, where two gentlemen from the Royal Household, Michael Weir from the Foreign Office, and ten senior Embassy staff as well as myself, receive him. The Prince, whom I am now meeting for the first time for five years, has grown tall and bears a striking resemblance to his father at the same age. His English is okay.

I drive with him in the official car to Windsor Castle, his ADC, Colonel Ahmad Oveisi, seated in the front. I deposit them in the care of Sir Peter Ashmore.[1] I change into my dinner-jacket in the hotel room at London Airport I have taken for that purpose, and get back to Windsor punctually at 8.15.

Unbeknown to me the occasion also marks the Waterloo Dinner, which requires the Duke of Wellington to kneel before the Queen at some stage and, in a ceremony lasting no more than ten seconds, to present her with a French tricolor as symbolic rent for the mansion he now occupies. The ceremony, the Duke explains, is the

[1] Master of the Queen's Household.

191

requirement of an Act of Parliament passed after the Battle of Waterloo.

I am assigned to take the Duchess of Gloucester into dinner, while the Queen is taken in by the Crown Prince, who sits on her right, and has the Queen Mother on his right. My two ladies are Princess Anne and the Duchess of Gloucester, and the *plat de résistance*, not surprisingly, is Boeuf à la Wellington.

After dinner we listen to Cleo Laine and Johnny Dankworth, then return to more drinks in the Grand Reception Room. Although it is nearly four in the morning Tehran time, the Crown Prince shows no outward signs of fatigue. The Queen comments approvingly on this, and shortly afterwards they leave; and so do I.

Wednesday, June 21

Moinzadeh, my security liaison, rings early in the morning to say that the dissidents have decided in the course of a meeting last night to mount a demonstration today to coincide with the Crown Prince's arrival at the Ascot races. Because of the traffic it takes Manuel an hour and twenty minutes to drive me to Ascot, but I eventually make it to Roger du Boulay's[1] lunch for the Crown Prince's entourage. We then watch the arrival of the coaches bearing the Royal Family and the Crown Prince, as some fifty-odd demonstrators chant anti-Shah slogans in the background.

We proceed to the Diplomatic Enclosure, and after the fourth race are invited to the Royal Enclosure for tea with the Royal party. I am placed at the Queen Mother's table, and she sweetly reminisces about her visit to Shiraz and Persepolis. She adds that Prince Michael and his bride will be going to Iran for part of their honeymoon, and she is going to write 'the Shahbanou' a note about their trip. She, too, praises the Crown Prince's impeccable conduct 'last night'.

After the last race, Prince Philip takes the Crown Prince to watch polo. We take our leave, and as I walk to the car park to look for Manuel, I hear the familiar chant: 'The Shah is a murderer.'

Thursday, June 22

I rise at 7 and drive to Windsor to collect the Crown Prince, whose stay at the Castle ends at 9, when he is to fly by helicopter to the

[1] Vice Marshal of the Diplomatic Corps.

192

Royal Naval College, Dartmouth. Prince Philip and Prince Charles are there to say goodbye to him. On the helicopter I see that the popular papers carry photos of both the Prince and the demonstrators.

Captain Paul Greening, whom we met at the dinner last night, welcomes the Prince at Dartmouth. The Iranian national anthem is played and a guard of honour inspected. A series of mildly interesting lectures on how the college is run then follow, the impression conveyed being that the end product is as much a miniscientist as an officer.

The Prince then meets and chats with the 24 Iranian naval cadets at the College, who look impressive. Lunch at Captain Greening's house. We then go on a tour of the river before returning to the Captain's house for tea, and finally emplane for the hour-long flight to Odiham. During the 35-minute drive to Godalming, near which Stilemans, the Imperial estate, is situated, the Prince, who has been complaining of a mild attack of plane-sickness, and now of car-sickness, becomes ill-tempered, and speaking more to his ADC than to me, asks why the helicopter had not been told to land at Stilemans. Colonel Oveisi professes not to know, but hazards the unfortunate guess that considerations of security or a desire for anonymity might have had something to do with it. Whereupon the Prince, pointing to the Iranian tricolour on the car, demands to know whether that explanation is offered 'as some kind of a joke'.

I ask the representative of government hospitality, who is in the car with us, to stop the car and remove the flag, and give the Prince an air-sickness tablet brought along for myself. But he goes on grumbling about 'not having thought of the obvious in planning the arrangements for the day', a matter, he says, 'that I must bring to the attention of my father'.

We reach Stilemans without further incident, and as soon as the Prince sees the familiar faces of his school-mates there assembled and has changed into jeans and a pullover, his mood improves noticeably.

I sip champagne and chat with Roger du Boulay while the Prince speaks with his father in Tehran and, according to an obviously relieved Oveisi, tells him everything had gone very well.

Saturday, June 24

Cyrus Ghani, telephoning from the Forest Mere health farm, wants to know whether the rumours about my recall to Tehran are true,

193

and I say that I have been told nothing officially.

'How will you react if they are true?'

'Naturally, I will do what I am told.'

'It will be a pity to leave the Embassy.'

'Yes, but Tehran has always had its compensations for me.'

He still thinks I should stay in London.

I see from the Persian papers that Pezeshkpour, one of the more outspoken members of the Majlis, has announced that while he remains faithful to the principles of Rastakhiz, he sees no reason why he should remain faithful to a political organisation which, according to the Shah himself, has failed to achieve its objectives. He therefore intends to revive his own Pan-Iranist Party. Others have followed his lead and are about to found parties of their own, while Homayoun, the Information Minister, has denied that membership of the Rastakhiz is compulsory.

I find it all utterly amazing. We had sunk so low, certainly when I was in Tehran, that failure to agree with everything HIM said and did was equated with treason. Now *Kayhan* editorials speak of distinguishing between criticism and disloyalty; and Nahavandi, the Empress's Principal Secretary, and his group of intellectuals have even gone as far as to say that the Shah–People Revolution, like any other revolution, suppressed all opposition in its initial stages, and this meant that many patriotic and able Iranians were prevented from serving their country.

We have come a very long way in a very short time, with political tolerance showing a sudden, unexpected and massive enlargement. *Pourvu que ça dure*!

Monday, June 26

The Empress telephones me from Tehran to ask about the Crown Prince's stay at Windsor, and I assure her that even by independent accounts his demeanour had been unexceptionable.

A perceptive, well informed article about the medieval bigotry of the mullahs in the *Guardian*, written, *not* by Thurgood, but by Martin Woollacott.

Tuesday, June 27

Tony and Sheila Parsons, on home leave, come to lunch. Everything from the BBC, the recent disturbances, the changes at Savak, to Rastakhiz and Tony's own future prospects is discussed. Sheila, who is quite outspoken in her loathing for the nouveau riche aspects of life in Iran, believes, as do so many others, that rapid industrialisation and the onset of the materialistic rat race have led to the alienation of youth and a search for refuge in traditional values such as those of religion. Tony thinks that, if the power of the mullahs is still as immense as the authorities fear, then obviously the progressive reforms of the past fifteen years, or indeed of the past fifty years, have failed in their intended purpose of bringing about a change in attitudes. Hmm!

Thursday, June 29

Manuel drives me, on a gloomy rainy day, to Stilemans where I am to escort the Crown Prince, who leaves for America today, to the airport. The Prince has so enjoyed his stay, Behbahanian tells me, that he has been urging his parents to come and spend a few days there, and a number of security officers will in fact shortly be arriving to inspect the house.

On the drive to the airport I tell the Prince that some members of the Royal Family had been impressed by the fact that on the night of his arrival he had stayed up so late without showing any signs of weariness. The Prince looks surprised at first. Then, with an air of bemused resignation, he says: 'I just don't understand what impresses the English'.

Angus Ogilvy comes to lunch, tête-à-tête. He praises HIM, but also asks about the spread of corruption and contingency plans if anything should happen to the Shah. He mentions, more than once, that if I should ever wish to see someone in the Government through other than my formal diplomatic channels, he would be very pleased to arrange such informal contacts. He strikes me as genuinely friendly and very helpful, with an admirable capacity for mid-day drinking.

Monday, July 3

Today is *Mab'ath*, the anniversary of the day in 610, when Mohammad heard the Lord's call appointing him as his messenger, and as such, one of the most important in our religious calendar. Yet the traditional ceremonies in the presence of HIM will again not be observed, because he 'has a cold'. I wonder whether the initiative not to hold official ceremonies comes from HIM, or the mullahs!

Tuesday, July 4

Amir Mas'oud Mirfakhrai, an old friend and a former colleague from my days at the Oil Company and the Prime Minister's Office, and now an aide to AAH at the Court Ministry, comes to see me. I have known him and worked with him for far too long not to trust him completely. He says my report of April 21 to the Court Minister (in which I had demanded an end to the activities of the Revenge and Vengeance Committees) had unleashed commotions of stupendous magnitude and secrecy, with senior representatives of Savak and the Special Bureau meeting in seemingly endless discussion with the Ministers of Information and Justice and others. He confirms that AAH is encountering stiff resistance in making even minor changes in the Court Ministry, an office where greater value is attached to loyalty than to probity, and that his reputation had therefore suffered.

Denis Wright comes to lunch. He has seen George Lenczonski's latest book on Iran, and has heard that Lesley Blanch is writing one on the Empress. He wonders when we shall realise the futility of such sycophantic approaches to public relations.

Denis says previous Iranian Ambassadors were wrong to ignore Nancy Lambton 'because every British Prime Minister, after reading his FO dispatches, would ask her round for a chat to learn her opinion on the matter. She is, after all, a cousin of both Alec Douglas-Home *and* Harold Macmillan'.

Nancy Lambton, I reflect when Denis has gone, was Press Attaché at the Embassy in Tehran during the war, and so a witness to the Tehran Conference, attended by Churchill, Roosevelt and Stalin, in December 1943. Then the Allies were emerging victorious in their war against Germany, and Lambton was part of the winning team. The Shah, on the other hand, had seen his father deposed by the British two years previously. He was the youthful and inexperienced King of an invaded and impoverished country, at the mercy of the occupying powers, at the nadir of his political and military influence.

The fluctuating fortunes of the two countries in the course of the subsequent decades have not obliterated or even modified Nancy Lambton's initial impression of the Shah. The fact that he is now omnipotent inside Iran, and courted outside, is in possession of vast oil riches and a sophisticated military arsenal, make him seem to her arrogant and vainglorious. That is indeed how she must appear to him, a rankling reminder of a humiliating chapter in Iran's history, an anachronism whose country, no longer in possession of its vast empire, is struggling to arrest its own rapid economic decline.

After the institution of the Shah's reforms in Iran in 1963, Lambton, by now Professor of Persian at the School of Oriental and African Studies, wrote a book critical of the most salient feature of the Shah's 'White Revolution', i.e. land reform, and thus brought upon herself the Shah's permanent displeasure. Lambton has undoubtedly been a person of influence in forming British political attitudes towards Iran, but no Iranian Ambassador who consorted with her could ever be sure of retaining his post for long.

Wednesday, July 5

Despite the cloudy and gloomy weather outside, the sun shines in my heart as I read in both *The Times* and *IHT* that AAH has succeeded in obtaining HIM's approval for establishing a code of business ethics for members of the Royal Family that would in effect end their interference and influence-peddling in major contracts.

Friday, July 7

From York House, where she has been lunching with the Duchess of Kent, I pick up Princess Fatemeh, and with Manuel at the wheel follow the royal procession to Wimbledon at nerve-racking speed. From the Royal Box we watch Martina Navratilova, in an exciting match, beat Chris Evert. After the ladies' singles and tea, the Princess, who is not as demanding as some other members of her family, wants to leave. None of us, however, can locate our respective cars and drivers, but there are plenty of taxis around, and she decides to take one.

'Do you go to London?' she asks a cabbie.
'Where in London do you want to go, lady?'
'Hyde Park Gate.'

'You see, at this time of day, with traffic being what it is, it's going to cost you six or seven pounds, lady.'

'That's all right.'

'Are you sure, lady?' the cabbie insists.

'Yes, I'm sure,' she says, unable to control her laughter any longer. Poor, innocent cabbie. I expect the real joke is on us.

Saturday, July 8

A favourable article in the *Guardian*, *not* by Liz Thurgood, entitled: 'The Shah shoves Iran towards Freedom.' There are references to improvements in the condition of political prisoners, an end to torture, and a greater climate of political freedom, all of which puts me in a good frame of mind when Parviz Mina takes me to the BP tent at Wimbledon for lunch, and then to watch the men's finals. In four thrilling sets Borg obliterates Connors.

Tuesday, July 11

Go to an exceedingly elegant dinner, followed by dancing, at the Heinzes'[1] Ascot Lodge, and stay till 2 a.m. Amongst the many familiar faces which appear after dinner is the one belonging to that socially ubiquitous monkey, Bianca Jagger.

Edward Heath says he met a number of mullahs in Mashad. When I ask whether they had succeeded in illuminating his thoughts, he beams his shark's smile and, shaking with laughter nods his head repeatedly.

Wednesday, July 12

An interesting tête-à-tête lunch with Eldon Griffiths at PG. He has just returned from a visit to America and Cuba, having in Washington seen Ardeshir, who had expressed a desire to return to Iran before the end of the year.

'Not to take up gardening?' I ask. Eldon remains silent.

'To be appointed Court Minister?' I persist.

'That's a possibility.'

[1] Mr and Mrs Jack Heinz.

With impressive command, he ranges far and wide over the international scene, expressing particular concern that so many American senators are now being assisted by completely inexperienced university graduates, many of whom are even more Left-leaning than the Tribunites in Britain. He speaks of Castro's projection of himself as 'the liberator of the colonial peoples', and of the Cuban economy's virtually complete dependence on the Soviet Union; of America's ability, given the political will, to squeeze the Russians out of Cuba by manipulating the wheat, credit and technology valves, now flowing open to the USSR; and of his deep and urgent concern with the economic and military plight of Turkey.

The visit of the British Parliamentarians to Iran had gone very well, he says. One or two of the more influential among them had contacted the *Guardian* on their return; had warned that it would prove counter-productive to ridicule or criticise the changes wrought by the advent of liberalisation in Iran, as this would only encourage the more irresponsible, radical and disruptive voices, and had urged the assignment of a more open-minded correspondent to Tehran. This has led to Martin Woollacott's being sent.

On internal developments in Iran he makes the astute observation that 'only if your Western allies, and America in particular, are willing to give you cast-iron guarantees on your external security and territorial integrity, should you pursue a policy of unlimited liberalisation'.

Monday, July 17

Hossein Eshraghi, in London on a visit, comes to see me. He praises the Embassy's work in London, and says he knows my standing with HIM is very high. Despite his habitual scepticism he feels HIM's policy of liberalisation is sincere and the reins have been visibly loosened. A reporter from the *N.Y.Times* who had recently interviewed the Shah had told Hossein privately that, whether it was through vanity or timidity, the Shah projected a loveless, severe, power-obsessed image, and had asked 'why can't he be a little more like Sadat'.

As Hossein speaks on, my mind wanders and my thoughts revert to what the New York Times reporter had said about the Shah.

From what I know, the Shah is a man of simple, even of Spartan tastes. His dislike of caviar is well-known and he hardly ever drinks. Contrary to appearances, his eating, dressing and living habits are devoid of luxury. He is in fact, a military man at heart, in his element in an atmosphere of military discipline. I remember an interview he had given a number of years ago to an American journalist in which he had remarked that if he hadn't been King, he would very likely have ended up as a general in the Iranian Air Force.

All of which is, of course, fine and admirable. The trouble is, however, that no one knows this aspect of the Shah's character. Instead, ever since those beastly celebrations at Persepolis, the media has not missed an opportunity to portray him as possessing a penchant for extravagent living.

There is also his shyness, which doesn't allow him to come out of his shell, in his contacts with people, to show warmth and affection, and thus dispel the impression of a harsh and unapproachable man. And because he is so sensitive, he becomes as much the creator as the victim of his own image.

Wednesday, July 19

There is an early morning telephone call from Manuchehr Zelli, the Number Two at the Ministry in Tehran. Associated Press has sent a story from Tehran to the effect that in the course of a press conference in Tehran, Mehdi Bazargan has asserted that torture is still rampant in Iran, and a man called Rezai has alleged that seven members of his family have been killed by the security people in Iran. HIM has given instructions that 'Radji should reply and call their allegations lies'.

A sudden irrepressible wave of anger and frustration engulfs me, but I control myself sufficiently to explain that the London Embassy is hardly the appropriate authority to refute allegations made about Savak to the Associated Press in Tehran. 'To whom should I issue this denial? What do I say, apart from stating that the allegations are lies? What are the details of the charges? Who are the Rezais? Have any of the Rezais, in fact, been killed? And if they have, why?' Reluctantly, Zelli agrees to raise the matter again to see if my instructions can be modified.

200

Thursday, July 20

Bryan Magee and Colin Phipps[1] come to lunch. They listen patiently as I draw what I believe to be an honest picture of the political situation in Iran. They show full appreciation of the problems and the dangers involved and seem particularly interested in the question of the succession. Magee says that a recalcitrant Shah-baiter like Stan Newens actually thinks Iran's record of human rights violations is far worse than the Soviet Union's. We all agree that the Iranian authorities' aggressive approach to public relations and use of hyperbolic language are much to blame. 'But,' Magee observes astutely, 'it is one thing for us to tell you what's wrong with your public relations; it's quite another for you to convince your superiors in Tehran.'

Back at the office after lunch, I discover that HIM's instructions on the Bazargan/Rezai interview have now been cabled to the Embassy. My orders are to describe the allegations as 'dirty lies that are politically motivated'. The text of the interview has not been supplied, and there is not one word on who the Rezais were, or why and how they were killed.

My anger turns to resignation. I ask Kakhi, whose ability to write effective, pithy, forceful, lucid Persian is, I realise, erratic, to prepare a draft reply suggesting, in language of unfailing courtesy but irrefutable logic, that denial of the allegations ought to come from the government spokesman in Tehran and not from the Embassy in London.

I leave him to work out the phraseology, change, and go to Buckingham Palace for the Garden Party. In the Royal Tent Her Majesty speaks of her forthcoming trip to Canada, which begins on Wednesday. I say we are looking forward to welcoming her to Iran in February, and she indicates that her visit to Saudi Arabia later on in the same journey 'will be delicate' for it involves a woman Head of State being received by the Saudis for the first time.

I rush back to change again and to examine Kakhi's draft, conscious that it will be the second time in as many months that I am asking HIM to revise his instructions. The draft doesn't please me and I postpone the project till tomorrow.

Friday, July 21

Kakhi's final draft still not satisfactory, so I write a cable in my
[1] Labour MP for Dudley West, 1974–79.

own hand which I think will do. But, before I have time to send it off, a six-page cable arrives from Tehran. This gives details of the various incidents referred to by Bazargan and Rezai, but makes absolutely no concessions on any of their charges, and instead of a detailed refutation of the allegations condemns the Bazargan interview in hysterical tones, describing it as 'an exercise in Islamic Marxism'. After much honest indecision, I decide to send off my cable, pretending that it had been dispatched before the Tehran cable had arrived. Once again, the waiting begins.

Saturday, July 22

No news from Tehran.

I take Lizzie to dinner at the Montpeliano. I tell her about my increasing emotional involvement with the events in Tehran and the distinct possibility that I may not survive my full term of office in London and be recalled to Tehran mid-course. She should not, therefore, regard our existing arrangement as indefinite, and when I return from Tehran some time in mid-August, while I would certainly love to see her, it would be with nothing like the regularity of the past. I tell her that there isn't 'someone else', and that even if there were, she is so gentle and unobtrusive that I would not have considered her an impediment. A more understanding companion, a more harmonious parting of the ways, one could not have hoped for. There are no histrionics, no tears, not even sadness. The sole sentiment she expresses is to wish me well.

Sunday, July 23

David Housego has reviewed the Lesley Blanch book on the Empress: 'This painfully sweet eulogy diminishes the Empress's stature by omitting the pressures on her which help to explain why she is a remarkable woman. It will be lapped up by the Court which has an insatiable appetite for Royal panegyrics.'

Before I set out for Bledlow Manor to lunch with the Carringtons, Khakpour rings to say NBC's man in London has telephoned to ask 'if you know anything about an attempted assassination of the Shah on the Caspian'. I tell him to deny the rumour and regard it as an exercise in the war of nerves.

The Carringtons' guests include Lord and Lady Hartwell, who

own the *Daily Telegraph*. Lady Hartwell refers to her acquaintance with Ardeshir and offers the opinion that 'the stronger and more powerful a country becomes, the more it should be prepared to accept criticism'.

'No quarrel with that,' I say.

Lady Hartwell introduces me to her husband, who tells me that on one of HIM's visits to England, Afshar who was then the Ambassador, had presented him to HIM, and HIM had complained of something the *Daily Telegraph* was supposed to have said about him. Lord Hartwell, taken aback by this unexpected complaint, had said nothing at the time, but had written subsequently to Afshar to deny the statement attributed to the *Telegraph*, and to demand an explanation. Both this letter and a follow-up one remained unanswered.

On the drive back I wonder whether there has been a reply to my cable and, if so, what it says. But there is no cable. Khakpour reports he has heard on the radio that the 'Shah has *not* been wounded in an accidental shooting' on the Caspian.

Monday, July 24

There are references in the papers to 'the Shah not wounded' story, but nothing official on the Embassy telex. There is still no news about my cable, and my fears begin to subside as I see that later cables have been answered. I begin to hope, with enormous relief, that maybe I am over the hump yet again.

Tuesday, July 25

Forty people are reported killed in clashes with the police in Mashad. The violence was sparked off during the funeral procession of a mullah who had allegedly died in a road accident, but who, the opposition suspected, had met his death in a more sinister fashion.

Wednesday, July 26

Lunch at the House of Commons with the Irano-British Parliamentary Group. Before it is my turn to speak Eldon Griffiths, who

203

is seated next to me, whispers: 'You can afford to be more aggressive.' This makes me wonder whether all those accusations of too apologetic an approach may not after all be justified. The subsequent question and answer period is fairly subdued.

In the evening I give a stag dinner at PG for Hushang Ansari, who is passing through London again on his way to America on some mysterious errand. Edward Heath, George Jellicoe, Charlie Douglas-Home, David Steel of BP, Christopher Soames, Roberto Campos and Peter Carrington are the others.

The conversation, never lacking in interest or excitement, remains nonetheless general, and does not degenerate, thank goodness, into yet another tiresome monologue by me about Iran and its problems. Indeed, with the prospect of early elections looming, the talk is mostly about British politics, with Christopher again supplying much of the relish. He tells how he accompanied Giscard d'Estaing on his first flight aboard the Concorde, at the end of which Giscard embraced the test pilot. 'What,' he says, 'I asked myself, would Ted have done in his place?' Ted shuffles uncomfortably in his seat. When George Jellicoe speaks about the possible composition of a future Thatcher government, Soames says: 'I don't know why *you*'re so interested in the outcome of the elections.'

It's only when the others have gone that Hushang and I, standing next to the marble balustrade of the residence, manage to have a forty-five-minute talk about Iran. I accuse him of having encouraged HIM's penchant for wild exaggerations; he confidently asserts that I've got it all wrong.

Thursday, July 27

Lunch with Denis Wright and two of his Shell colleagues at the Travellers. Denis praises David Housego's review of the Blanch book, repeats his dislike of 'commissioned books', and reveals that the English princess the review says the Shah wanted to marry was Princess Alexandra, then still unmarried.

Monday, July 31

Princess Margaret comes to dinner. I tell her about my current reading of Frankie Donaldson's biography of her uncle, Edward

VIII. After securing her permission to speak about members of her family, I ask whether, with hindsight, the treatment Edward VIII received from his parents – all those so-called 'character building' exercises, the total absence of any affection, the constant bullying, even when he was forty, over such trivial matters as his clothes – weren't responsible for reducing him to the pathetically insecure character that he turned out to be.

'They all received that kind of treatment, including my father,' she says.

She says she found the Donaldson book fascinating and 'couldn't put it down' till she had finished it. I get the distinct impression that she is not an admirer of her late uncle, who 'liked the Nazis; can you imagine?' – or of his wife. The Princess, who incidentally observes that 'this time we have no demonstrations', also speaks about the EEC leaders she had recently met in London. Giscard d'Estaing, she says, had been by far the most elegant and impressive. 'I'm not the Queen; I'm not important or anything. But he was so graceful in his manners that I felt very special. Not like Jimmy Carter,' she adds, 'who walked into the room and his presence was insignificant.'

Tomorrow, I reflect with pleasure tinged with anxiety, I return to Tehran.

Tuesday, August 1

Peter Temple-Morris is aboard the same flight and we chat briefly. Otherwise, I concentrate on Edward VIII. Farhad awaits me at the bottom of the landing steps. On the drive to the Hilton he tells me that HIM looks unhealthily thin on television, and a heart specialist friend of Farhad's had recently been asked to go and see him, but the ECG had apparently shown no abnormalities.

How lovely to be back in unlovely Tehran.

Wednesday, August 2

In the car Farhad has lent me I drive to my house in Niavaran. As I turn up the steep slope of Roshan Avenue and approach the outer wall of the house, with the rhododendrons lushly overhanging it, I see the extension Michel has built on to the original structure.

Workmen are busy everywhere as I go from room to room to see what changes have been made.

I then drive to Parvine's house. Apart from the Filipino maid and the Indian cook, no one is at home. For an hour or so I sit by the pool, enjoying the warmth of the sun on my pale, shrivelled skin, reading the Donaldson book. I go to Mother's for lunch. I have many enemies at the Foreign Ministry, she tells me, all waiting for me to chance my luck with HIM's uncertain patience once too often, thus bringing disaster upon myself and creating a vacancy in the London Embassy.

On the drive back to the Hilton I try to take in as much as I can of the changes in the silhouette of Tehran, the mushrooming skyscrapers, the newly-completed highways linking the south to the foothills in the north, all the ugly, amorphous disorganised structures that are rapidly turning Tehran into a municipal Gomorrah.

In the lobby of the hotel I see Mostafa Elm, about to leave a message for me in my pigeon-hole. Having been recalled as ambassador to the Sudan over allegations of embezzlement, and just released from jail on a thirty million rials[1] bail, he is downcast and disheartened and seeks both sympathy and help. He denies all allegations of wrongdoing.[2]

I tell him, in soberingly commanding tones, to get a hold of himself, to shake off his apathy and attitude of helplessness, to believe in the justice of his cause, and to mobilise all the available means to exonerate himself. 'Even if you have committed the offences attributed to you,' I say, 'I don't believe you should go to jail, because so many bigger fish are still swimming freely. Remember, though, that *you* are not in a position to say that. All you can and should do is insist on your innocence.' He leaves, I believe, greatly encouraged.

Thursday, August 3

I am invited to lunch with AAH on Saturday, Constitution Day. I see from the *FT* and *IHT* that Dariush Homayoun, the Information Minister, has said that altogether in the recent rioting six people have been killed, including two in Tehran.

In the afternoon I play tennis at the Imperial Country Club. During the game an Air Force helicopter lands on the Club's helipad, which is close to the courts, kicking up a huge cloud of dust

[1] About £250,000.

[2] Elm was aquitted of all charges against him in 1980.

in the process. Shortly afterwards servants carrying shirts and suits on hangers rush down the flight of steps leading to the court and hurry off in the direction of the changing rooms, while from the opposite direction waiters bearing slices of water-melon and fruit juices covered with aluminium foil speed towards the No. 1 court. Four security men follow the servants, placing their hands on their bulging revolvers as they come down the steps. They position themselves at each corner of the court, conspicuously trying to appear inconspicuous. A minute later a bow-legged man in his late forties, wearing tennis clothes and displaying a slight paunch, descends the steps and walks on to the court, which has been watered, swept and rolled since the early afternoon for his exclusive use. He is General Hossein Rabii, Commander of the Iranian Air Force.

In the evening I speak with Saipa. She doesn't beat about the bush and, with the changed political climate in mind, plunges straight to the heart of the matter: 'Well, is this what you wanted? Are you happy now?' she asks, with as much earnestness as good humour. My attempt at a reply is drowned in a shower of friendly abuse. 'HIM is physically well but worried,' she says. We are to meet at Hushang Ansari's on Monday.

Saturday, August 5

Today is the seventy-second anniversary of the signing of the Iranian Constitution. In an hour-long speech to mark the occasion HIM has adopted a tone which is conciliatory and concessionary, but there are one or two silly promises (more later).

I lunch with AAH at the former Government guest house which is now the official residence of the Court Minister. He is in sports clothes, it being a public holiday, looks well and appears in expansive mood. As soon as he sees me he observes: 'You've aged a little.' He compliments me on my performance in London, but adds that 'the mischief in between the lines of your cables is clearly discernible'.

We soon move to the adjacent dining-room, where caviar is served for the first course. I listen intently as AAH speaks. 'The Government is paralysed, Rastakhiz is dead and buried, and policy is non-existent.' HIM, whom he had seen over the weekend, 'is a worried man', and now realises that the choice of Amouzegar for Prime Minister was a mistake; but Hushang Ansari, with his lavish life-style, would have been wrong too, 'and there is no one left'. Everyone is now 'riding his own donkey' and there is no 'control centre'. The Government has adopted the tactic of 'hiding under HIM's skirt', placing the credit, as well as the blame, for everything squarely on 'HIM's instructions'.

It is not true that Amouzegar had offered to resign several times, but only once. This was after he had said that Iran would stop its assistance to Pakistan if Bhutto were executed, a statement that had later to be denied. He blames Amouzegar for pursuing the narrow aim of reducing inflation which has meant that all funds have been cut off, not only to the bazaar but also to the mullahs, who now feel left out and are agitating for their share of the oil money. The mullahs, he believes, have to be resisted at all costs, but some accommodation with them ought to be found whereby they would lend their support, albeit in religious language, to the régime's more progressive aims.

Corruption at the top is rampant on a shameless scale, he says. 'Along the Caspian coast three casinos are now in full operation. Two are owned by relatives of the Shah, and a third by the Pahlavi Foundation.' After a moment's reflection he adds with a chuckle that he had insisted on the omission of a passage in HIM's speech this morning calling for a campaign against corruption. 'Your Majesty,' he had said, 'people will laugh.' The whole town, he goes on, is aware of the scandal involving a member of the royal family and a group of French contractors, while accusations and counter accusations are being publicly hurled by them at one another.

He says he raised the subject of corruption very many times with HIM over all these years, but HIM simply does not seem to understand the moral – as well as the social and the political – arguments for the need to stamp it out.

He believes things will come to a head next spring, when the election campaigns for the Majlis begin, and repeats his concern that 'there is no control centre'.

He describes Nahavandi, the Empress's Secretary, and the group of French-educated intellectuals surrounding the Empress, as highly ambitious and says they are using the protective umbrella of the Empress to score political points against their opponents. Nahavandi may now be going to leave the Empress's bureau and go to the Central Bank, so that he can pursue his political ambitions free from any apparent Court connections. His opponents are circulating a photograph, which Nahavandi claims is a fake montage, purporting to show him burning an Iranian flag while a student in Paris.

In the midst of all this AAH suddenly stops, looks at me intently, and asks: 'Would you like to become the Empress's Chef de Cabinet?'

'I am complimented to be asked,' I say, after some quick thinking, 'and I think she is a lovely person, but Saipa would never forgive me.'

He smiles, and, gently nodding his head, says he understands. 'You've got two years still in London, which is a marvellous city, with so many intelligent people to deal with.'

Thinking that AAH might actually have spoken of me to the Empress as a possible successor to Nahavandi, and anticipating that she would rightly feel offended at my refusal, I say: 'Can we agree between ourselves that you never offered me that job?'

'Absolutely.'

I raise the scenario suggested by a friend, namely that HIM should keep control of the armed forces and foreign policy but leave the day-to-day affairs of the state to the government. HIM, he says, would never relinquish any power voluntarily, even though he thinks 'now that the dam has been cracked' a return to the old order will never be possible.

Fereydoun Mahdavi[1] has been in touch with Matin-Daftari and his National Front associates 'who will be permitted to operate as a political unit', but if they make 'cacophonous noises,' says AAH, 'they will be told to shut up in no uncertain terms.' He agrees that the army, which 'is loyal', holds the ultimate guarantee of the régime's survival, 'even though the Russians have a theory that all our arms purchases are intended to allow the Americans storage facilities' for use against them, and that in an emergency plane loads of American pilots and other qualified personnel would arrive to activate our war machine.

Then he wonders, to my bewilderment, whether all the recent disturbances haven't been engineered by 'our Western friends' as part of a bigger plan to secure the transfer of some of the Shah's absolute powers to our civil institutions, thereby making them more responsible and effective should HIM wish to surrender the helm. I find no less bewildering his speculation whether HIM isn't still engaged in his old game of playing everyone off against everyone else, in order to retain power for himself.

When I mention some of the points I want to raise with HIM during my prospective audience, including our embarrassing sensitivity to the BBC, AAH says, 'You will find him listening more than before, whatever the subject.'

In all the years I have known and worked with AAH, I have

[1] A former member of the National Front who later became a minister in AAH's cabinet.

rarely seen him more forthrightly critical or more outspokenly condemnatory of the conduct of HIM and members of the Royal Family. His disgust at the unethical dealings of some of the Shah's relatives, which have been conducted so blatantly and arrogantly, drives him to desperation. He is deeply anxious about there being 'no policy, no control centre'. Whether speaking about HIM and his family, or about the resurgence of dissident political activity, AAH never minced his words, and though he reverted to English on occasions to make a particular point, he did not, as I did, take the slightest notice of the presence of the waiters in the room throughout our protracted luncheon discussions. Yet his mood was not any the less sanguine for all his worries. He seemed imbued with a fresh spirit of combativeness, of forceful energy, in an arena where he could not consider himself an idle bystander. With immense confidence and an impish twinkle in his eye, he had spoken of the forthcoming Majlis elections and of the delicate task, this time, of 'manipulating' them. As always, he seemed not only to know what was wrong, but to be confident that he also knew what needed to be done.

Sunday, August 6

My audience has been scheduled for ten on Tuesday. I read HIM's Constitution Day speech in detail. Three-quarters of it is devoted to an account of Iranian history in two world wars, to the oil nationalisation and events leading up to the 'Shah–People Revolution', 'many of whose provisions exceed, in progressiveness of outlook, anything existing in the world's most advanced countries'. All this is territory that he has covered often before. Then we come to his new concessions. The people's right to assemble for political purposes will be respected, and the next elections, which will be 'absolutely free', will allow for the participation even of those who are opposed to his concept of the 'Great Civilisation'. 'Political liberties as understood in European democracies' are now promised after the spring elections. This assurance, in my opinion, is needlessly offered and impossible to fulfil.

Monday, August 7

I spend the morning at the Foreign Ministry, play tennis in the afternoon, and at seven punctually present myself at Saipa's newly re-decorated Saadabad home.

Seated alone on the sofa that faces the entrance to her drawing-room, she moves forward to allow me to kiss, first her hand, then her offered cheek. She is elegantly dressed and sports a faint smile that could almost be one of composed resignation.

'I am going to make you very unhappy by telling you two things I want Your Highness to hear,' I say, 'so please brace yourself, and don't get angry. Remember, I am on *your* side.'

'You always do say things that make me unhappy,' she says, her expression unchanged.

I say I have heard Lord Chalfont is to be asked to do a book on her, and have come to implore her to abandon the idea. Her role in the 1953 overthrow of Mossadeq, while complimentary to her courage and loyalty, would emphasise the relative lack of these qualities in some of the other principals; and in any case a friendly biography at this particular time would be ill-advised and even provocative. She denies that the book is intended to be an adulation of her social and political activities and insists that it can contain as much criticism as is necessary. She has a right to tell the story of her life, especially as it is a story worth telling.

I move on to my other topic. HIM, I say, has embarked on a policy of liberalisation. He will be surrendering a measure of his political powers in order to ensure the emergence of durable political institutions that would guarantee, not only the continuation of his own rule, but the preservation of the monarchy after him. One predictable outcome of such a development would be the inevitable reactivation of the Majlis and a less restrained press, both of which could start criticising members of the Royal Family. She herself may be attacked, and she may consider it prudent to go abroad for a while, until things cool down. I see a sudden rush of blood to her cheeks as I utter my last sentence, but she retains her composure.

'My name,' she says calmly, 'has never been associated with any business and I have no involvement in any deals.' She strongly maintains her innocence, and says it is 'stupid circulars' like the one 'your former boss' has issued[1] that give members of the Royal Family a bad reputation.

The others arrive, dinner is served, and I leave early to prepare for my audience tomorrow with HIM.

---

[1] A reference to the code of conduct for members of the Royal Family made public by Hoveyda on July 5.

Tuesday, August 8

Not completely trusting the Hilton operator I leave my curtains undrawn and consequently awake at 5.30. I am at the Air Taxi terminal by 8. Manuchehr Ganji, the Minister of Education, arrives soon afterwards, and by 8.30 we are airborne for the 15-minute flight to Nowshahr. The waiting car drives us to the pier which forms Their Majesties' Nowshahr residence. After two identification checks we drive to the end of the pier, where we disembark and are led to the small waiting room with its air-cooler on full blast. Some Imperial Guard officers, and one or two civilians, stand up as we go in, and tea is served. At about 10.15 Ganji is called in. I shuffle my papers and in my mind go over the sequence of what I want to say for the umpteenth time.

At 11.15 my name is called and I go in. Wearing a sports shirt and shorts, HIM stands in the middle of the room, and as I bow and approach to bow again and kiss his hand, the huge great dane barks half-heartedly and is told to shut up. HIM sits down at a card table and points to the chair opposite him, which I proceed to occupy. Contrary to the current gossip, I find him looking well if a little thinner, with his bluish grey hair neatly combed back.

'Well', he says with a half-smile, 'what is it?'

I have come as always, I say, to seek HIM's instructions and guidance on a number of issues in order better to carry out his wishes. I mention the BBC and 'respectfully submit' that 'the conscience of the media lies to the Left of centre, a state of affairs we must accept', and to over-react to every uncomplimentary mention of Iran will not get us anywhere. 'Apart from instances of obvious bias or misreporting we should, in my judgment, generally ignore what they say.' He dislikes my use of the word 'over-react' but otherwise seems, to my surprise, to agree. With this ready and unexpected agreement, all the additional, supportive arguments I had prepared to defend my case suddenly appear irrelevant and superfluous.

I mention the provision of information on, and media access to, those held for political reasons and say a great deal of adverse criticism and hostile suspicion is generated by our mishandling of such cases. I can see as I speak that it is not a topic that interests him greatly. He bears with me for a minute longer, then suggests that, if I have any proposals for improving the procedure, I should convey them to the Prime Minister.

As I speak, I see him gaze intently at me at some stage, with enlarged, unblinking eyes, in an effort, I suppose, to assert psychological ascendancy or simply to intimidate – an exercise that I find more intriguing than disconcerting. But this does not last long, and after a few moments he resumes his normal expression. I proceed to other topics – Amnesty's request for clemency for religious extremists condemned to death in Esfahan;[1] the possibility of a visit to the Sassanid ruins at Bam in eastern Iran by the Queen and Prince Philip in February, and the advisability of a quick settlement of our legal wrangles with Tate and Lyle[2] which are damaging our credit-worthiness in the City as a trading partner.

When I mention the possibility of the Queen's visit to Bam, his mind seems to wander, and he utters almost inaudibly, as much to himself as to me, the name of a religious activist who has 'created so many problems in Kerman'.[3] But he recovers almost immediately, and with a confident chuckle asserts: 'But, of course, the army cooks by themselves would be capable of taking care of him.'

Ironically, however, it is HIM who brings up domestic affairs. He speaks of the genuine concern many people feel over the inflammatory utterances of the mullahs. Some of it, he has no doubt, is 'the work of the KGB, which has directed its efforts over the past thirty years to penetrating the clergy'. But, he asks with as much curiosity as uncertainty, 'do our Western friends', in my opinion 'also have a hand in the current disturbances?'

'I can't possibly think of any reason why they should want to do so,' I reply, desperately trying to conceal my surprise at his question, and feeling perhaps for the very first time included amongst the esoteric few with whom HIM is prepared to share his innermost worries. I speak of the vast community of interests and objectives we share with our Western friends, of the highly laudatory statements Carter had made publicly about the Shah during and after his Washington visit, and assure him that 'he needn't worry about the British, because were it not for North Sea oil they, if he will forgive the expression, wouldn't be able to pull their own trousers up'.

Nodding his head gently, he says it is certainly true that few American presidents have shown the degree of personal friendship and public praise towards him that Carter has shown, whom he quotes as saying 'our military alliance with Iran is unshakable'.

[1] The Hadafi group.
[2] Over allegations of bribery in a sugar contract with the Ministry of Commerce.
[3] Bam is in Kerman Province.

Encouraged and emboldened by the exchange so far, I say our friends in the West are full of admiration for the remarkable flexibility HIM has shown in permitting a freer climate of political activity. I cite the Shcheransky and Ginsberg [Soviet dissidents] trials in an attempt to illustrate the greater degree of forbearance that characterises the current climate of opinion in the world, and foolishly add that 'we can't, of course, swim against the current'.

'I am not swimming against the current,' says HIM

'I know you're not, Sir, which is what makes your initiative so admirable.' I go on to say that a society which, thanks to HIM's enlightened policies, has reached the degree of economic prosperity and social awarness of Iran today, 'must distance itself from the harsh discipline of the past'.

He interrupts to say that he has held that belief for a long time, and has himself said so on numerous occasions: 'If the institution of monarchy is to continue after us – and, for the sake of the country, it must – then change is necessary.'

'The tolerance shown towards the opposition by Your Majesty has the support of the Iranian middle classes,' I say.

'Tolerance, yes, but to what degree?' he asks rhetorically.

I go on to say that what in my judgment we ought now to be thinking of is how to sow seeds of division in the ranks of the clergy by lending support to a religiously acceptable and popularly respected figure. Someone untainted by the brush of Bahaism or Westernisation, a good public speaker, well versed in the Koran, who could come forward to engage Khomeini in debate, albeit indirectly and through the international media, and in doing so demonstrate that Khomeini's interpretation of Islam is incompatible with human dignity and unsuited to the conduct of the affairs of a country like Iran, which needs industrialisation.

Finding HIM, as AAH had predicted, 'in a listening mood', I continue, and say whoever the person is that fits the role of intellectual standard-bearer for progressive, enlightened Islam – 'and it could be someone like Shariatmadari' – all the machinery of the state, from unlimited funds to the massive propaganda apparatus, should be made available for the dissemination of his arguments. We would have to bear in mind that such a person must be considered 'a dispensable figure', as there would be a considerable likelihood of an attempt on his life. At the same time, accommodation should be sought with the more moderate political and religious elements.

'On all this,' HIM asserts, 'people are now working', particularly on finding some degree of accommodation with the more moderate clergy.

214

My audience lasts for just under an hour, at the end of which I am offered the raised hand, which I kiss, and, bowing, take my leave.

I see Her Majesty for a brief moment as I come out, seated amongst some of the royal children on the terrace of the pier, kiss her hand and proceed to the airport. Any anxieties I may have had about the rising turmoil in the country, or HIM's genuine concern at the turn events have taken, are momentarily submerged by the elation I feel at my own performance. But I soon begin to chide myself for not having seized this unique opportunity, with HIM in so receptive a mood, to have said more, and to have put forward the scenario whereby HIM would voluntarily withdraw from all but the military and foreign policy aspects of government, or to have pleaded for a less belligerent and exaggerated tone in his public utterances. Yet, as I go over in my mind the various exchanges during the audience, looking out from the oval window of the Falcon as it soars above the cloud-covered Alborz mountains, I am, I judge, quite chuffed.

Thursday, August 10

The morning at the Foreign Ministry in Hossein Eshraghi's office, where I go over the cables received from and sent to London during my absence, and a delightful evening at Haideh Hakimi's enchanting country home at Pounak. As the lights of Mehrabad Airport shimmered in the distance I sank into an armchair to take a first sip of my ice-chilled Soltanieh vodka, as well as to take in the loveliness of my surroundings. My thoughts turned to Harold Nicolson's description of a similar evening in Gholhak fifty years earlier: 'The owls, that moon-soaked night, answered each other from tree to tree: the crickets shrieked an undertone, continuous bleaching, as if an emanation of the dry and crackling sun of noon. Between the trees, the mountains glimmered, as if lit by the headlights of some vast motor. A pond, under the oleanders, gurgled sullenly.'

Where else in the world, I wondered, would one find the same delicate, almost fragile, cool breeze as in the summer nights of Tehran?

Friday, August 11

The first item of news on the World Service of the BBC is a statement by HIM that 'only armed insurrection can prevent the

215

political liberalisation of Iran, and then only temporarily'. In an interview with Andrew Whitley he also asserts that Savak had become a state within a state, a situation that couldn't be allowed to continue. There are assurances about the freedom of the next elections.

In the evening I learn that, as rioting has broken out in Esfahan and several persons are reported killed, the city has been placed under martial law.

Saturday, August 12

I go to see Dariush Homayoun, the Minister of Information, in an effort to coordinate the handling of information on political detainees. Having watched his impressive performance on television the night before, when he had defended the imposition of martial law in Esfahan and provided seemingly accurate statistics about the number of casualties on both sides, I compliment him warmly. 'You should say these things to the Prime Minister', he says. Apparently Amouzegar is continually blaming his Ministry for provoking HIM's displeasure.

Sunday, August 13

There is a call at 8.30 from Afsaneh Jahanbani: 'The boss told me to ask you to stop by at the Court Ministry during the morning at your convenience.'

'When is a good time for him?'

'Between 9 and 11.'

I go to the Ministry at 9.30. AAH is his usual ebullient high-spirited self as he comes into Afsaneh's room to see out his previous visitors and to ask me into his study. He closes both doors behind him before slumping into his usual spot on the sofa. 'How did it go?' he asks.

I provide a much shortened account of the exchanges with HIM, and end by saying that, judging by his interview yesterday, I very strongly suspect that HIM has not distinguished in his own mind between 'liberalisation', which ought to mean an end to the omnipotence of Savak and a stifled press, and Western-type democracy, which would be singularly unsuited to Iran's present condition and needs.

216

AAH says he had had an audience lasting three hours yesterday. The events of the past three months have taken their toll on both HIM's and the Empress's nerves. At no time was the need greater for HIM to detach himself from the internal political scene and let others place their heads on the executioner's block. But he can't, and is constantly projecting himself into the centre of things. He is giving another interview on Thursday. The Empress is no different, and having tasted the exercise of power she too finds it difficult to resist. Amouzegar seems reluctant to enter the political arena effectively.

He harks back to the compulsive theme of corruption. 'It is,' he says, 'like a gangrene, as if these were the last days of the régime', with certain people 'filling their pockets with a greed that cannot be believed'.

Describing the régime's reactions to the disconcerting trend of political developments as 'piecemeal', he says he told HIM during his audience yesterday that 'the world, which Your Majesty used to address lectures to until three months ago, now wants to know why there is continued rioting throughout Iran, and why Esfahan is under martial law'.

As he walks me to the door to shake my hand, he says, with a huge smile on his lips: 'Ultimately, we shall all walk around with one of those poison capsules in our mouths; or the lucky ones may get away in time.'

I drive down to the city for my midday appointment with Amouzegar, who greets me, as always, with warm cordiality. He says he notices from my cables the direction in which I try to push things. After I have handed him my memos on the media and political detainees and on the Tate and Lyle affair, he asks me how I view the situation. I say I applaud and approve of the loosening of tight control, but am not at all sure whether there is any overall policy which would make it clear, at least to those at the top, how far along the road of liberalisation we want to go.

He says the Rastakhiz Party and its policies ought to provide both the direction in which the country should go and the machinery for going there, but, instead of uniting in the face of the various opposition groups now that the grip has been eased, each wing of Rastakhiz is trying to pull the party towards support for its own selfish interests, with the current chaos as the consequence. He believes that the main strength of the opposition comes from the machinations of the communists, and that the Khomeinists and National Front leaders lack any significant degree of popular support. 'Elections in Iran are always won by three groups – the workers, the peasants, and the guilds – and the sympathy of all

217

three is overwhelmingly with the system.'

I say I was surprised that HIM had wondered whether 'our Western friends' had a hand in the current disturbances. He says that while he doesn't think the British Government has a hand, and has no shred of evidence that any other British-connected group has, 'one must remember the historic connection between them and the mullahs, and a man like Shariatmadari can very easily be influenced by what the BBC says, so that the picture isn't quite as black and white as all that'.

I mention that, of all Iranian Ministers of Information I have known, Dariush Homayoun is the only one who, in my view, has had any real understanding of the issues involved. Surprised, he says he wished I had said that to His Majesty, because HIM is constantly referring to 'that wretched Ministry of Information'. I reply that my idea of effective propaganda is closer to Homayoun's than to HIM's.

Tuesday, August 15

The Khansalar restaurant, reported to be Bahai-owned, has been blown up by a bomb, and the commander of the Khorassan garrison has been shot dead by a soldier who had apparently gone berserk and shouted 'Allah, Allah, Allah ...' as he fired his gun.

Wednesday, August 16

I lunch at Hushang Ansari's mansion, close to my own house in Niavaran.

He is in a subdued, dejected mood and lets me do all the talking. I say that, as far as I can judge, the situation is deteriorating day by day, and that the increase in sporadic violence, the rising spate of bombings and the closure of the bazaar are all strengthening the hands of the extremists, neutralising the more moderate ayatollahs, and, most damaging of all, sapping the morale of the régime's supporters. Khomeini's tapes calling for the violent overthrow of the Shah are selling quite openly like hot cakes, and leaders of the National Front now concede privately that things are moving out of their control. With the universities starting up in October, and the month of religious mourning [Moharram] beginning in December, we can expect events to take a distinct turn for the worse. For the moment, HIM should keep his cool and allow the drift to continue, giving as much publicity as possible to acts of mindless violence, perpetrated by the opposition, in an effort to shock the middle classes out of their complacent torpor and into a rude realisation of the danger of mob rule. Then, when he judges that everybody's nerves have been sufficiently frayed, he should seize upon one particularly violent act of death or destruction by the mob, and make a dramatic and confident gesture, bringing in the army for a complete crackdown, with as much ruthlessness as may be necessary. But this is only the first thing he ought to do. Simultaneously with the crackdown, he should exile all but his immediate family in an effort to disarm his more vociferous critics and gain a breathing space. Lastly, he should call in someone like Ali Amini, acceptable to the mullahs, to the National Front and to the general public, and ask him to form a government of national reconciliation. Only then will he be able to count on the absolute loyalty of the army, which would of course remain under his control.

Hushang says that, knowing HIM, he might do the first thing I suggest, would never do the second, and only do the third if it was imposed on him. I reply that to resort to force without at the same time making what, after all, is an overdue concession, or fail to seek political accommodation, would be a sure recipe for disaster.

As he walks me to the door, I try to bolster his sagging morale – an ironic reversal of roles compared with our conversation on the steps of the Embassy in London nearly two years ago. You must remember, I say to him, that the opposition is cast from the same mould as ourselves and can be relied on to be as incompetent as us, if not more so. So, while we must view the future with uncertainty, and even anxiety, there is no need for panic.

Friday, August 18

An article in the *Guardian* quotes the story of one of HIM's confidants telling him: 'No one ever dared to tell a lie to your father; no one has ever dared to tell you the truth.'

HIM has given another press interview, and his nervousness comes across. He admits he is surprised at the extent and persistence of the disturbances his liberalisation has unleashed. The Islamic Marxists are to blame for everything.

Saturday, August 19

A last call on AAH before I take my leave. I am returning to London, I tell him, no clearer in mind than the day I arrived about the sort of explanation of current events in Iran I should give to our friends, let alone to our enemies.

He says HIM is determined, whatever his reasons may be, not to abandon the process of democratisation – a policy we both agree is the right one. But he is critical of the Government's vapid inactivity. Why, for instance, he asks, haven't the various women's organisations staged, or been urged to stage, demonstrations against the diminished status women can expect if the mullahs came to power?

I earnestly urge him to beg HIM to appoint as Prime Minister someone with political acumen and mass appeal who can step into the vacuum and divert some of the flak from the throne, and so allow tempers to cool, halt the present slide and provide a breathing spell.

He says he has indeed mentioned the need for such an appointment to HIM, who actually agrees that this move would be judicious. But old habits die hard; HIM finds it impossible to keep out of the limelight, and the day after he agrees to do so he starts projecting himself into the middle of some new controversy. We embrace and say goodbye, promising to keep in close touch.

Sunday, August 20

Oh my God! 377 people have been burnt to death in a fire in a cinema in Abadan. The Government says sabotage by those 'benighted elements' who consider cinemas places of corruption is responsible. The four exits from the cinema hall were apparently locked, and the fire deliberately started.

I telephone Mirfakhrai at the Court Ministry to suggest to AAH that a mullah of prominence should be brought in front of the television cameras tonight to denounce such mindless savagery as contrary to the laws of God.

I lunch with Mother to say goodbye. Farhad and Hossein Eshraghi see me off at the Pavilion for official guests, and from their general observations I gather that the cinema fire incident is rapidly mobilising support for strong-arm measures. Perhaps, I think to myself, a few more such incidents are needed before the ultimate crackdown.

220

In London in the evening I watch horrifying news films of the mass burials at Abadan.

Monday, August 21

A perceptive, informed, balanced and, as always, well-written article by Lord Chalfont in *The Times*, called, 'Who is behind the violent unrest in Iran?'

There is much excitement amongst Embassy colleagues on my first day at the office over current developments in Iran. The unrest, I tell them at a staff meeting, is an inevitable consequence of the deliberate policy of loosening the reins. Indeed, it would have been surprising if there had not been any manifestation of public discontent, and we should expect things to get a bit worse, but the army can ultimately be relied upon to restore law and order. Externally, Iran is too important to be allowed to become communist; and the mullahs, everyone agrees, are too stupid, too incompetent, too lacking in organisation ever to gain, much less to retain, political power.

Wednesday, August 23

I brace myself for lunch with Mostafa Fateh, one of the Shah's most vociferous and intelligent critics, now in total disfavour, and himself the subject of repeated arrests and house searches by Savak. Since I can't ask him to the Embassy, we lunch at Claridge's, and sure enough as soon as we sit down at our corner table, he fires away in his eloquent and quite captivating manner. 'This time', he assures me, in a tone almost of jubilation, 'his tail has been caught in the trap.' The pressure on the Shah to mend his ways came from the Americans, says Mostafa, but so advanced is the putrefaction of his régime that 'this time he will be toppled'. The Shah, he says, has a remarkable visual memory 'but otherwise he is unimaginative', totally incapable of any flexibility. He has always regarded the Iranian masses as a bunch of cretins who understood only the language of force. 'Some members of the Tudeh Party, after much assiduous and detailed research have come up with a quite fascinating statistic. It puts the number of political deaths during the Shah's reign as 18,000.'

With little respect for my long and well-known association with AAH, he says that, of all the Shah's advisers, 'Hoveyda is the most intelligent, the most able and the most insidious', being mainly responsible for the Shah's love of flattery and for his detachment from reality. 'The only person in all that lot for whom I feel genuinely sorry,' he says, 'is poor Farah'.

'You', he tells me, with genuine solicitude, 'are too closely associated with the Shah's régime to be liked by those who will soon succeed him – whoever they may be. Lighten your commitments in Tehran, sell your possessions, and prepare to live outside Iran. You know I am motivated solely by concern for your well-being when I say this'.

To end our conversation on a lighter note Mostafa, now seventy-five but never one to forgo an opportunity to boast of his sexual powers, offers a word of fatherly advice. 'The secret of long life', he asserts authoritatively, 'lies in sleeping with as many women as often as one can. Remember that,' he observes emphatically, 'and remember that everything else doesn't matter.'

Thursday, August 24

Hats off to the mullahs! They have succeeded quite brilliantly in shifting on to the government blame for the Abadan fire. Ten thousand people have demonstrated against the Shah in the city, and the Government hasn't even sent a minister to conduct an investigation. No wonder Liz Thurgood's *Guardian* article predicts 'Abadan fire could topple the Shah' in a huge banner headline.

Friday, August 25

Two articles, in the *New Statesman* and the *Economist*, replete with flak, plus an anonymous telephone call that a bomb has been planted at the Embassy, keep me edgy. I lock myself for an hour in my room, pace up and down the magnificent Kerman carpet adorning the floor of the huge office, and lecture myself on the sterling qualities of steadfastness and courage, on the need to suppress my mounting anxieties, on the need to pull myself together and not set a bad example to those I am meant to inspire. My morale *must* not sag; my psyche *must* not crack.

Whatever the shortcomings of HIM's rule, and despite the vitriolic propaganda directed by the liberal press against him, he must not go. Ghoreishi is surely right when he says that with HIM removed, 'we would become worse than Iraq'. Am I stupid and credulous enough to believe, as the liberal opposition predicts, that the hidebound theocracy of the mullahs will never be acceptable to the majority of Iranians, and that sanity and moderation will ultimately prevail, once Khomeini and his gang come into power? No; HIM should stay if he can, retain command of the armed forces, but be politically emasculated.

Sunday, August 27

[On a four-day holiday in Ireland] I learn from Radio Dublin that Amouzegar has resigned, i.e. been told to go, and that Sharif-Emami has been appointed to succeed him. Amir Khosro Afshar is the new Foreign Minister.

Monday, August 28

Before setting off from Cork I buy the *Daily Telegraph* and see that the Imperial calendar has been abandoned in favour of the Islamic one, and that consequently we have reverted overnight from the year 2537 to 1357. HIM has declared that respect for the tenets of Islam is to be the cornerstone of the new government's policies; there will be a fresh campaign against inflation, and all the political parties will be legalised and allowed to take part in the next general elections.

Wednesday, August 30

Of the mass of messages awaiting me on my return to London, one freezes me in my tracks. 'Mrs Mostafa Fateh rang to speak to you. Her husband passed away last night and she needs your help urgently.' At the particular moment in his life when he would have enjoyed seeing his old foe engulfed in the most serious challenge to his reign, Mostafa's recipe for longevity has failed him.

223

Thursday, August 31

I ring Tehran and speak to Hossein Eshraghi. He knows about Mostafa's death, so I am not the bearer of ill tidings. Afshar is overjoyed at being the new Foreign Minister, he says. They are coming to London on September 21 for a few days before going to New York for the General Assembly. We agree I should ask Afshar to 'stay at his old home' while in London, an offer Afshar will most probably refuse. Hossein says AAH is under pressure from the mullahs to resign, on account principally of his allegedly Bahai father. Perhaps to reassure me, Hossein adds that 'no changes are foreseen in our diplomatic posts abroad'.

From the office I speak to Farhad in Tehran. The law and order situation has deteriorated, he says, and only yesterday he had seen a group of demonstrators carrying a placard proclaiming 'Long Live the King; Khomeini is our King'. Hoveyda's position is precarious, 'and so is yours', he says, according to the gossip making the rounds. Saipa is now in Paris and has apparently been told to stay there. Farhad is coming to London on September 10.

I lunch alone, and in the early afternoon ring Saipa in Paris. She sounds deeply dejected and pessimistic. The slide towards the precipice will not be arrested by Sharif-Emami's appointment, she says, adding that 'for us – and by us I mean the Pahlavis – it is virtually over', it being only a matter of time before a republic based on Islamic principles is proclaimed. 'His Majesty will never agree to be King in a country where Khomeini or Shariatmadari exercise the ultimate power. He will never have anything to do with the mullahs.' She is bitter about the Iranian people 'who are incapable of gratitude after all that my father and brother did for them', and blames it all on Hoveyda 'who lied to my brother for fourteen years and did nothing to arrest the thieves'. She keeps asking how the present situation came about. Why did we let things reach their present state? Then she curses Carter. When I say I don't think she should go back to Tehran now, she says she wants to be with her brother in his hour of difficulty.

Later in the afternoon I call on Mostafa's widow. Pari, his daughter, his son and some other relatives, all dressed in black and red-eyed, are assembled. Apparently Mostafa suffered a massive coronary stroke while in a dentist's waiting-room, never regained consciousness and died shortly afterwards. Mrs Fateh says she had rebuked Mostafa for having spoken to me about the Shah in the way he did during our lunch together, adding, 'He had no right to be so impertinent'. Despite the solemnity of the occasion anxieties about current developments in Tehran quickly take over the conversation. *Le Monde*, I am told, has ridiculed Sharif-Emami for closing, as Prime Minister, the casinos he was operating until yesterday as head of the Pahlavi Foundation.

As Ronald drives me back to the office I begin seriously to think that the reign of the Pahlavis may well be drawing to an inglorious end. I find my own thoughts and sentiments confused and divided, yet within me I feel the sort of calm that can only come from a sense of resignation.

Friday, September 1

The Tehran press is notable for two new and important developments: for the first time huge pictures of Khomeini are splashed across the front pages, and he is referred to as 'his reverence the Grand Ayatollah'; and already there is speculation that Sharif-Emami's government, having failed to stop the bloodshed, may not last. Some 50,000 people have demonstrated in Mashad, 40,000 in Qom, and three have been killed.

Tuesday, September 5

Varying accounts of huge (up to 250,000) demonstrations in Tehran yesterday, to mark Eid-e-Fetr, in all the papers. The demonstrators have pelted the soldiers with flowers, crying, 'Brother doesn't kill brother.' This evokes, in my mind at least, images of the anti-war demonstrations during the Democratic National Convention in Chicago in 1968, and I wonder whether the introduction of effective new forms of propaganda, such as roses in gun barrels, isn't just a little above the ingenuity of the mullahs!

The Tehran papers carry pictures of yesterday's demonstrations. The police are shown in force, but otherwise a sea of turban-covered heads.

Thursday, September 7

Dariush Oskoui and General Jam come to lunch, but it remains a generally uninspired occasion, with Jam expressing concern in subdued terms over the responsibility of 'foreign elements' for the current disturbances. It is only when I, pointing to myself, say that much of the blame for the tragic events now unfolding lies with *our* generation, which was too supine and obsequious, and so failed to prevent many of the régime's political follies, leaving it to the congenitally cretinous, lice-ridden mullahs of Qom to become standard bearers of liberty, that Jam lets his guard down and refers to some of the régime's mistakes. Throughout, however, he remains respectful of the person of HIM.

In the evening I ring the Princess, who is now back in Tehran after a cultural engagement in the Soviet Union. Her arrival in Tehran and her helicopter trip from the airport to Saadabad had coincided with the huge demonstrations then in progress, and she had seen 'several hundred thousands marching in protest'. She then tells me: 1) Hoveyda, sensing the pressure for his removal, has asked HIM to relieve him of his post; 2) Their Majesties' proposed State visits to East Germany and Romania may have to be postponed; 3) She doesn't know whether Ardeshir will succeed AAH at the Court Ministry, but Hushang Ansari, too, is under much pressure to go.

My attempts to inject a note of levity into the conversation and extract a laugh from her prove singularly unsuccessful. I skip dinner, introspect, and sleep early.

Friday, September 8

Martial law has been declared in Tehran, and General Oveisi has been appointed martial law administrator. 'Many', according to Radio Tehran, have been killed in the ensuing clashes. *The Times* has an editorial entitled 'Grave crisis in Iran'.

Unsmiling, even ashen faces greet me at the office. Mahdavi is quite beside himself with excitement and worry. Twice he bursts into my office to announce that news from Tehran 'is very bad' and that there have been 'many dead'.

A report from Richard Oppenheimer in Tehran on the BBC one o'clock news speaks of ten killed and two hundred wounded. According to him a soldier, ordered to fire on a crowd, had shot his commander first, then himself. When asked whether he thinks the imposition of martial law will restore order Oppenheimer replies that, judging from the hysterical anger of the people, he doesn't think so. He repeatedly uses the expression 'very grave' to describe the turn of events. By five o'clock the figure for the dead has reached three hundred.

After lunch I ring Tehran and speak to Farhad. 'Thank God they've brought in martial law,' he says. 'It's preposterous to believe a few bazaaris could have been persuaded by the mullahs to put on such an impressive display of organisation and discipline. The demonstrators are all professionals.' The sound of intermittent gunfire had kept him up from early morning, he says. A group of demonstrators in the vicinity of Mother's house had knocked on her door as soon as the police appeared to ask her for water for *vozzo'e* [ritual washing before prayers], then asked for cigarettes and the 'right' to use the telephone. They are well provided with food and grenades on the back of their motorcycles, he says. He also says there is a scramble to get out of Tehran, and there are no seats on any plane leaving the city until the 28th.

I then speak to Mother and tell her she should come and stay at the Embassy for a while 'before I am told to hand over to someone else'. That last comment produces a hearty guffaw from her, which leads me to reflect that Mother's and my own sense of humour are not quite identical.

I watch films of the events in Tehran on television: mobs throwing stones, burning cars, looting offices, buildings ablaze. This has been a dreadful day, and I am glad it's over.

Saturday, September 9

I awake latish, having slept surprisingly well, considering. I pull back the curtain to see what the weather is like, and notice a pile of metal barriers and two policemen nearby, in conversation. Largish demonstrations due, I suspect.

The papers are filled with lurid descriptions of yesterday's events, with the *Financial Times* commenting that some diplomats in Tehran think HIM hasn't acted forcefully enough, and that the authorities instead of imposing a total clamp-down should have dealt with each incident separately as it arose. The BBC commentator, on the other hand, observes that some people think the Shah has over-reacted at a time when the opposition was beginning to show signs of disunity.

The news at ten reports Hoveyda's resignation, describing him as a 'key adviser to the Shah and one of the most powerful men in Iran'. There are no reports of any further clashes.

The Embassy demonstrators, larger in numbers, more violent in temper, more virulent in their slogans, pass by, and I wonder

227

whether our respective roles as spectator and demonstrator may not soon be reversed.

My loathing for the mullahs and everything they stand for has not changed and never will change. If anything, the reassertion of their views in the Tehran press before the recent clamp-down, their demands for strict literal adherance to everything the Koran says, their degrading primitiveness and misplaced self-righteousness, their nauseating bigotry and sanctimonious hypocrisy, have only served to confirm my contempt for the values they claim to represent and uphold. Theirs is a creed that, by demanding unquestioned acceptance of the contents of a book, requires the abdication of thought and reason. I cannot imagine what will happen if they should ever come to power. The country will be set back a hundred years, and, initially at least, there will be violence, lawlessness, vandalism and, worst of all, the ugly vengeance that inevitably accompanies the overthrow of an authoritarian régime.

The Social Democrats and the educated liberals will be swept aside at the very beginning, and either the Tudeh Party or a military junta, the only groups with any organisation, will take over. But what troubles me at this stage more than anxious speculation about the future of Iran is the question whether, in the innermost corners of my mind, in the depths of my consciousness, I believe the Pahlavis have reached the point of no return

Could it be, or at least be seen to be, that HIM's hands are now too full of blood for him to be worth saving? Does anyone, inside Iran, still view him with affection or sympathy? Have not his false priorities and disastrous economic policies, his military grandiosity and obsession with everything that flies and fires, his unquenchable thirst for flattery and his breathtaking insensitivity to the feelings of his own people, his vainglory and ceaseless lecturing – have these not dissipated any remaining reserves of national and international goodwill towards him?

Mostafa is surely wrong; the Shah has not killed 18,000 people. Even if he had, one ought not to feel unduly squeamish about such statistics. HIM's political opponents, had they been in power, might have killed many more. A cursory glance at the contemporary history of countries all around us is sufficient to prove that point.

But my doubts persist. Isn't it fair to inquire what will happen when he lifts martial law? Two hundred people, it is now estimated, died yesterday. How many more would have to die? How many more would have to die, not as HIM would argue, so that Iran should be saved from communism, but so that a few should be able to continue feeding their insatiable appetites?

And yet, and yet – shouldn't I be ashamed of even entertaining such thoughts? Would I dare look Saipa in the eyes if ever she should read these lines? I, who have shared with her so many moments of tender affection; I, who owe her so enormous a debt of gratitude, for the office that I hold, for the munificent generosity with which she has treated me! Is there no such thing as the milk of human gratitude, of loyalty? Did I not know about the régime's shortcomings when I agreed to represent HIM in London? Why didn't I speak out then? Isn't it beneath contempt to drive in the Embassy's Rolls Royce, drink its Dom Pérignon, spend its lavish allowances, go to Buck House and mix with British Royalty on HIM's credentials, but then draw back when it comes to defending the less reputable of the régime's activities? Questions that gnawingly, exasperatingly persist, and to which I find no answer.

A leader in the *Daily Telegraph*, under the menacing title 'The Shah Endangered', speaks of the need to protect the West's military and economic investment in Iran.

Sunday, September 10

Tehran, says the BBC, has had a quiet night. The military are in control and good old censorship is back in force. When Sharif-Emami had been about to present his government to the Majlis, Pezeshkpour, leader of the Pan-Iranists, stood up and accused the government of already having too much blood on its hands, and walked out. Sharif-Emami replied that extreme measures had been forced on the government because the newly-granted liberties had been abused, thus endangering national security. An early end to martial law and the lifting of censorship are promised, in a speech which is conciliatory and shows flexibility.

While I am having lunch Mahdavi telephones to report that Scotland Yard has just rung to say an aeroplane bearing members of Iran's royal family is due to land at Heathrow in half an hour, and do we know anything about it? I tell him to reply that, since we know nothing, the information is probably incorrect. He rings fifteen minutes later to say Princess Shams, Mr Pahlbod and a number of companions had arrived on what appears to be a private visit. Is the royal exodus on, I wonder?

Monday, September 11

Lords Weidenfeld and Chalfont come to talk about a possible authorised biography of Saipa, and, as George puts it, 'the story of the Pahlavis'. This would be an analytical history of their rule over Iran, and Chalfont would spend up to three years researching and writing it.

I say that while I think the Princess, given her symbiotic relationship with her brother, her childhood experiences with her exiled father in South Africa, her role in the 1953 crisis, and her commitment to raise the status of women in Iran, would make a fascinating subject for a biography, the timing for such a book is now singularly inopportune. I also say that we celebrated fifty years of Pahlavi rule last year, an occasion which was marked by, *inter alia*, the appearance of numerous books on HIM, on the Empress, on Reza Shah, and on the dynasty, and that it is difficult to see what there is left to say.

In the afternoon, Mohsen Tayebi, newly arrived from Tehran, stops by to see me. Saipa, he says, is leaving Tehran for Paris tomorrow, and the mood in Court circles is one of unmitigated gloom. I feel an inner sinking sensation when he says at Saipa's house in Tehran the pictures were being taken down, the carpets rolled up.

Tuesday, September 12

My optimism and confidence now return. There is an editorial in the *Washington Post* and a cover story in *Time* magazine, both undeniably pro-Shah. I reason to myself that our Western friends have at last realised that more than the Pahlavi régime is at stake in the survival of the monarchy, and that, whatever reservations they may have about the Shah's person or the nature of his rule, they have now decided to lend him all moral support. HIM, I conclude, is over the hump, and while he may never again rule in quite the old manner, he has weathered the crisis, and learnt a chastening lesson in the process. From now on he will not only be a better king but a better man as well.

Wednesday, September 13

Mother and Farhad arrive.
All is quiet on the Eastern front.

Thursday, September 14

As the Majlis debate continues, the Government comes under incessant attack, some of it quite venomous, but I interpret it all as a desirable letting off of steam.

Lord Chalfont telephones to say he has received a telex from Tehran to the effect that the book project is still very much alive. I have heard no more, I say.

Saturday, September 16

AAH rings to thank me for a cable I had sent him to assure him of my continued devotion and loyalty. I say the impression here is that the worst could be over. He is not so sure and is hesitant about making any predictions. The connection is an exceptionally bad one and our conversation is brief.

The Sharif-Emami Government, I learn from the radio news, has received a vote of confidence in the Majlis by 176 to 16, and guerrillas dressed as soldiers have attacked a security post in Tabriz and killed nine people.

Before going to bed I hear news of an earthquake in Iran.

Sunday, September 17

Extensive coverage of last week's events in the papers. Callaghan has written to HIM to express sympathy as well as the hope that liberalisation will continue; and Stan Newens and a few other MPs have taken him to task for doing so and even demanded that the Queen's visit next year be cancelled.

The death toll in the earthquake centred on Tabas is now put at 15,000, and TV films of the devastation make grim viewing. Is this, like the Abadan cinema fire, another sign of divine displeasure with the ways of the régime, I wonder?

Tuesday, September 19

The death toll in the earthquake disaster has now risen to 22,000 and the Empress, on a tour of the stricken areas, has been heckled over the shortage of doctors, nurses, tents and blankets. Indeed, persistent press reports of the mishandling of the relief work prompt me to cable Afshar with a warning of the possibility of political exploitation of the situation, and suggesting the immediate appointment of some capable person to supervise relief work.

Expressions of sympathy and offers of assistance pour in from individuals and institutions on a quite staggering scale, confirming my belief that the British are at their best at times of disaster.

Wednesday, September 20

I go to the airport personally to welcome Mirfendereski, dismissed in 1973 by HIM as Acting Foreign Minister but now rehabilitated thanks to Afshar, and en route to New York after a two-day stopover in London. He is more confident and composed than I have seen him recently, and we agree that HIM should stay, because the alternatives would be too terrifying to contemplate. We both believe that he has pulled through again. In confidence, he says Afshar had urged him to write to Moinian, HIM's Bureau Chief, to express thanks 'for His Majesty's forgiveness', but he had refused to do so, because, as he had told Afshar, 'it would break me as a man, and broken I am no good to anyone, including myself'.

Thursday, September 21

I go to the Airport to welcome Afshar. On the drive to Claridge's Afshar says AAH is in 'serious trouble', and Shariatmadari has asked that he be brought to trial for the mismanagement of recent years, a demand HIM has so far strongly resisted, saying that 'to try Hoveyda would be tantamount to putting the whole régime on trial'.

I take leave, noting that the Minister retains his rooms at Claridge's but moves to his own apartment in Kensington where, he says, he will be more comfortable.

'I am not going to push anyone who is already going downhill' is how Afshar described his sentiments towards AAH. When I mention this in confidence to Mirfendereski before his departure for New York, he says I shouldn't allow Afshar's feelings for AAH to interfere with my own relationship with Afshar, who had told him in Tehran that he would not recall me from London unless HIM instructed him to do so. This leaves me wondering whether Afshar *could* in fact recall me without some sort of a nod from an albeit enfeebled HIM.

Mirfendereski is surely right, I tell myself afterwards. Whatever the differences between Afshar and Hoveyda, they are surely no concern of mine, and can probably be attributed to their common past, to careers that have spanned so many decades of various diplomatic assignments, to the petty rivalries and jealousies of their unequally successful lives, and to the change in fortune these lives now seem to be undergoing.

I attend a reception at the Saudi Arabian Embassy, where I again receive innumerable expressions of concern, and go to Claridge's for lunch with Afshar. Afshar says Amini is continuing his activities against the Government, but the danger there is that the army's loyalty is to HIM alone, whereas Amini's condition for accepting the premiership was that all power, including the armed forces, should be placed under the control of the Prime Minister. This could split the army, and so lead to civil war. The Americans are pushing both the anti-corruption drive and liberalisation, and the American Ambassador had telephoned to congratulate Afshar on the Government's adoption of a recent anti-corruption measure. He also says that the mullahs are going to put forward the names of some twenty leading religious figures, from among which the Prime Minister would choose five, and these would form the Council of Clerics which would pronounce on the compatibility of all legislation with the tenets of Islam, as required by the Constitution. There is no other way but to make concessions to the mullahs, he says, but the hope is that the five eventually selected will be moderate and progressive in their outlook. Afshar then makes an oblique criticism of Hoveyda.

'Can I say something to Your Excellency?' I ask in as calm, courteous, but firm a tone of voice as I can muster. 'Nothing that you, or anyone else, may say will detract in the slightest from my high respect and admiration for Hoveyda. Whenever Hoveyda's name or record of service are attacked I shall defend him, whoever his detractor may be. Whatever justification there may be for your resentment against him, I cannot be expected to share it, and if you have any consideration for my feelings you will be good enough to refrain from criticising him in front of me.'

'All right,' he retorts, red with anger. 'I grant your wish. In any case I have no intention of kicking a man who is down. But there is one thing I must say to you before closing the subject – everything he told you was a lie.'

Told me when? In what context? About whom? I long to ask, but say nothing to avoid a more damaging escalation.

Monday, September 25

Later in the morning Afshar comes to the Embassy, with Hossein in tow, bringing with them a huge file of excerpts from the BBC's Persian language broadcasts. I must, he says, on the massive evidence of these monitored broadcasts, protest to the BBC about its lack of impartiality. Hossein nods his approval.

I shall do as I am instructed, I say, but if I am allowed my personal view – and at this Afshar says 'of course' – I should like to give my reasons why I believe protesting will not succeed. It would be virtually impossible, I say, to prove 'wilful partiality'; and while the BBC would be willing to correct, and express regret over, instances of obvious misreporting, they would never admit to bias, nor would we be able to substantiate such a charge. The Foreign Office would never lean heavily enough on the BBC, because that would lay it open to attack by left-wing MPs, who are closely in touch with dissident Iranians, both in Iran and in London. So, while we would certainly fail to bring about any change in the BBC's policies and practices, we would only be once again demonstrating our morbid over-sensitivity and excessive vulner-ability to its transmissions.

Afshar says the Government's instructions are perfectly clear and leave no room for ambiguity. Furthermore, the Prime Minister had said to him personally, 'I know I can rely on Radji to make an effective protest.'

Will he allow me to put my objections in writing so that he may have a closer, more detailed look at them, I ask, before making the protest. Of course I can, he says.

Tuesday, September 26

A dejected and worried Hossein comes to see me at the office, alone. He speaks of the all-pervading uncertainty in Tehran. No one knows what is going to happen next, and there is no consultative body composed of sensible committed individuals, which could be trusted with the task of thinking out the various options and making recommendations to the Government. Everyone seems to be looking after his own interests, with no consideration for where the country is going. HIM has resisted demands to remove his two sisters from the presidencies of the Red Lion and Sun and the Organisation for Social Services, and obviously still doesn't appreciate the strength of the opposition his policy of liberalisation has unleashed.

A cable from the Foreign Ministry announces the appointment of Ardalan as Court Minister and states that members of the Royal Family may no longer engage in business activities of any sort, and must immediately surrender to the Government the chairmanship or presidency of any organisations, charitable or otherwise, which they hold. There go HIM's two sisters.

In the evening I speak to Cyrus Ghani, just back from the States. He has it on good authority, he says, that the Americans have now all rallied round HIM, realising suddenly the disaster a Government headed by Khomeini would be. Carter's recent telephone call to the Shah was intended to demonstrate not only America's continued support, but also tangible proof of that support to the Iranian army brass, just in case they should begin to think of going it alone.

Wednesday, September 27

Tony Parsons, I see to my utter amazement, has said, in remarks at some ribbon-cutting ceremony, that 'the British Government supports the Iranian monarchy'. To dispel any suspicions HIM may have entertained, I suppose!

Lunch with Mother and Farhad. Mother says she is unhappy here and wants to go back 'to my home', in spite of all the uncertainties.

Ten thousand workers in the oil industry in Khuzestan have gone on strike, ostensibly for higher wages.

Friday, September 29

I ring Saipa in Juan les Pins. She immediately protests that I have been neglectful, and calms down only when I say that I have purposely refrained from telephoning because of not wanting to afflict others with my own brand of moroseness. She speaks of 'the loss of face' suffered by members of the Royal Family by the issue of the recent circulars and, as always, protests her innocence.

She praises Sharif-Emami's courage and considers Afshar's appointment 'curious'. She is going to New York, she says, 'but not to make any speeches'.

A call from Fereydoun in New York. There is a paralysis of will, a total lack of imagination and a complete absence of initiative in everything that emerges from Tehran, he says. Far from sharing my admiration for Sharif-Emami, he says Shariatmadari's primary objection is to the person of the Prime Minister himself, but adds that Shariatmadari is a nobody, and the only voice that is listened to now is Khomeini's. He has spoken to AAH, 'who is not worried about his own skin' and has enough documents stashed away to clear himself from any accusations that may be levelled against him. He criticises Ardeshir, however, who is going around boasting to everyone that the new Prime Minister, the new Foreign Minister, and the new Court Minister all owe their appointments to him.

Monday, October 2

A particularly scathing article by James Cameron in the *Guardian*, castigating Callaghan for his support of the Shah. There is a reference in the papers to an amnesty ordered by the Government for all students hitherto engaged in anti-state activities abroad, on condition that they respect the Constitution on their return to Iran. I am surprised we have heard nothing about this directly from Tehran, and when Kakhi suggests we should circulate news of the amnesty to the universities in Britain I suggest we ask Tehran for details.

In the afternoon I ring Hossein in New York to inquire, *inter alia*, about the fate of the BBC protest. Afshar, he says, has had a meeting with David Owen and raised with him the question of the BBC's Persian broadcasts. Afshar had said that, while he fully appreciated the BBC's independence from Government, not every-one in Iran was aware of that independence. People in the bazaars and the countryside found it incomprehensible that a radio station bearing the name of the British Broadcasting Corporation could put out news bulletins and commentaries that did not reflect the views of the British Government. Owen's response had been 'arrogant and undiplomatic', he says. Hossein also says that I must make my protest to the BBC.

Tuesday, October 3

Lunch with Mark Dodd, head of BBC's Eastern Services, to whom I hand an unsigned letter of protest, addressed to the Director General. I have refrained from signing the letter, I tell him, so as not to elevate our numerous complaints to the level of a formal protest, but the facts speak for themselves. The BBC's Persian Service has become an effective instrument for disseminating the views of a man who is openly preaching the violent overthrow of the legally constituted government of Iran, and were it not for the Persian Service, Khomeini's revolutionary call would never have enjoyed the massive audience that it does today.

Dodd replies that 'Khomeini is now an important factor in the political equation of Iran, a fact which the BBC cannot ignore'; that the Persian service has never broadcast those of his utterances that were mere exhortations to revolution, devoid of any news content; and that many Iranians have written to the BBC to say that for the BBC not to lend whole-hearted support to the massive popular movement now expressing itself in Iran would be tantamount to a betrayal of those same principles of democracy and liberty that the BBC has always claimed to uphold. The BBC had, of course, not broadcast this correspondence.

Wednesday, October 4

Julian Amery, confessing that he and his colleagues in the Conservative Party are 'rather confused at the turn of events in Tehran', comes to lunch. He says he believes one should go to the help of one's friends when they are in trouble, and is prepared to use the excuse of his daughter's presence in Tehran to fly out there for an exchange of views with HIM, with the Prime Minister, with Afshar, and 'with my old friend, Hoveyda'. Reflecting on the basic decency of such a gesture, I promise to convey his wishes to Tehran and to let him know its reaction.

Friday, October 6

Industrial unrest, strikes and clashes with the police have continued throughout the country, and I read in *Iran Post*, a none-too-reliable Persian weekly published in London, that Sharif-Emami may resign and Amini, Sanjabi, or even General Jam take over as Prime Minister.

I read also that, because of harassment by the Iraqi authorities, Khomeini has decided to leave Iraq. Kuwait has refused him entry, so that he may go to Syria or Algeria. Why not to Libya, I wonder.

I ring AAH in Tehran to tell him about Julian Amery's forthcoming trip and wish to see him while he is in Tehran. There is little hint in his voice of his habitual ebullience or cheerfulness, but he does sound even-voiced and firm. He is reluctant to talk about himself and asks about the British reaction to events in Iran. I say Callaghan's letter expressing support for HIM's policies, written at a time when his party has a majority of minus nine in Parliament, and when he knows it is certain to invite a hostile reaction from his own left wing, speaks for itself. Tony Parsons's unprecedented public praise for the Iranian monarchy, I add, leaves little doubt, at least in my mind, about the British Government's position. He agrees.

There is nothing, he assures me, I can do for him from my end. Now is the time to be thick-skinned, I permit myself to say to him, and while everyone is naturally worried, all will be well in the end. 'Ensha'allah' ('If God wills'), he replies.

Saturday, October 7

An editorial in the *Washington Post* reprinted in *I.H.T.*, argues that HIM, while corrupt and oppressive, is better than a dictator the Americans don't know, whereas Samoza of Nicaragua is so corrupt and oppressive that anyone would be better than him.

I drive to the airport to welcome Afshar and entourage. As we wait for his suitcases to be claimed and placed in the car, the Minister gives me an account of his activities at the UN.

238

Both the World Service and Radio Iran carry accounts of continued rioting and shootings in a number of Iranian cities, and of spreading work stoppages, which now affect the telephones.

Hossein comes to see me in the afternoon, both of us reluctantly aware of a certain *froideur* that the difficulties in my official dialogue with the Minister have created. The Minister, I remind myself, is Hossein's former boss and long-time friend, whereas I can look upon myself as an anachronistic hang-over from a clique whose more prominent members have already been sacrificed on the altar of political expediency.

'What about the Minister's various meetings in New York?' I ask in an effort to facilitate conversation. Hossein says that in his opinion David Owen lacks the polish a Foreign Secretary ought to have. He had referred to HIM as 'His Imperial Highness' throughout his meeting with Afshar, and had pre-empted the subject matter of the discussions by being the first to raise the question of the BBC broadcasts, saying he agreed with any criticism Afshar might make, but that he, Owen, was powerless to influence the BBC. As for the attitude of the British Government, however, there could be no doubt of its whole-hearted support for the policies of the Iranian régime. Michael Weir had been present at the meeting.

Vance, too, had claimed to be totally committed to HIM's continuing in power, and had dismissed as lacking in any significance the American Embassy's recent contacts with members of the National Front in Tehran, saying they were intended to keep the Embassy informed of developments and in no way implied support for the opposition.

Hossein also says that some while ago we approached the Iraqis, *sotto voce* and in absolute confidence, to remind them that it was contrary to the spirit of the friendship and good neighbourliness they professed towards us to harbour on their soil a political agitator against the Iranian régime, like Khomeini. The Iraqis, as much from fear of the implications of Khomeini's teachings for their own secular socialism as from a desire to please us, had tightened the noose around Khomeini and some of his supporters. Khomeini had reacted by saying he would leave Iraq altogether. We both agree that it would be a blessing if Khomeini were to die in Paris and, that whether he died of natural causes or otherwise, 'Savak would be blamed for it'. Khomeini's death would, he agrees, make a martyr of him, but the focal point of the opposition would then have disappeared, and until a new leader emerged much needed time would have been gained.

239

Monday, October 9

As the strikes and demonstrations have continued, the Government has agreed to a hundred per cent rise in almost all wages and salaries.

Shapour Bahrami telephones from Paris and wants to speak to Afshar. The French authorities, he says, have privately informed him that Khomeini has been told he can stay in France as long as he does not engage in any political activity against the Iranian Government. That, I tell Bahrami, does surprise me.

At a tea party at the Embassy some fifty colleagues and their wives, along with General Jam, turn up to meet the new Foreign Minister.

Though I don't hear it myself, I am later told that a spirited exchange takes place between Afshar and Jam on the advisability or otherwise of legalising the Tudeh Party.

Lord George-Brown comes to the residence at 6.30 to see Afshar, who asks me to attend as well. G-B says that, as a former Foreign Secretary, his powers are limited, but as a writer and broadcaster he hopes he still commands some influence, particularly in the United States. He has been deeply worried about Iran, 'a country of extreme importance to the West', and has written to Ardeshir to express his anxiety, and wants to know whether there is any way he can translate his anxiety into an active, helpful role. He is willing to go to Tehran to talk to HIM, to the Prime Minister, to the mullahs, and on his return to write and speak about his experiences, emphasising the Shah's indispensible role. Afshar, who through Ardeshir already knows about the letter, thanks G-B for his friendly sentiments and promises to let him know about HIM's reaction through the Embassy.

Wednesday, October 11

With Hossein I drive the Minister to the airport, 'respectfully' saying to him on the way that he must tell Sharif-Emami that, while no one minimises his enormous difficulties or the considerable courage he has shown in facing them, he *must* continue in office, whatever the hardships and the indignities, because his departure would mean that we had failed to reach a political solution on HIM's terms. Whoever succeeded Sharif-Emami would

240

dictate to the Shah rather than listen to him, thus leaving him with only one last card to play – the army. This would be an exceedingly dangerous position for HIM to be in.

The military have taken over Tehran's two leading papers only a week after Sharif-Emami had been rash enough to promise publicly full freedom for the press and the media. The journalists have gone on strike, and there is speculation whether this indicates that the military are taking matters into their own hands. I hope he won't resign. Shoot-outs at Tehran University have left at least three dead.

Thursday, October 12

My unmitigated gloom is not diminished by seeing a front page picture of Khomeini in the *Herald Tribune*.

There is a cable from Tehran asking for details of the State of Emergency legislation 'in Northern Ireland and Cyprus'. What State of Emergency can one superimpose on martial law, I wonder?

Friday, October 13

At the office I struggle with the rough draft of remarks I shall have to make at the Iran Society's annual dinner in a fortnight's time, but get bogged down in the first paragraph.

Mohsen Tayebi, back from Tehran, comes to lunch. He confirms that members of the Royal Family have all been told to leave and not come back for the time being. Shahram and Niloufar[1] have been allowed to stay, and now live at Saipa's newly decorated house. Mohsen had dined there recently. There had been no sign of the army of servants and drivers that used to be a feature when the Princess was there. Shahriar, Saipa's other son, dining there one night, had looked round the now bare walls of the dining-room and spotting the one remaining picture on the wall, had said, 'There's one they forgot to take'.

Mohsen also says that Shahram had said to him 'that stupid Radji in London can't handle the newspapers the way Ardeshir in Washington can'. Mohsen's answer had been that few voices were still willing publicly to defend the Pahlavi name, so that he had better be careful in his accusations.

[1] Saipa's son and daughter-in-law.

241

Saturday, October 14

The Government has bowed to the demands of the striking journalists and ended censorship.

A letter from Gerald Mansell, Deputy Director General and Head of External Broadcasting, discussing points raised during the Dodd lunch, in which he says:

'It is, I believe, incontrovertible that in recent months Ayatollah Khomeini has emerged as a factor on the Iranian political scene. He has, therefore, become a man whose statements and activities are "copy" for the world news media including the BBC External Service.

'The criteria applied by the BBC External Service News Room have, however, been stringent and not more than half a dozen short news stories have been written and broadcast reflecting Ayatollah Khomeini's political statements since mid-May. During the same period there were some 460 stories about Iran in the Persian Service News, including 23 in which the statements and activities of other Ayatollahs in the country were reported. I find, therefore, that I cannot accept that the extent of our reporting of Ayatollah Khomeini's views could fairly be described as providing a "mouthpiece" or "tribune" for the Ayatollah.

'Although I share your belief that the Persian Service reaches a substantial audience in Iran, I cannot conceive of it as the principal disseminator of the Ayatollah's views.'

He goes on to admit that the BBC was at fault in one of the instances of 'tendentious reporting' I had complained about, and concludes:

'You will always find us ready to look into detailed criticism of our coverage. Although we may not in every case see eye to eye with you, particularly in matters in which journalistic judgment is involved rather than the plain reporting of facts, I hope you will accept my assurance that our response will always be straightforward and that when we are satisfied that we have erred we shall always be ready to acknowledge it.'

I cable the entire text to Tehran.

Tuesday, October 17

I lunch with Dr Fallah, back from Tehran. He had seen HIM in

242

Tehran, 'looking thin but in a slightly better mood', and he had spoken to him of the country's financial problems. No one, it seems, had either calculated or foreseen the cumulative effect of the massive financial commitments entered into over the past few years. The deficit this year will be in excess of fifteen billion dollars, and all the cutbacks in the nuclear reactor programmes and in military purchases will do nothing to solve the immediate problem since they can have an effect only after 1981. At the same time Sharif-Emami, with his back to the wall and facing an unprecedented public outcry for the immediate remedying of long-neglected grievances, is accepting unconditionally all demands for huge increases in wages. As things are going now, in eighteen months our inflation rate will reach 150 per cent. 'Sharif-Emami will go through the six or so billion dollar reserves,' says Fallah, 'and then print as much money as is necessary to meet demands.' The one ray of hope in this picture of financial insolvency is that the oil companies, expecting OPEC to raise prices again, are increasing their liftings. It is this increase in liftings that he is going to raise with the oil companies in London.

Wednesday, October 18

An interview with Khomeini in *Le Monde*, in which he says a solution of Iran's problems is possible only if the Pahlavi dynasty is removed. The tone is utterly uncompromising and recalcitrant, the content crude and misinformed.

General Nassiri, the former head of Savak, to my amazement has returned to Tehran from Rawalpindi, apparently to stand trial. How can his trial be anything but a monumental embarrassment for the régime, with the finger of accusation pointing in only one direction? My God!

Saturday, October 21

There has been a massive demonstration at Tehran University by left-wing students, shouting anti-Shah slogans and demanding an end to martial law and the release of political prisoners. The security forces, present in force, have watched and not interfered, leading the BBC commentator to express surprise at the extent to which things have changed in Iran.

Dinner with Farhad, who returns to Tehran tomorrow. I say to him that I shall go back to Tehran when my assignment in London ends, or is ended, because though I would almost certainly now be miserable in Tehran, I know I would be infinitely more miserable anywhere else. But I tell him that he ought to consider living where he would like best, including the US; that he is not, and never has been, politically involved in Iran, and might be harassed there simply because of being my brother. He says he will make his mind up once he has returned to Tehran.

Sunday, October 22

I watch an hour-long programme on ITV's *Weekend World* on Iran. The presenter, Brian Walden, replete with mispronunciations, speaks as if he has a hot potato loose somewhere in his mouth. But the programme is redeemed by the interview with David Owen, whose forthright defence of the Shah I find commendable. The Shah, he says, has shown flexibility on human rights and, considerations of British national interests apart, he is preferable to either the benighted mullahs or the communists, both of whom have worse records on human rights than he has.

Tuesday, October 24

The Foreign Secretary's comments have opened the floodgates of counter-attack from, *inter alia*, the *Guardian*, which has no fewer than three articles, including a leader, on Iran; also from a three-man fact-finding delegation of Tribunite MPs just back from a visit to Tehran. Their spokesman, Russell Kerr, is vitriolic in his denunciation of the 'Shah's bloody tyranny'. Meanwhile, according to the BBC, disturbances are spreading throughout Iran and the death toll is mounting.

Wednesday, October 25

More violent demonstrations are reported from Iran in the 8 o'clock news, and David Owen has been attacked in both the British and the Persian press for lending support to the Shah. A report from Andrew Whitley in Tehran describes the armed forces as at 'full stretch'.

Lunch with Peter Tapsell[1] at James Capel and Co. Chapman Pincher is there along with a few others. Luckily for me Tapsell does most of the talking, taking the credit for much that is right with the Conservative Party. He says: 'If the Conservatives win, Carrington will probably be the next Foreign Secretary, which would mean Douglas Hurd would be spokesman on foreign affairs in the Commons.' But given that 'Margaret's experience of foreign affairs is limited', and that someone like Healey as shadow Foreign Secretary 'would refuse even to consider a person like Hurd, let alone speak to him', the problem will be a difficult one. The solution is to make Tapsell himself spokesman in the Commons, but he thinks he will only be given 'something like the Social Services'.

An article in the *Figaro* by Thierry Dejardin describes his recent conversation with HIM in Tehran: 'A lean, pale man, with drooping shoulders', who in the course of the interview had used the word '*décourageant*' more than twenty times.

Khomeini has also given an interview, in Paris, in which he says that compromise with Iran's present régime is not possible; that the people should wage 'a war of attrition' against it, and that 'an elected government of the Moslem people' is the only acceptable system.

Thursday, October 26

Today is, of course, HIM's birthday, which because of the Tabas earthquake – and one or two other reasons one can think of – we are not celebrating. Michael Fitzalan-Howard, attired in morning dress, comes to drink HIM's health. We talk about the current situation in Iran, about the Queen's visit in February which he says 'she hopes is still on', and about the London diplomatic scene generally.

At 12.30 my security officer rings to say that our 'Paris Embassy, or one of the employees working there' is to be attacked, and will I immediately notify our ambassador in Paris, 'but in no circumstances to use the embassy telephone' to do so.

Does that mean my telephone is bugged, I ask myself. How can it be? Who by? Or is someone eavesdropping? My initial agitation, however, is soon replaced by calmer thoughts, as well as by a tinge

[1] Conservative MP for Horncastle since 1966.

245

of scepticism about the melodramatic manner and content of the
message.

Friday, October 27

Julian Amery, back from Tehran, telephones to thank me for the
arrangements made for his visit. He had seen 'everybody' and had
found the scene somewhat depressing. There had been long silences
during the audience with HIM, and a good deal of carpet-gazing.
AAH was putting up a brave front and, now deprived of his army of
servants, had made them coffee at his new apartment. We arrange
to meet.

Farhad telephones in the afternoon from Tehran to say 'the old
boy looks a goner'. The strike by the oil industry workers is
designed to paralyse the movement of army vehicles, but soon there
may not even be enough aviation fuel for commercial planes to take
off. I tell him he should make arrangements to get out, and when he
mentions 'the old lady', I say she can manage without him but that
he should definitely leave, conveying the impression that I have
some sinister inside information.

Saturday, October 28

A soldier has been arrested in the town of Jahrom after shooting the
police chief and the town's martial law administrator, and violence
has continued at Tehran University where the students have
escalated their political demands and now ask for the removal of all
portraits of HIM.

Sunday, October 29

Frank Giles, in the *Sunday Times*, writes that Britain would be
'poorer' if the Shah went. There is a telephone call from Cyrus that
he has it on first-hand authority that even people like Bazargan and
the National Front leadership are becoming increasingly worried
about Khomeini's intransigence.

I lunch with the Lord Chamberlain and Lady Maclean at St

James's Palace. The Swedish and Portuguese ambassadors are there, as well as Sir John Hunt, Secretary to the Cabinet, and one of those impressively elegant military men who, on state occasions, walk ahead of, or behind, the Queen, perfectly conscious that their sole contribution to the occasion lies in the splendid pomposity of their deportment.

The occasion is apolitical; Lady Maclean is charming; and the food, and particularly the bread, is simply delicious.

Tuesday, October 31

I read in *Le Monde* of the 'nearly full accord' reached between Khomeini and Sanjabi,[1] who has gone to see him in Paris, and wonder whether that can mean anything other than agreement on HIM's departure. The BBC reports a noticeable escalation of violence and the complete stoppage of oil exports. The *Washington Post* has a leading article calling for support for the Shah.

On the powerful radio at the residence I listen to the raging Majlis debate, horrified at the virulence of the personal attacks on present and former ministers, particularly on AAH, and appalled by the inflammatory over-emotionalism of the speeches, as speaker after speaker tries to establish his Islamic credentials by distancing himself from the Court and attacking the Shah's governmental associates. At 6 pm I hear that the army has taken over the country's oil installations and given the strikers three days to return to work or face dismissal. Each day of the oil export stoppage will cost the country sixty million dollars. More have died in continued violence in the provinces.

At the Lebanese Ambassador's valedictory cocktail party, many hands are outstretched in sympathy and support. Frank Giles, back from Washington where he had seen Ardeshir, says Ardeshir had insisted that Giles should, as a friend, tell him what, in his opinion, the authorities in Iran were doing wrong. Giles, after some hesitation, had replied: 'Ardeshir, it might help if the soldiers didn't fire live bullets into unarmed crowds so readily.'

'Really, Frank? You think that's important?' Ardeshir had inquired, registering genuine astonishment rather than callous indifference. 'I shall inform His Imperial Majesty of this immediately.'

[1] The National Front leader.

247

Wednesday, November 1

At the State Opening of Parliament, where my diplomatic colleagues receive me with what I consider to be equal dosages of curiosity and sympathy, I hear the Queen say her trip to Iran, scheduled for February, is still on.

I rush back and change to go to the Algerian National Day reception, where again I find myself the object of friendly solicitations. On the drive back to the office I hear an anonymous member of the National Front, speaking on Radio Four, express the view that 'it is up to the Shah how much longer the violence continues'.

George Jellicoe and Christopher Soames both telephone. George wants to know whether there is anything he can do about the BBC Persian Service, about which Tony Parsons has spoken or written to him. I paint an objectively grim picture of the situation, adding that Radio Tehran itself is now just as inflammatory, but welcoming any muzzle he may be able to put on the BBC.

Christopher wants to know whether there is anything in particular we want him to say during the Lords debate on foreign affairs next week. I mention the flak David Owen had received for his remarks on television recently, and say the problem is essentially an internal one. All of this he already knows, so the choice of what to say is left to him.

Iran Air, too, has gone on strike, and according to Andrew Whitley the oil strikers have stiffened their demands because of the army's intervention. The Government, meanwhile, has promised to release the remaining 600 'criminal' political prisoners on December 3.

Thursday, November 2

The National Front has now suggested a referendum on the monarchy, which, in effect, means their abandonment of the 1906 Constitution. There is a nondescript leader in *The Times*. Ten thousand people have marched through Tehran and Qom, but the security forces have held their fire.

I lunch alone, go over my Iran Society speech to be delivered in the evening and persuade myself to give a convincing performance at the dinner.

At St James's Palace I join a long queue of distinguished people lining up to offer their congratulations to the royal newly-weds,

Prince and Princess Michael of Kent. Among the 400-odd guests, circulating like everyone else without any fuss being made of her presence, is the Queen.

My own guests at the Savoy dinner are the Saudi Arabian Ambassador and Mrs Alheglan, and David and Ann Steel. The guest speaker is Lord Barber.

Carrington ends his amusing remarks by a reference to 'the dark clouds that have appeared on the political horizon of Iran' and wishes us well. Lord Barber stresses Iran's strategic importance to the world community and commercial importance to Britain as a trading partner. Then I do my bit. I say that we had expected the social and economic strides of the past decades to have created within our society elements of stability and responsibility, but that we underestimated the shattering effect which genuine public discontent, released by a policy of liberalisation, had had on the fragile framework of our institutions. After references to a disregard for traditional values and a too tolerant attitude towards pervading corruption, I emphasise 'the quintessential beneficence' of the régime's ambitions for Iran, and end by saying that, while the road ahead will be a difficult one and we may hiccup again, 'there is not the slightest doubt in my mind that our setback is a temporary one; that sanity and moderation will ultimately prevail, because to the overwhelming majority of thinking Iranians, the realistic alternatives to our existing Constitution are totally unacceptable'.

As I sit down, I think to myself that I have probably spoken for the last time as Patron of the Iran Society.

Friday, November 3

Perhaps because I have seen an oblique reference to a possible change of government, I experience an inexplicable surge of optimism, convincing myself that Amini will be the next Prime Minister with Sanjabi a prominent member of his Government; and that, with an alliance between the National Front and 'respected individuals', the bazaar and the universities can be placated. And if *they* are placated moderate public opinion will be also. My sole worry remains the strike of the oil workers.

I lunch at Julian Amery's, with Billy McLean and George Gardiner.[1] Julian is far more pessimistic about the outcome of events in Iran than I am. He says HIM was 'very depressed' during his audience and there had been prolonged periods of silence during which Julian had tried to leave but had been

[1] Conservative MP for Reigate and Banstead since 1974.

motioned by the Shah to stay. Julian understandably shows greater concern for the strategic and global implications of the fall of the Shah than for what it might mean for Iran itself, but this irritates me.

Back at the office I send a cable to Afshar:

'At the Iran Society dinner last night, in the course of a conversation with two senior members of the Foreign Office, I detected a sense of profound anxiety over the future course of events in Iran which, I must respectfully submit, they felt arose directly from HIM's attitude. They felt that the persistence of such an attitude posed a serious danger, as it could adversely affect the morale of others. In language that was faultlessly courteous and discreet, they said they felt that HIM had to some extent lost his patience and perseverance. I also derived from them the impression that it is precisely in the throes of the present crisis that those qualities of resolute firmness and determination, which they know HIM to possess, ought to be demonstrated.'

The rest of the cable deals with the views expressed by the 'two officials' on the manner of confronting the demonstrators and the advisability of the use of tear gas and rubber bullets rather than live ammunition to keep the death toll down.

Saturday, November 4

A 'thank you' note from David Steel, congratulating me 'on a most courageous speech, delivered with such poise and sensitivity', re-charges my vanity, but my new-found optimism quickly evaporates when I hear of more shootings at Tehran University. The 1 o'clock news confirms the speculation that 'a coalition government of national reconciliation', which would include Sanjabi, may be in the making.

General Jam, whose name is being mentioned with increasing frequency as a possible army chief or Minister of Defence in a new coalition government, asks us to send a coded cable to HIM to the effect that, despite the rumours, he seeks no position, and his loyalties remain with his Sovereign.

An article in *Pravda* asserts that the Soviet Union would not support the coming to power of Khomeini. Khomeini himself says he will never compromise, and may even call for a civil war, and that any group – meaning principally the National Front – that

250

cooperates with the Shah's régime ranges itself against him and against Islam.

After a distracted game of tennis at Queen's, I return to hear that HIM is to make a TV broadcast, and immediately toy with the idea of sending a cable to suggest that in it he announces the turning over to the Government of the Pahlavi Foundation. But when I hear, in a later bulletin, that Sanjabi, still in Paris, has said that he has patched up his disagreement with Khomeini and has no intention either of meeting the Shah or of participating in a coalition government, my heart sinks, the clouds descend, and I am robbed of the will to move.

I wish to God I weren't a witness to this chapter of Iran's contemporary history.

Sunday, November 5

Judging by radio reports, the mob is loose on the streets of Tehran.

The *Sunday Times* says the National Front's refusal to join a coalition government leaves only the military option, and estimates that the military and the Americans now seem strongly against any further concessions to the mob. Outright comments that HIM has lost his nerve and is no longer in control appear in the papers. Amini has been to see the mullahs in Qom but, with the National Front witholding cooperation for fear of *takfir* (excommunication), it is difficult to see what he can accomplish.

Telecommunication workers in Iran have now gone on strike, and Mahdavi rings me at home to say that one direct line has been established between Paris and Tehran for urgent telexes only, and we should telephone the Paris Embassy and read them our cables, if we have any.

Later in the day I get through and speak to both Farhad and Mother, and as I speak to Farhad he tries to draw my attention to the noise of the choppers in the background, firing tear-gas canisters. He is getting out if he can within the next forty-eight hours.

Later news reports speak of attacks on foreigners and the British Embassy, which has been set on fire. Sharif-Emami is resigning and the Shah is in conference with his top civilian and military advisers.

Monday, November 6

The morning papers show the mob at work in Tehran, and the *Times* article is headed 'Tehran is burning'. General Azhari is the new Prime Minister and Afshar, I see, has been retained as Foreign Minister.

At 10 I listen to the Shah's broadcast. He sounds calm, even under sedation, and uses 'I' instead of the royal 'we'. He is conciliatory, even apologetic, saying considerations of national security have forced the present government on him. He 'requests' the clergy to invite the people to show restraint, appeals to workers and students to respect the law, promises not to repeat past mistakes and excesses, vows to fight corruption and to bring in democratic government.

It is a sad, wretched performance, a grovelling supplication which one knows will be rejected by Khomeini. The Shah has now played his last card – a military government – and if this should prove ineffective – and I don't see how it can succeed – the end for him, and those associated with him, must be nigh.

David Alliance, a successful Iranian businessman now resident in Manchester, comes to tell me that, through his influential contacts in the business community in London, he is bringing pressure on the BBC to tone down their Persian broadcasts. And George-Brown, he says, is going to Paris to see Khomeini. That does surprise me.

My cable to Afshar about HIM's lack of firmness and determination has been seen by HIM, without comment. He is now taking it from everyone, including me, poor man. And there is a reply to General Jam's cable, which says simply: 'From you, we would not have expected otherwise.'

There is a telephone call from Afshar to inform me that John Graham will be the next British Ambassador to Tehran. When I ask about the events of yesterday, he says, 'Last night was the first time I slept soundly in weeks;' and hints that if the army hadn't intervened little would have remained of Tehran. 'They already have their President and Prime Minister,' he says, referring to the mob, 'and both are in Paris.' With the military in, HIM has regained his confidence, he assures me.

I ask about my cable, and whether HIM had found it somewhat impertinent. 'Loyalty to His Majesty requires frankness at times,' he says pompously, without answering my question.

The late news speaks of continued rioting in parts of the country. From Paris, I hear that Khomeini has reiterated his intention to topple the monarchy, and stated that he will now do so by appealing to the soldiers to lay down their arms.

Tuesday, November 7

Relative calm has returned to Tehran, even though some shooting has been heard. The bazaar is still shut, as are the banks and schools, and queues outside petrol stations are getting longer. Kakhi informs me that Radio Iran, now under military control, has reverted to its former tiresome panegyrics, praising HIM's every action and utterance to high heaven. I ask him to prepare a cable to Afshar, reminding him that, unless Radio Iran retains some semblance of credibility, everyone will tune into the Persian Service of the BBC and the whole miserable circle of protest and denial will start all over again.

As I walk from the Chancery back to the residence, I see some thirty or so people demonstrating against the Shah's rule.

When I return to the office a distraught Nadereh tells me Farhad had telephoned to say Hoveyda had been arrested, along with several former ministers, and that General Khademi, head of Iran Air, had shot himself and was gravely wounded.

Wednesday, November 8

For the first time in many days not only are we not the first item of news, but we are not mentioned in the news at all, for which Allah be praised.

Mahdavi tells me at the office that the telecommunications people have gone on strike again and the telex cannot be relied upon for instant communication with Tehran. With Iran Air on strike there is no pouch either, so we are reduced to the telephone. Ironically, the last coded message from Tehran is not from the Foreign Ministry, but from HIM's Private Bureau chief, instructing me to inform those members of the Royal family who may be in London not to return to Tehran without HIM's explicit prior permission.

Kakhi, who has been working on a cable suggesting the transfer to the government of ownership of the Pahlavi Foundation, comes in to say HIM has just instructed the Minister of Justice 1) to investigate ways of transferring the Foundation's assets to the ownership of the people within a month; and 2) to look into the sources of the wealth of members of the Royal Family, both in Iran and abroad.

There is a telephone call from Michael Weir who says Tony Parsons had seen HIM last night and had found him to be in a far better mood. HIM had spoken of his determination to fight corruption. AAH had also been mentioned, and HIM had said that Hoveyda would never be tried 'because that would mean putting the régime on trial'. Michael, who has just returned from Washington where he has been discussing Iran, says he is speaking to the BP people in the afternoon.

There is a call from Peter Temple-Morris 'to offer solidarity', and one from Agha Khan Bakhtiar to say that Hushang Ansari has left Iran and gone to the States.

At 5 Afsaneh Jahanbani (AAH's secretary) telephones from Tehran. Hoveyda, she says, *has* been arrested. Before the knock on his door, HIM had spoken to him by telephone and told Hoveyda that he would be taken to a place 'where your safety could be ensured'. AAH had been given time to pack a few things, including books, and had remained calm and composed, according to Ali Ghaffari and Fereshteh Razavi, who were with him. The arrest had been made by a Lieutenant-General in civilian clothes, accompanied by two other officers, all of whom had appeared courteous but solemn.

Afsaneh also tells me that Khademi had certainly not committed suicide, but had been shot in the head by two as yet unidentified men who had jumped over the wall into his house.

Two letters, one from Natasha and Stephen Spender, and the other from Lizzie, offer sympathy 'at this difficult time'. On the 8 o'clock news I hear Shahram Chubin describe Hoveyda as a 'Bahai' who has been made a scapegoat, but who is not personally corrupt.

I am so terribly, terribly sorry for Hoveyda.

Thursday, November 9

A telephone call of kind words from John Leahy, and a visit from Dadresan, the Iran Air representative in London, who brings his newly-appointed successor for an introductory meeting. He confirms to me that, from a conversation he has had with the General's wife, and despite an official cable from the Ministry telling us that it was suicide, Khademi has in fact been murdered.

I send a cable to Afshar to remind the military authorities, now arresting the ringleaders of the opposition, to observe a minimum code of ethics in their treatment of detainees, so as not to expose us once again to the hysterics of human rights organizations abroad. When, with Mahdavi and Kakhi, I lunch later with Martin Ennals, I tell him of my action, hoping to pre-empt his predictable

254

objections. He, curiously, wants to know whether there is anything his organisation can do for AAH.

Fereydoun, whom I ring later in the afternoon in New York, is distraught. Amir Abbas's life is in danger, he tells me, and I should immediately contact Ennals and ask him to set the wheels in motion. 'This is the second time the Shah has tricked my brother,' he says, leaving me wondering which was the first. 'The Carter administration is under enormous pressure from liberal elements not to support a military government that is arresting and killing people,' a pressure which it will sooner or later have to heed, 'and that will be the end of the road for all of us'. Amir Abbas's sole concern should now be his own survival, says Fereydoun.

Charlie and Jessica Douglas-Home come to dinner. Charlie is going to Iran shortly, and I speak to him quite candidly about what I see to be the situation. Eldon Griffiths telephones to say the Irano-British Parliamentary Group of MPs have issued a statement expressing support for the Shah, and would I see that HIM is apprised of their statement.

A muddled, confused, worrying, unhappy day.

Friday, November 10

On his return to Tehran from Paris, Sanjabi has declared that there is agreement between him and Khomeini on the need for the formation of a truly national government, and that until such a government comes into being the strikes and the campaign of civil disobedience should continue, with Sunday declared a day of nationwide strikes. Meanwhile it appears the oil workers have not all gone back to work and our lack of financial liquidity is becoming increasingly recognized.

Lord and Lady George-Brown are my guests to lunch. During his audience George-Brown had found HIM 'very dejected', and had said what he could to bolster his morale. HIM had to make up his mind what it was that he wanted, he had told the Shah, and if his decision was to stay on, then he ought not to be too squeamish about the methods employed to keep him in power, including more frequent use of the military, and the offer of scapegoats 'like Hoveyda and Nassiri'. When HIM had been taken aback by what George-Brown had said and had even disagreed with the suggested course of action, George-Brown had told him that 'there is no point in having soldiers and tanks out in the streets if they aren't going to do anything', so planting the seed, I think to myself, in HIM's mind, of forming a military government.

I ask if Tony Parsons regarded HIM's survival chances at about fifty-fifty.

'Tony, without wishing to be unfair to him, thinks they are less than fifty-fifty. I had thought they were rather better than fifty-fifty until what you have now told me about Sanjabi's remarks this morning.'

He had met and was much impressed by Amini and Sharif-Emami, and had driven to Qom to meet Shariatmadari who, 'sporting a shrewd smile', had four times referred to 'your Dr Owen', wounded at the Foreign Secretary's label of 'reactionary mullahs' to describe Iran's religious leaders during his now infamous TV interview. The opposition figures he had met, and particularly Shahpour Bakhtiar, had no illusions about Khomeini's shortcomings. At the same time, he had been impressed by the moderation of the secular opposition.

When I mention Tony's impending departure from Tehran, George-Brown says that 'would be no bad thing', as people who stay on in a particular job for some years tend to go 'soft', but that I mustn't think him a brute for saying so. His remarks over Capital Radio on the damaging effects of the BBC's Persian language broadcasts had brought a telephone call from Gregson, the Comptroller, and they are meeting on Monday, with Mansell there too, to discuss it further.

Later in the evening I speak to Saipa in New York. Fereydoun, she says, has gone completely wild and was now saying the strangest things about the Shah's treachery to his brother to all sorts of people. She doesn't appear unduly disturbed about the turn of events in Tehran, saying martial law could remain in force for five or six years. When I do mention AAH's treatment by her brother, she says, with no trace of any sympathy that I can detect, that it had been Hoveyda who, for the last six years he was in office, had misled HIM, and so created the conditions for the present upheavals. It is useless to argue, I immediately recognise.

She asks about the opinion of 'your friends in England'.

'They think HIM has a fifty-fifty chance of survival.'

'Fifty-fifty? Is that all? No more?' She asks with genuine curiosity, as if haggling might improve the odds. She speaks with injured pride and genuine resentment of HIM's recent actions on the Pahlavi Foundation, the exile of the Royal family, and restrictions on the sources of their wealth. She doesn't know where Hushang Ansari is, though she knows he has left Tehran. We promise to keep in touch.

256

Saturday, November 11

I pull the curtains back to discover that it is a dull, overcast day. The presence of two policemen at the corner of the Embassy enclave reminds me that it is Saturday and that there will be demonstrations again.

Mrs Afshar, wife of the Foreign Minister, a pretty, charming, likeable woman, comes to lunch; and Princess Fatemeh, who had said she would join us for coffee, arrives just as we are starting to peel our artichokes. The *Herald Tribune* has had a large photo of Khomeini on its front page in the morning, and the damage done to the morale of the ladies is perfectly apparent. The Princess asks about Hoveyda, and I say the prospects look grim for him, no matter what happens now. 'Will they kill him?' she wants to know, wiping a tear from her eye as she asks that question.

'I hope not. I don't know.'

We speak about Homayoun Mazandi[1] who, at her own expense, has hired a TV crew and gone to Paris to interview Khomeini; of her considerable courage, of her unorthodox methods and muddled convictions, and eventually break up to go our respective ways.

The 3 o'clock news reports that Sanjabi, about to address an invited press conference, has been 'arrested by a general and some plain-clothes men of Savak'. It all sounds rather East European.

Sunday, November 12

We dominate the news in the Sunday papers again, and feature on Brian Walden's 'Weekend World'. I do wish he would make an effort to pronounce names of people and places correctly.

After lunch I come back to the residence to talk to Homayoun Mazandi about her interview with Khomeini. By her own account, the intense emotional excitement of the occasion and her lack of professionalism had turned the meeting into something of a farce. She had been accused of being a 'Savaki', and told to leave. On the steps outside the Ayatollah's house she had broken down and cried for a long time, before eventually making her way back to Paris. She hands me what there is of her filmed interview with the Ayatollah, and I promise 'to think about what we should do next'. I admire her good intentions, her willingness to take action, and her quite considerable courage.

[1] An Iranian hostess living in London.

The 9 o'clock news speaks of relative calm in Tehran but of shootings in the provinces. The oil strikers have not gone back.

Monday, November 13

Farhad reports from Tehran that, while the general situation appears calmer, there seems to be a breakdown of discipline among the Tehranis, with people generally more aggressive, restless and rude than normally. 'One-way streets no longer exist,' he says, 'and if you raise your voice to protest, you face a lynch mob.'

There is a leading article in *The Times*, which I judge to be more descriptive than prescriptive.

I lunch with Michael Weir at Overton's. Tony Parsons and Bill Sullivan have been seeing HIM on an almost daily basis, with Tony, according to the Sullivan cables that Michael had seen in Washington, doing most of the talking. Great hopes had been placed in the formation of a coalition Government of National Unity, originally to have been headed by Abdollah Entezam and, after his refusal on genuine reasons of health, by Amini, and to have included Sanjabi, Bazargan and Shariatmadari's son. But the National Front reneged at the last minute. 'Sanjabi is a weak man and he stayed far too long in Paris,' says Michael, 'and now, of course, there is no one left to talk to.'

Do I have any ideas, he wants to know. Half-heartedly, I mumble something about the imperative necessity of finding a political solution, adding that I consider the assessment of the Foreign Office too pessimistic.

'You're not exactly bursting with optimism yourself,' says Michael.

In desparation, Tony is now suggesting a temporary government of trusted and respected individuals, even of non-politicians, 'but one immediately comes down to the question of names'. 'We are,' says Michael a minute later, 'now reduced to prayer.'

We move to John Graham's appointment. David Owen apparently was not getting on well with him over the handling of the Rhodesian negotiations, while on the other hand he has great respect for Tony and wanted Tony within reach. So John goes to Tehran and Michael will go to Cairo. Perhaps out of politesse, he says he would have preferred to have been posted to Tehran.

I see Parviz Mina in the afternoon. He says the foreign exodus is on, and he had secured a seat on a plane leaving Tehran only through string-pulling. The winter months, he says, are the time when the oil industry must work at full capacity both for the domestic and export markets. Unless there is a settlement of the strike of oil workers, the accumulated fuel reserves will run out in fifteen days, and there are bound to be shortages, even if the workers return to work tomorrow. General Oveisi had asked him for advice, which he had given, but the demands of the oil workers are political in nature, and he had come abroad so as not to be asked to run an ailing industry whose disease is political.

On the early evening news there is an interview with an Iranian, Siamak Zand, claiming to be a high official of the Court Ministry, and seeking political asylum in England. He calls the Shah corrupt and responsible for all the killings now going on in Iran; 'He is a butcher.' When Peter Snow, the ITV interviewer, asks how he can justify the term 'butcher', Zand says because on 'Black Friday' the Shah was aboard a helicopter that had fired on the demonstrators. I immediately decide to prepare a statement denying Zand's accusations.

Tuesday, November 14

Radio Tehran, now operated by the military, reports that the oil workers have all gone back to work, and I wonder whether it is true. Telephone calls of sympathy, and many requests for information about relatives in Iran, pour in. At 11.15 one of my security liaison officers rings up to say that a group of eight people, posing as passengers, have entered the Iran Air office in Piccadilly and vandalized it, tearing up portraits of the Shah, pouring acid on them and hanging up Khomeini's pictures instead, covering the walls with graffiti.

There is a telephone call from Afshar in the evening re the Zand allegations. I stress that we shouldn't over-react, and tell him the Embassy is preparing a release to the Press, denying the charges.

The news, before I go to bed, speaks of more shootings in Tehran.

Wednesday, November 15

The Diplomatic Corps assembles at 11 at St James's Palace to pay its respects to the visiting President Eanes of Portugal. My paranoia, about being the object of glances of sympathy alternating

259

with stares of curiosity from colleagues, is revived. When, speaking to de Perinat, the Spanish Ambassador, I refer to the innumerable letters of support I have received from British friends and strangers over the events in Iran, he says he never knew 'a people who *wrote* as much as the English do'.

Thursday, November 16

Tony Alloway of *The Times* reports feverish political activity by HIM to find a solution that would install the National Front as Iran's civilian government. The World Service of the BBC hints that the Americans have said they will agree, if need be, with the Shah's departure and the establishment of a republic, provided it is led by a military figure, 'like Numeiry of Sudan', ruling out, in effect, both Khomeini and free elections for the foreseeable future. A miracle if it works, I think to myself.

I attend the Annual General Meeting of the British Institute of Persian Studies, where David Stronach, the Director, provides a quite fascinating account of the Institute's activities in Iran. The occasion, as always, is well-attended, and also, as always, as soon as the lights go out and the slides appear the sound of snoring becomes audible. I suppose it is the discipline of attending which is regarded as more important than the content of the lecture. I shall never understand the ways of the Islanders.

Friday, November 17

A telephone call from Farhad warns, in language as cryptic as possible that 1) I should exercise extreme caution in my telephone conversations with Tehran; and 2) I should address my more important cables to Moinian at HIM's Private Bureau. All this he has put down in a letter which our friend, Alireza, leaving for Paris today, will mail on once he gets there.

For the rest of the day I am plunged into speculation as to what it all means. The *Herald Tribune* has a story by Johnny Apple of the *New York Times*, quoting Zand to the effect that a number of Western journalists were given substantial gifts by the Iranian government in return for laudatory articles on the Shah.

Monday, November 20

The World Service refers to the American response to Brezhnev's call yesterday not to interfere, 'specially militarily', in the affairs of Iran. Cyrus Vance has said that, while the US supports the Shah, America does not intend to interfere in the internal affairs of Iran.

How does one remain loyal to a rat? Whatever the problem, becoming a rat oneself is surely not the solution. Despite some initial reservations about sticking my neck out so far and so late in the day by assuming the role of the régime's principal defender, the lengthy and, I believe, quite credible Embassy statement refuting the Zand charges is sent out to all the papers, including the representative of the *New York Times* in London, Johnny Apple. While I know Tehran has too many things on its plate to worry about Zand's allegations, I do very strongly feel that his charges have to be refuted. Since Tehran has not supplied one single line of instructions as to how to approach the problem, the refutation of the allegations can only be done by destroying Zand's own credibility as a witness. I accordingly drafted a press release in which I pointed out that 'Mr Zand's position was that of a relatively minor official in the press department of the Court Ministry and not, as some sections of the British media have described, that of "a close confidant of the Shah of Iran"'. I went on to point out 'glaring inconsistencies' in his account, and noted that 'on his "defection" flight (but nobody tried to stop him from leaving) Mr Zand was apprehended by Frankfurt police on November 2, after a complaint of his disorderly behaviour on the flight'. I concluded: 'From what appears in certain sections of the press, Mr Zand seems to have been approached, and coached, by journalistic circles whose hostility to the Iranian régime has long ante-dated his "defection" and is well documented. Mr Zand's credentials better suit him in the role of a self-serving opportunist who blows with the current wind.'

I lunch with Abdul Reza Ansari at PG. HIM's treatment of AAH is brought up, and we both agree that there is a name for people who treat their loyal and faithful aides in such a manner. Abdul Reza believes HIM's action will only hasten the desertions from the ranks which are already taking place, and thus weaken rather than strengthen HIM's hand. He also says he will not return to Tehran because he would never be given a fair hearing, although the public accounts of the Imperial Organization for Social Services, over which he presided, will stand up to any scrutiny.

What he wants from me specifically is to change his diplomatic passport to an ordinary one. He will write a letter stating that he has lost the briefcase containing his passport and formally asking for a new one, to make it easier to me. I say I will speak to my Consul-General, but expect no difficulties.

I dine with Sir Harold Wilson at the Athenaeum. Apart from Marcia, there are three fortyish, rich, seemingly self-made businessmen. Sir Harold, who assures me at the outset that I am 'in the company of friends and can therefore speak quite freely', is too kindly motivated in goading me to place the blame for all that currently ails Iran on 'the Russian communists'.

When one of the other guests mentions the ordeal of Jeremy Thorpe, the current talking point in town, Sir Harold says Peter Bessell, the main prosecution witness, had written to him when he was Prime Minister asking for a Labour seat at the same time that he had written to Ted Heath to ask for a Tory seat.

But we soon revert to Iran, with Sir Harold believing that perhaps I am not capitalising on the 'help and support of Iran's innumerable friends in this country'. He asks: 'When did you see the Foreign Secretary last? When did you see the Prime Minister?'

I say that I am indeed grateful for the assistance and understanding of our many friends here, but that our difficulties are essentially internal in character. 'What about the Communists?' he asks.

Marcia strongly condemns the Shah for sacrificing his trusted friends.

Tuesday, November 21

I receive a strongly worded cable from Afshar about 'the malicious and provocative broadcasts of the Persian Service' and am instructed to listen to every broadcast each day and to protest as often as possible.

I issue Abdol Reza Ansari with an ordinary passport and, as required by routine regulations, instruct the Consul-General to notify Tehran of our having done so.

In the evening Ardeshir calls from Washington to say that the Embassy press release on the Zand allegations has caused trouble in Tehran. Reuter, only quoting the paragraph speaking about the Middle Eastern custom of giving gifts, has interpreted that as confirmation of Zand's allegations of bribery.

Ardeshir says Tehran has been unable to contact me because of the strike of the telecommunication people. He sounds excited but friendly, and grows considerably calmer in the course of our conversation. I read him the relevant passage, explaining that the reason for its inclusion was to protect ourselves, 'just in case gifts had been given'. 'It's a minor thing, in any case,' he says, adding that if I want to send a reply I can do so through his direct line to Tehran. I do.

Wednesday, November 22

The promised letter from Farhad, taken by Alireza to Paris and posted from there, finally arrives.

In it, he warns me that my telephone conversations with Tehran are probably tapped; and that Afsaneh had specially asked to see him the other day to say that she knew 'from absolutely reliable sources' that some of my cables are deliberately withheld from HIM; and that, if I have anything important to say, I should cable it to Moinian. Afsaneh had spoken to AAH, whose only complaint had been his loneliness.

The *Herald Tribune* has printed the Embassy's reply to the Zand allegations, but it has placed alongside it a cartoon showing the crumbling of the guns which have been the pillars upholding the Shah's throne. 'Balanced reporting' they would call it. And *Le Monde* carries an advertisement demanding the release of AAH, signed by some prominent Frenchmen. I suspect it's Fereydoun's doing. Good luck to him.

I remain tense and worried the whole day. My new instructions, namely to monitor the Persian Service daily, determine instances of tendentious reporting, and protest vigorously on every occasion, displease me, even though I am fully aware of the headaches these broadcasts are causing Tehran. Then there is the telephone conversation with Ardeshir. With nothing to go on, a refutation of the Zand allegations had been prepared and circulated which I would have thought was a creditable effort. Instead, one paragraph in it has caused HIM's displeasure, and there has been no reply to my subsequent cable of explanation sent through Washington. And, of course, now there is Farhad's letter, casting a pall of suspicion on the loyalty – indeed the good will – of old and formerly trusted friends.

I receive a strongly worded cable from a Director-General of the Foreign Ministry demanding to know why, in contravention of the Ministry's quite clearly stated instructions not to change passports without its prior permission, the Embassy has done so in the case of Abdol Reza Ansari.

I ask to see the circular to which the cable refers. The instructions are explicit, clearly stated and unequivocal in intent; and we, by which I mean Mahdavi, my Number Two, and Javaheri, the Consul-General, who actually provided the passport, have acted against them. How is it possible, I ask myself, that neither Mahdavi nor Javaheri, hesitant as they were, ever mentioned the existence of the circular? They claim, that they too, like me, had simply forgotten about the Ministry circular.

My many 'friends' at the Ministry will be quick to point out, and rightly so, that I stand in flagrant breach of specific instructions, and will no doubt attribute my motives for having done so to a desire to help out a co-member of the 'Ashraf clique'. I have supplied my 'friends' at the Ministry with the smoking gun they have all along been looking for.

I work on a cable to Afshar, expressing deep regret over the issue of the passport and assuming full responsibility for the affair, but asking him to understand that an inadvertent disregard of the circular, rather than any sinister wish to help out a crony in distress, underlay the entire unfortunate episode. I try to make its tone as little grovelling as possible.

I find and speak to Ansari at midnight, and explain Tehran's inquisitorial tone over the affair, asking him to send back the new passport. He indicates that he is not alone, changes the subject to the *Herald Tribune* reply, and says he will speak to me tomorrow.

A troubled night.

Thursday, November 23

When I am finally able to talk to Ansari he says the last thing in the world he wants to do is to create additional headaches for me. 'I found the briefcase containing the old passport before leaving the hotel, and will therefore be sending back the newly issued one,' he says conspiratorially. I thank him deeply for his understanding and cooperation, wondering what I could have done if he had said quite simply that he wouldn't return the passport. Abdol Raza Ansari is an honourable man.

My post-mortem with Mahdavi and Javaheri about the passport

affair reveals no new information. In my cable of explanation to Afshar I now insert a concluding paragraph to the effect that 'Mr Ansari has, incidentally, found his lost briefcase and diplomatic passport, and will be returning the ordinary passport to the Embassy by registered mail'.

Later in the day I receive the Foreign Minister's cable on 'HIM's displeasure' over the paragraph referring to the giving of gifts to journalists, referred to in the Embassy reply. How, HIM has demanded, could the Embassy have issued a statement on such a sensitive issue without seeking the permission of the Ministry first. Afshar, according to his cable, had replied that the need to act urgently, coupled with the dislocation of communications, could perhaps explain the Embassy's action. 'I have no doubt,' goes on the cable, 'that in future you will not undertake any action on similar sensitive matters without first seeking instructions from the Ministry.'

I ring Hossein in Tehran. Afshar had stood by me and defended my action over the offending paragraph in the reply, says Hossein, and I should telephone to thank him. When I begin to raise the passport affair, we are cut off. Two hours later we speak again, and he promises to apprise the Minister of my explanation. He warns me rather cryptically that I should be extremely careful of what I say to people privately, 'and that includes everyone', because 'everybody is out to settle personal scores'.

King Constantine comes to lunch and brings a number of envelopes destined for Their Majesties in Tehran. He says King Hussein had privately predicted the events in Iran several years ago, and if the rest of his predictions come true, Riyadh would be the next to fall.

I don evening dress and proceed to Buck House for the Queen's reception. When my turn comes to be presented, Her Majesty, expressing concern over the events, asks what the situation is now. I reply that the month ahead will be a difficult one but that ultimately all will be well. 'It all happened so suddenly,' she observes, with genuine bewilderment. Prince Philip says: 'You seem to have bouts of national insanity every fifteen years;' while Prince Charles and the Queen Mother express their good wishes for a happy outcome. Princess Margaret, looking sun-tanned and much thinner, remarks that 'the noise of the demonstrations echoes through my house every Saturday'.

When we leave our formal positions to circulate in the larger reception rooms I chat briefly with the Foreign Secretary. I tell him I am sorry that he had been attacked by his own party for supporting the Shah, and he says the National Executive of the

Labour Party should be told to shut up from time to time, but what he hadn't quite foreseen was the strong Iranian reaction to his remarks. I say we must go on trying for a political solution while the military restore law and order.

'With a minimum of force,' he says, adding that Tony Parsons will be kept on in Tehran throughout the month of Moharram, and return to London in January. He would have liked to have gone on talking, I feel, but is called away to be presented to the Queen. 'Cheer up,' he says as he leaves, causing me to wonder whether my despondency is so poorly concealed.

Friday, November 24

I swallow much pride, speak to Afshar, and thank him for his support over the affair of the circular, an expression of gratitude which he accepts unhesitatingly. He then raises the subject of the BBC, which has broadcast Khomeini's call for the non-payment of taxes and for strikes during the month of Moharram, as well as his appeal to the younger officers and conscripts to switch their loyalty to him. He has spoken to Tony and to Andrew Whitley, telling the latter that as far as the BBC is concerned matters have now reached an intolerable climax.

'Is there any hope?' Whitley had asked. Afshar had told him the government had already made up its mind to expel him. It was only the timing of implementing that decision that remained to be decided.

He says General Azhari's address to the Majlis and Senate had been well received by the people, who had now come to see that the main issue was not whether the régime should continue or not, but the very real danger that Iran would disintegrate if the monarchy was toppled.

I make no mention, nor does he, of the passport affair. He does say, however, that he may soon be visiting London again.

Shahbazi, an old colleague from my days at the Prime Minister's office, stops by for a chat. He says that, on AAH's advice, he had left Tehran the day before Hoveyda's arrest. Former Prime Ministers, ex-ministers, senior government officials, ambassadors and other politically prominent people now have to obtain 'special permission' to leave the country. Amouzegar, he says, had been detained at the airport, and only his telephone call to the Palace and HIM's specific instructions had secured his release and subsequent departure. It would be stupid of anyone to return now, he says, because one would be thrown into jail, there to languish for two or three years before anyone did anything even about preferring charges.

Sunday, November 26

At PG a message awaits me to call a friend who has just returned from Washington. When I do, we stay on the line for well over half an hour. 'The Americans,' he says, 'are desperate about the situation.' A State Department friend had told him that 'short of landing the marines, we are willing to do anything to stabilize Iran'.

Then he had met a senior American military figure who had said: 'All of us were relying on the Shah. He was the focus of stability and the source of our strength in the entire area. We depended on him, and supplied him with all the equipment he cared to ask for. Yet, when Carter spoke to him the other day, all he could manage was a feeble "yes" and "no". What's the matter with him? Has the Shah lost his manhood? And this man in Paris – you mean to tell me you can't neutralise him?' My friend had started to mention the efforts that were being made, in cooperation with other ayatollahs, to isolate Khomeini politically, when the American interrupted impatiently to say: 'Hell no! I mean can't you physically eliminate him?'

He had also seen and spoken to a high official of the former Administration, who had told him that Tony Parsons was a socialist at heart who didn't like the Shah, and his wife Sheila was an even more fiery left-winger, who loathed the Iranian royal family, while Bill Sullivan, the American Ambassador, who had gained a reputation as a hawk while serving in Laos, was now trying to ingratiate himself with the trendy liberals of the Administration. These two, with the more articulate Tony to the fore, were the people the Shah now most relied on for advice – even for guidance – on how to stem the tide of Iran's revolution. The Shah should have acted with resolute firmness from the start. 'The worst kind of dictator is a weak sulking one,' he had told my friend.

Before I go to bed I hear radio reports of widespread disturbances all over Iran.

Monday, November 27

A fat, largish envelope, covered in French stamps and clearly marked 'from AR Ansari', brightens my day. The much-awaited passport is inside it, together with a formally written note from Ansari saying that his mislaid briefcase had been found, with his old passport in it, and he therefore has no need of another. How many people would have acted so unselfishly, I wonder?

The news speaks of continued fighting in the streets of Tehran. Amini has given an interview in which he has condemned Savak, praised the clergy, and called for national unity to save the country.

Ahmad Ghoreishi comes to lunch. The régime, he says, is rotten at the core, and to hope that it will be kept in power by popular acclaim is complete nonsense. The only way it can stay in power is by the exercise of force. 'And if he can't use force, he ought to go. There's no alternative. You can't be a dictator and a constitutional monarch, a soft-liner and hard-liner, all at the same time.'

Ahmad also says that while in Tehran, Afshar had told him Sharif-Emami had asked that 'Radji be removed from London' because of his links with Hoveyda and Ashraf, but Afshar had resisted, replying that he couldn't find anyone better for the moment.

In the evening papers I read an item that the striking employees of the Central Bank have circulated a document accusing two of the Shah's nephews and an army general, plus a few others, of having recently transferred 2.4 billion dollars to banks outside Iran. Oh God, No!

Tuesday, November 28

Lengthy accounts of the recent money transfers appear in all the papers, those accused being amongst some of HIM's closest civilian and military associates. The scandal, whether true or not, must, I fear, be so enormously damaging that all subsequent denials will fail to erase it from the public mind. It may well prove to be the kiss of death for the régime. The Persian Service, claiming the subject to be a legitimate item of news of great public interest, will disseminate it with much relish, and all Khomeini's most exaggerated and odious accusations will now be assumed to have been substantiated.

There is a cable from Afshar, in code, informing us of what we have just heard on Radio Iran, namely, that the Foreign Minister has protested to the British Ambassador about the persistent tendentious reporting of the BBC's Persian Service.

Later, there is a call from Hossein to say that he and Afshar would be coming to London on December 7 'for seven nights'.

The reports of the money transfers are grossly exaggerated, he says, and the storm over Ansari's passport has blown over, 'although the episode would not have ended there had you not retrieved the passport'.

Wednesday, November 29

In the penultimate issue of *The Times* before it suspends publication[1] there is a leading article on Iran. It argues that, while HIM has served Iran well throughout his reign, he should now, for the sake of Iran as well as for his own sake, plan his departure, so that a constitutional monarchy may in time take over. I wonder if Charlie has written it.

Later I receive a call from him. Yes, it was he who had written this morning's leader, and what did I think of it? I say I agreed with everything he had said, and admired the friendly sympathetic tone in which he had said it, but disagreed with his conclusion: The Shah's departure would not usher in an era of constitutional monarchy but mean the end of the monarchy. We arrange to meet soon.

I send off a letter of protest to the BBC in which I say that, being now able to monitor the Persian Service's transmissions, the Embassy is 'frankly astonished at the undisguised bias that is an ever-present feature of its broadcasts, and the compromising light in which they place the Government's efforts to restore stability in Iran ...'

After giving details of three separate instances of biased and misleading reporting, I continue:

'My Government is well aware that the BBC will claim a right and duty to pursue the truth in the interest of the free flow of information, and that it will deny a charge of partiality in its reportorial function. But from ample existing evidence, any fair-minded person would be bound to deduce that the publicising of insurrectional doctrines clothed in Passion-play rhetoric, the brandishing of rumour as fact, and the preoccupation of the lèse-majesté outpourings of known groups opposed to the monarchy amount, at best, to a species of selective impartiality which leaves little doubt as to the BBC's partisan attitude towards the régime in Iran.

[1] As a consequence of industrial action.

'A continuation of the Persian Service's reportorial activities in Iran in such a vein can only be viewed by my Government with the gravest concern.'

In the evening I speak to Saipa in NY and tell her that at the bottom of my heart I know that somehow all will be well in the end, and feel that she has cheered up. Ardeshir, she informs me, has returned to Tehran, HIM has not yet fully regained his composure and confidence, and Hushang Ansari is 'genuinely ill' and in a New York hospital.

Thursday, November 30

Seyyed Hossein Nasr, the new head of the Empress's Private Bureau, comes to see me at the office. Although he doesn't quite say so, I gather he is in London to make use of his university contacts to enlist pressure from academic circles against the BBC. I show him the Embassy file on our correspondence with the BBC; say we could arrange for him to talk to Mansell or anyone else he might wish to see, and tell him of the sort of answers the BBC would predictably produce. After our chat I discern a slight dampening of enthusiasm for the mission he has been entrusted with.

In the evening a visit from Khosro Eghbal. He says that early in September Giscard d'Estaing had sent an eminent representative in the person of Antoine Pinay[1] to HIM to assure him of France's continued support. Khosro had seen Pinay in Paris after his return from Tehran, had told him 'all there was to know' about the shortcomings of the Shah, his family and entourage, but had firmly impressed upon him that, despite all the drawbacks, 'the Shah is the glue that holds the army together', and that his departure at this time would be a catastrophe.

He says there is a desperate need to create a force of moderates, of people the public could find acceptable, to fill the gaping vacuum between Khomeini and the army. A certain Najafi, the Minister of Justice in the present government, is now regarded as such a person, and he ought soon to find some pretext to leave the military government. He confirms that HIM had offered the premiership to Entezam, Sorouri, Najm-el-molk, even to the pro-Mossadeq Sadighi, but none of them had seen his own premiership as a solution to the present crisis. Nevertheless, the only sensible plan remains to urge unity among the moderates, and to put pressure on an unbending Khomeini to return and end the killings. Many people who have had enough of the present disruption to their daily

[1] A former French Prime Minister.

270

lives, who are weary of the continuing violence, who fear the dire economic consequences of a prolonged industrial paralysis, would wholeheartedly lend their support to such a plan. The silent majority, so to speak, would then be mobilised.

It is when Khosro starts speaking about American contingency planning that I begin to feel a degree of scepticism about the picture he paints. The Americans, he says, have drawn up plans to occupy southern Iran, employing troops at present in Germany and using Israel as a staging-post, should the authority of the government in Iran collapse. Having secured the oil installations and safeguarded the sea routes of the Persian Gulf, they would then be in no position to object to Soviet intervention in the north, so in effect tacitly acquiescing in yet another partition of Iran.

Friday, December 1

There is a cable from Afshar calling my protest to the BBC 'timely', and informing me that 'the BBC representative has been summoned to the Ministry tomorrow to explain his misrepresentation of facts in reporting the money transfers. For your own information, his expulsion seems probable'.

I inform Afshar of our second protest in as many days to the BBC, but advise against Whitley's expulsion on the grounds that it will not silence the Persian Service, but merely create hostile reactions in the media.

I now toy with an idea that has been in my mind off and on ever since an Embassy colleague, quite by chance, mentioned it some time ago. Last year, my colleague had said, severe storms had so badly damaged the gigantic transmitter on the island of Masirah, off the coast of Oman, which is used to relay the BBC's Persian and Arabic Services, that for over three months, while the transmitter was being repaired, the Persian programme was hardly audible in Iran.

The Iranian Navy is familiar with the coast of Oman. There are teams of Iranian frogmen who are probably over-paid and under-worked, and an improvised storm, if properly created, would be difficult to detect. In any case, it could always be blamed on the South Yemenis. This, surely, would be a far more effective and acceptable way of silencing the Persian Service than expelling Whitley.

I don't succeed in speaking to Afshar, but I do find his wife, and over a particularly crackling connection shout out my suggestion to

271

her to pass on to her husband. She says she has understood.

At ten o'clock I listen to the news. Moharram has already started in Iran and, according to Whitley, so has 'the revolt of the people to topple the Shah'. Thousands shouting 'Allah-o-Akbar[1]' have appeared on the rooftops and in the streets, in violation of curfew regulations, and the security forces have been using automatic weapons. Casualties, according to the BBC, are high and there are reports of widespread disturbances throughout the country.

Saturday, December 2

While the British have written in such impressive numbers to express sympathy and support for 'the difficult period you are going through', my own compatriots at every level have been pouring vitriolic obloquy on the fallen in general, and on Hoveyda in particular. Virtually no one has seen fit to express understanding, let alone sorrow or compassion, over the fate of those apprehended, who now languish in some dreadful hole, awaiting what can only be described as a terrifying fate. Indeed, instead of showing some sign of humanitarian concern, they ask, 'Why hasn't so and so been arrested yet?' I suppose this proves something or other.

There is a telephone call from Iraj Amini, son of Ali Amini, in Paris. After resigning his post as Ambassador to Tunisia he had been persuaded by colleagues at the Foreign Ministry to take his leave less dramatically than he had originally intended. He is now going back to Tunis to make his farewells, and will thereafter retain his association with the Ministry in the semi-honorary role of adviser. He says that many people who had heard of his plan to resign had telephoned to ask 'whether Radji would now do the same' – the connection being the lumping together of two 'Ashraf ambassadors'. Yesterday in Tehran he had spoken to HIM and told him about the disservice rendered to his cause 'by those who have wanted Your Majesty to rule and not reign', a remark that HIM had apparently listened to without comment. He says that Sadighi, a respected university professor in his mid-seventies and a former Mossadeq cabinet minister, is due to take over the premiership once the crucial days of Moharram are over.

Perhaps, I reflect after our conversation, my thoughts about some of the characteristics of my compatriots had been premature.

[1] God is great.

272

Iraj's telephone call had been a spontaneous gesture of kindness – that of a man who, sensing the end was near, was trying to tip the scales on the credit side.

Yesterday's casualties have been high, and the papers are full of lurid accounts of helicopters machine-gunning the demonstrators from the air, to the constant scream of ambulance sirens rushing to and from hospitals.

Surely, one other casualty of the recent events in Iran has been our sense of national pride. I must confess that, while I certainly do possess that pride, I hope that, unlike some overzealous Iranians, I do not possess it to excess. But, even by these more modest standards, I don't see how HIM, and all of us in his camp, can claim to have retained any vestige of national pride after all our supplications for Western moral support, at a time when we are being disowned by our own people. This total dependence on Western backing as a determining factor in the future of the régime, this inexplicable faith in the capacity and the ability of our European and American allies to put it all right by waving a magic wand, and the attribution of all that happens in Iran to some sinister plot concocted behind our backs in London or Washington, credits our Western friends with far more influence and ability than they have ever deserved. But old attitudes are hard to shake off, and our excessive respect for the West really amounts to a national inferiority complex.

Sunday, December 3

The evening news, after reporting high casualties again, says some demonstrators had fired on troops and placed bombs under their vehicles. It says Khomeini has called on the soldiers to rise against 'the oppressor of the age', and that continuous discussions are going on at the Palace to bring in a civilian government and decide the future of the monarchy.

My cipher clerk rings up to say that, as from tomorrow, Iran Air will be on strike again.

Monday, December 4

A cable from Mohsen in Tehran informs me that Farhad will be arriving on Wednesday from Kuwait.

I lunch with some of my more senior colleagues at the Embassy. Pourdad, NIRTV's London representative is there too. The expression on their faces ranges from woebegone to desperate. I suggest the desirability of mounting counter-demonstrations in London that would be more anti-Khomeini than pro-Shah. Khakpour totally, and Dastegheib partially, are the only two who think the idea worth while. Kakhi thinks it important to know who would lead the demonstration, as the fortunes of those following would depend very much on the political reputation of the leaders, while Gitty believes that, if the turn-out was low, the demonstrators 'would lose face'.

I say that there are many Iranians in London who want to express their opinion about the future of their country in its present turmoil; and that, while I believe the Embassy ought to avoid the sort of active involvement which subsequently proved so embarrassing for our Washington Embassy during HIM's last visit there, we would be failing in our duty if we didn't provide the anti-Khomeini forces with the help they wanted. The discussions end on a note of seeming unanimity.

In the afternoon there is a call from Jamshid Amouzegar in New York. He is wounded by having been named as one of those alleged to have transferred large sums of money abroad, and has gone to great lengths to obtain a denial from the Central Bank in Tehran, which he has printed in the New York papers. He now wants to know whether similar allegations have appeared in the British press, and, if so, whether his denial could be printed in the relevant newspapers. I say that, because of the strict libel laws here, no names have been mentioned in the British papers, although some Persian language papers published in London have mentioned his name. I will see if they can be made to retract, or at least to print his denial.

Later I speak to Fereydoun. He sees Saipa almost nightly, and is outraged by her open assertion, even to him, that AAH is responsible for the state in which the country now finds itself. He had spoken to AAH on Friday and had found him in good spirits. He says there is little doubt in his mind now that AAH's arrest was Ardeshir's doing, and should be seen as his revenge on the Prime Minister who had brought about his dismissal as Foreign Minister. Fereydoun sounds surprisingly calm.

Winston Churchill comes for a drink in the evening. Julian has been describing his audience with HIM to his Conservative Party colleagues, giving them the picture of total gloom and wavering leadership he had found. Winston wants to go to Tehran on Sunday, which would be Tassou'a[1], to see HIM and the others. 'It

[1] The ninth day of Moharram, and a day of deep mourning.

274

is all-important,' he says, 'that the Shah should stay in power.' I try hard to dissuade him from going on that particular day for considerations of safety and security but to no avail.

In the evening Kenneth Harris has arranged for me to be invited to the annual Astor-Goodman dinner at the Great Hall of Lincoln's Inn. When it comes to the speeches, Harold Macmillan is helped to his feet and stands with apparent difficulty, but his voice is richly resonant. He is angry and puzzled, he says, at the lack of will demonstrated by the western democracies. The situation is more dangerous than it was in 1936, and yet nothing is being done. 'Afghanistan was lost in the course of one afternoon while the British were discussing whether the pay increase should be five or seven per cent, and not a word was uttered by anyone. The weakest ever Administration is in power in the United States ... and if Persia should fall – if Persia should fall,' he repeats, pausing for emphasis and effect, 'that will be almost the end, my friends. Asia and Africa are the two lungs by which the West breathes,' he concludes, thus revealing the source of one of Julian's mercantalistic statements, 'and it is the responsibility of the West to maintain their stability.' It is, on the whole, a stirring if somewhat theatrical performance. Henry Kissinger is the next speaker. He cautions that détente should not be construed as appeasement. Iran is in trouble because 'while many local mistakes were made, the Shah tried to modernise, and no one can quarrel with the progress that comes from modernisation'. He speaks of the enormous geopolitical considerations involved, and stresses Iran's importance to the security of the West.

After dinner I go up to Kissinger, introduce myself, and thank him for his positive references to Iran. 'Please give my regards to the Shah,' he says, in his deep, rather nasal bass voice. 'You know how I feel about Iran.'

Tuesday, December 5

Sporadic violence has continued. I put in an appearance at the Thai Embassy for the King's vin d'honneur, and return to PG to lunch with Peter Temple-Morris. Julian's depiction of HIM's silent gloom seems to have caused more damage by way of loss of confidence in Conservative ranks than I had suspected. The Shah, says Peter, should bring in his trusted and loyal friends and start fighting back. He mustn't mind about the Western media. He should get on television, deliver a rousing speech to revive the sagging spirits of his demoralised supporters, and come out fighting. And he should do so, if not from a desire to save the monarchy, then in order to save Iran from possible disintegration.

In the afternoon I succeed in speaking to Farhad in Tehran. His nerves seem to have taken a battering in the past few days. He says he had stopped to thank a group of soldiers and officers, now to be found at all major intersections in the city, for 'saving Iran', offering to treat their children free of charge. Unshaven and red-eyed from lack of sleep, they had stared back at him in puzzlement and gratitude. 'We have always been scared in this country,' he says. 'First, of telling HIM the truth, then of Savak, and now of Khomeini. Is this the fate to which we are condemned?'

Wednesday, December 6

In the afternoon there is a call from Edward Heath's secretary to say that he wants to see me at 5. I go over to his Wilton Street home. 'I understand you have been having problems with the BBC, and I want to know if I can help,' he says. He is surprised that the French, despite their enormous economic interests in Iran, have allowed Khomeini to continue unhindered with his impassioned calls for revolution. He also asks about 'your former boss'.

I explain the nature of our problem with the BBC, pointing out that, far from wanting the corporation to abandon its attachment to liberal values, all we ask is that they do not disseminate Khomeini's calls for revolution, nor further inflame the passions already aroused.

He says he will have a word with Michael Swann.[1]

There is a dinner at the Saudi Embassy for ex-King Simeon of Bulgaria. At dinner I am placed on Queen Margaret's right and have Lady Bowker on my other side.

'I am very angry, Radji, at what happened to my friend Amir Abbas,' says Elsa Bowker, recalling her friendship with him since the days when he and Fereydoun were students in her native Beirut. 'You don't treat your Prime Minister of twelve years like that, Radji – a man who was the most intelligent, cultivated, able

[1] Chairman of the BBC.

276

and successful Prime Minister Iran ever had. I hate the Shah, Radji, I hate him.'

Thursday, December 7

Afshar will not be arriving today, I learn, but Hossein will.

Westinghouse and General Electric are pulling their employees and their families out of Iran, and the families of some American servicemen are also leaving on special charter flights. The queue to Mehrabad Airport is described by the BBC as half a mile long.

Sanjabi has been released from detention unconditionally, and in an interview has reiterated his opposition to 'a monarchy that stands in contravention of the law', a phrase which is wrongly translated by the papers as an 'illegal monarchy'. He has said the future of the Shah should be decided by the Iranian people, and the Shah should abide by that decision. He will participate in the march planned for Tasoo'a on Sunday, insisting on the peaceful nature of the demonstration and predicting that, if disturbances do occur, they will be the work of professional agitators or of Government agents.

Ahmad Ghoreishi comes to see me. He says aides from Haig's and Brzezinski's offices have been trying to contact him, but he is reluctant to speak to them because he wouldn't know what to say. Eventually he tells Nasr, who is due to speak to the Empress later, to ask for instructions. Some three hours later a Mr Mobasher, speaking from the Royal Palace at Niavaran, comes on the line. He says he has been dialling London unsuccessfully for over two hours. HIM, he says, has given instructions that Ahmad should speak to the Americans, listen to what they say, and report back to him. Then, as if Ahmad's conversation might be the determining factor in the fate of Iran, Mr Mobasher adds: 'May the protection of God be with you.'

Things must be pretty desperate, we all agree, if it takes two hours to dial London from the Royal Palace, and if such hope and importance are attached to a simple conversation of this nature.

Friday, December 8

The mullahs of Qom have issued a religious edict forbidding the soldiers to fire on demonstrators. The BBC Persian Service has broadcast the edict, so that the demonstrators, the potential demonstrators and the soldiers now know the score. Sunday and Monday are Tasoo'a and Ashura[1] respectively, and if the procession of marchers should move towards Niavaran Palace an 'interesting' situation will arise.

The matter seems to me sufficiently grave that I decide to communicate directly with HIM's Private Bureau. Accordingly, I send two cables for HIM through Moinian. After describing the impression of gloom and despondency which senior British officials feel has overtaken HIM, and the dangers this poses to the morale of others, particularly in the armed forces, I 'respectfully submit, at the risk of appearing impertinent', that on Sunday a ceremony be improvised to show HIM on television 'with a face that speaks of inner strength, of self-confidence, and of certainty over the future'. I also suggest that 'despite all the attendant dangers, HIM, displaying those same expressions, should attend the memorial service on Ashura at the Sepahsalar Mosque, as he traditionally has done on every Ashura. The resolve of all who love their country will thus be greatly strengthened'. In a second cable I urge the immediate appointment of someone to take charge of NIOC.

Hossein and Ahmad come to lunch with Farhad and me. Carter's remark in the course of a press conference yesterday, to the effect that he doesn't know 'whether the Shah can survive' the present crisis but hopes he does, enlivens our conversation. We curse Carter's asinine insensitivity, and agree that the effect of that statement on HIM's mind will be devastating.

Radio Iran says the ban on processions has been lifted to 'allow the observance of Islamic traditions of mourning during Moharram', thus quite sensibly averting a clash.

Saturday, December 9

I go over to Claridge's for a long awaited tête-à-tête with Hossein. If only because of our close association with AAH, both Fereydoun

---

[1] Ashura, the 10th day of the month of Moharram, commemorates the martyrdom of Imam Hossein at Karbela, and is the day of deepest mourning in the Shia calendar.

and I should now consider our positions as 'shaky'. There are various minuses on my side, such as my failure to tone down the Persian Service's broadcasts. Hossein mentions to me an alleged private comment from HIM . . . 'we must think of someone else for London.' Hossein is inclined to doubt whether such a remark was ever made, but I have no way of knowing the truth of the matter. Farhad and Patricia join us for lunch, but in the circumstances it is not surprising we eat in a heavily charged silence.

In the *Financial Times* I see a statement issued by Jody Powell expressing President Carter's anger over the misinterpretation of his comment on the Shah. There has been, says Powell, no change in US policy of support for Iran. Elsewhere, I hear that close on one million people are expected to take part in tomorrow's march in Tehran, a procession that news reports describe, to my intense annoyance, as 'the Armageddon that will decide the fate of the Pahlavis'.

When I return to PG I learn that some three thousand people had marched past the Embassy in a noisy demonstration against the Shah and the British and American Governments which support him.

I speak to a friend in New York. Michael Blumenthal, the US Treasury Secretary, who recently saw HIM in Tehran, had been appalled by his state of lugubrious dejection. George Ball – former US Under-Secretary of State, and elder statesman – has been brought in on the scene in an advisory capacity, and has been seeing many people with the aim of finding a solution that would keep HIM in power constitutionally. The Americans have also established contact with Khomeini in Paris, but have gotten nowhere.

Sunday, December 10

Five hundred thousand people, according to the BBC, are parading peacefully through the streets of Tehran, carrying pictures of Khomeini and chanting anti-Shah slogans. They are, according to the reporter, remarkably well organised.

As I sip coffee and pore over the papers the noise of metal barricades being dropped off a police van reminds me of the demonstrations planned for later in the day. At about 3.00, some six to eight hundred, mostly bearded and scruffy of 'our less fortunate but more verminous compatriots', as Farhad would say,

279

walk past the Embassy, waving their fists in the air and exhorting each other to say 'death to the Shah'.

I write a brief report to Moinian on the Zand circular, and enclose all the cables exchanged between the Embassy and the Ministry, explaining the motives and the reasoning for the particular course of action adopted by the Embassy.

Monday, December 11

Hossein Nasr comes to the office for a chat. He had spoken to Denis Wright about the BBC and Denis had told him Sharif-Emami was right when he had said that, instead of attacking the BBC, we should try to raise the standards of Radio Iran. He confesses to have been much taken aback by Denis's sturdy defence of the BBC.

I hand him my sealed report for Moinian and, after a brief reference to its contents, say that I am asking him to act as courier to avoid its accidental loss in the pouch.

'I have a request, too,' he says. 'When you next speak to Cyrus ask him to tell the Americans to put the emphasis in their public statements on the "law and order" and "stability" issues rather than on "democracy" and "liberalisation".'

Two million people, according to the BBC, have taken part in a demonstration against the Shah in Tehran on this day of Ashura. 'A seething carpet of humanity ... as far as the eye could see,' reports Geoffrey Robertson of the turn-out at Shahyad Monument.

My God! Two million people is an enormous figure by any standards! Two million people, united in a single common objective – that the Shah should go. In a sense the referendum the opposition has been demanding on the future of the monarchy has just been held, and the media with its 'populist' and 'democratic' sympathies, will be quick to interpret it as a massive rejection of the régime.

There is a cable from Afshar, declaring that 'the BBC has yet again shown its malice by giving the figure of one million for the number of demonstrators yesterday, whereas the actual figure cited by independent observers was 350,000'.

I watch a film of the demonstrations at night. Whatever the actual numbers, it is indeed a seething ocean of humanity that covers the length and breadth of Eisenhower Avenue as far as the eye can see. Gloom descends.

Tuesday, December 12

There is a report out by Amnesty International accusing the Iranian Government of the continued practice of torture. In view of the assurances given last year by the Shah that torture would end, the report calls HIM's promise an example of 'gross hypocrisy'. Bloody cheek!

There are news reports of helicopters firing on demonstrators in continued protests in Esfahan.

Afshar, who arrives tomorrow, telephones to confirm his appointments with Francis Pym[1] and David Owen. He asks about Hossein, and makes a number of supposedly amusing observations, to which I react coolly but correctly, I believe. I say he had better have something other than the BBC to talk about when he comes to London.

Mahdavi, a picture of unmitigated gloom, comes in to suggest that 'we do something' about Afshar's cable yesterday, which claimed that the number of demonstrators had been grossly exaggerated by news reports. 'Unless you do, Tehran is bound to feel you are more interested in defending the BBC than in carrying out the instructions of your government,' he says. I agree. But the *Daily Telegraph*, *Mail* and *Guardian* correspondents have all independently reported figures of over one million, so I can't attack the BBC on that score. Instead, I decide to reply to the Director General's last communication, and to reject his explanations and claims of impartiality as totally inadequate.

Farhad rings a friend in Tehran. In a tone of voice betraying greater hope than optimism, his friend speaks of a wave of counter-demonstrations in Mashad, Tabriz, Qom, Rezaeih and one or two other cities. As Farhad is speaking to Tehran, Ahmad Ghoreishi rings on the other line from Washington. 'Ayatollah Ghomi (one of the Grand Ayatollahs resident in Mashad),' Ahmad has learnt, 'has been visited in his sleep by the Hazrat (the coming Mahdi), who told him that the Shah's departure would be the end of Iran. While Ghomi was pondering this manifestation of the divine, the Hazrat appeared a second time to urge that, unless a move was made immediately, it would be too late to save the country. And so Ghomi has given the word, and people all over Iran have now risen to demand that the Shah does not abandon the country.' He also says Carter will say something today to rectify his infuriating solecism of a few days ago.

The Prime Minister, during question time in the Commons, has stated that he would not recommend the Queen to proceed with her

[1] Opposition spokesman on Foreign Affairs.

visit to Iran if the present troubles continue. When pressed, he said that if the visit does take place it should not be regarded as offering support to the régime.

At Ann Steel's cocktails John Sutcliffe of BP says that no matter what happens now, there will have to be fuel rationing in Iran this winter. I also stop by at Shusha's for a second cocktail, where trendy leftists and bleeding heart activists are over-represented, before proceeding to the Spanish Embassy for an elegant dinner. Charlie Douglas-Home is among the three hundred-odd guests, and appears surprised when I tell him that his commentary on Iran hasn't been broadcast by the BBC's Persian Service. 'Too friendly to us in tone, I suppose,' I say.

At the dinner table at the Embassy I am seated next to Petita Stilianopolous.[1] Petita has, she says, complete faith in astrology and knows 'a marvellous psychic astrologer in Madrid who had performed miracles with his predictions many times'. I ask her to telephone her friend in Madrid and ask about the future prospects of someone born on October 26. She promises to let me know the response.

Wednesday, December 13

The deteriorating economic situation in Iran is the first item of news on the World Service. As Radio Iran blares out the chants of pro-Shah demonstrators in Esfahan, I receive a cable from Afshar, who arrives today, reporting that oil production is down to 1.5 million barrels a day. Demonstrators have broken into the Consulate-General in Manchester, overturned furniture, torn up papers, scrawled slogans on walls and been arrested by the police. I speak to Jahan'nema, the Consul-General, who seems generally to have kept his cool.

There is a call from Khosro Eghbal in Paris. He confirms the view that the world has seen the Ashura procession as a referendum, with the verdict clearly for the Shah to go. The opposition is already claiming that some twenty million people took part in the anti-Shah demonstrations over the two days of Tasoo'a and Ashura, and that the figure adds up to nearly two-thirds of Iran's entire population. The Americans are desperate, as signs are beginning to emerge of a split in the army, some officers favouring an accommodation with Khomeini, others in favour of much

[1] Wife of the Philippines Ambassador to London.

tougher action. General Jam is being talked of as army chief, to preserve the unity of the officer corps, and George Ball has gone to Tehran to recommend the formation of a Council of Elders. HIM, says Khosro, would be required to go on vacation for six months or so, until a political solution has been hammered out.

'Will he ever return if he leaves, though?' I ask.

'The answer to that question can't be known,' he says.

There is a letter from Julian Amery 'asking for the favour of your diplomatic bag to transmit the enclosed letters to Tehran'. One of the letters is for HIM, one for Afshar and one for Hoveyda. 'If for any reason you think it inappropriate for me to write to Hoveyda in his present circumstances, I would of course be guided by you. As he has not yet been put on trial I imagine he is still free to receive correspondence but will leave this to your discretion.'

There is a manuscript postscript: 'Callaghan's statement in the House yesterday was a totally unnecessary stab in the back, designed to win him a couple of extra votes for tonight's division, I suspect.'

Afshar arrives, and Hossein and I welcome him. George Ball has *not* gone to Tehran, but HIM *is* showing signs of hopeless indecision, he says. All the talk about the formation of a civilian government has undermined the morale of General Azhari, the Prime Minister, and weakened his resolve to remain steadfast. Afshar also expresses surprise and annoyance over Callaghan's statement that the Queen's prospective visit should not be inter-preted as offering support to the Shah's régime. He says I should see Weir as soon as possible and make a formal protest to the effect that the statement appears to give clear indication of a change of policy. I say that I shall see Weir tomorrow and make my protest, but that I believe we are reading the signals wrong again, and that 'what Callaghan, or for that matter, Carter, says doesn't any longer matter, but what Khomeini says and what the generals do, does'.

'I agree with you,' says Afshar, 'but HIM attaches great impor-tance to the attitude of the British and the Americans.' He tells me that Hushang Ansari has formally resigned as Chairman of NIOC.

Khomeini has issued a statement in Paris declaring the Ashura turn-out a national referendum and warning all heads of state dealing with Iran not to support the Shah; if they do, they risk an oil and trade embargo when the Islamic republic is established. In a display of political ignorance, he has also called on the American Senate to impeach Carter for his support of the Shah.

All initiative now seems to have passed into the hands of the opposition. The Empress, who exercises considerable dove-ish influence on the vacillating Shah, has prevailed upon him 'not to spill blood'. Her comment after the Ashura processions was: 'If they don't want us, we should go.'

Thursday, December 14

John Holmes of *The Times* comes to speak to me about doing a special supplement on Iran to coincide with the Queen's visit in February. Three considerations, he agrees, would seem to make discussion of the project at this stage premature – the money for the supplement may not be available; *The Times* may by then still not be publishing; and the visit may not take place. With a halo of retrospective wisdom aglow about him, Mr Holmes withdraws.

At 11 I go to the Foreign Office to speak to Michael Weir. I say that the Prime Minister's remarks in the Commons are bound to leave a negative psychological effect on public opinion in Iran. Following my instructions from Afshar, I refer to the meeting in New York between the two Foreign Ministers, in the course of which David Owen had confirmed that the Queen would make a reference to her visit to Iran at the Opening of Parliament, and the assurance Owen had given that 'we do not withhold support from our friends when they are in difficulty, or abandon them when in need', an assurance that had been repeatedly expressed by the British Ambassador to Tehran as well. I add that the Prime Minister's specific remark, that the Queen's visit should not be seen as support for the régime, stands in contradiction to the previous assurances, and its dissemination over the Persian Service of the BBC will weaken the Iranian government's position. I point out that, in view of the traditional Persian suspicions regarding British intentions towards their country, the Prime Minister's comment will undoubtedly have an unfavourable effect on Iranian public opinion.

Michael says that, while he fully understands our point of view and will convey it to the relevant authorities, we must bear in mind that previous expressions of support from British government officials have given rise to waves of protest, not only within the Labour Party, but in Iran as well; and that an open expression of support by the British government for the policies of the Iranian government could leave an even worse impression on public opinion.

I say that it would exceed the bounds of etiquette for me to hold forth on what the Prime Minister should, or should not, have said, but if he had confined himself merely to the first part of his reply he would not have created new headaches for us in Iran.

As we move on to other subjects, Michael says Tony has reported that there are currently four centres of political influence at work in Iran: the clergy, the military, the National Front and such honest brokers as Messrs Entezam and Amini; and that while none of the four, at heart, wishes to see a change of régime, the fact that there is no contact or dialogue between the various groups makes it unlikely that a political compromise can emerge.

I return to the Embassy and write a report on my meeting with Weir, when Afshar unexpectedly turns up at about one. I hand him the just completed report, which he reads carefully, then scribbles something on it which I cannot see, summons the cipher clerk, hands him the report with his additions to it, and asks him to cable it to Tehran immediately, using the cipher for HIM's Private Bureau.

When he has gone, I ask Shams, the cipher clerk, to let me see Afshar's additions. He has left my text completely unchanged. What he has done has been to insert before my text the common but somewhat unctuous preamble of 'I kiss Your Majesty's hand and have the honour to submit the following report from Your Ambassador to London'. There is, however, one innovation – he has substituted the word 'foot' for 'hand'.

At 5.30 we go back to the Foreign Office for the meeting with the Foreign Secretary. Hossein accompanies us. Ivor Lucas meets Afshar at the door, and we wait for about five minutes while the Foreign Secretary concludes his press conference before going up to his room. Michael Weir and a younger man are with the Secretary of State.

Afshar raises the matter of the Queen's visit and the Prime Minister's remark, and Owen indicates that 'there has been no change in HMG's position', and that the visit still stands. Afshar then points to the danger of Iran's disintegration if the monarchy should be overthrown, speaks of the army's complete reliability, and of HIM's desire to rule as a constitutional monarch.

Owen refers to 'the staggering number of demonstrators' on Ashura, and of the need to employ 'the minimum of force' because high casualty figures alienate Western opinion. Then, as if to correct his previous remark, he says: 'But what we think in Western capitals doesn't matter. Forget about us. If we can help in any way, tell us, but it wouldn't be right for us to suggest solutions, even if we had any, for your domestic difficulties.'

Back at his suite at Claridge's, Afshar asks Hossein to write a report of the meeting – 'long hand and I shall summarise it myself'. While Hossein concentrates on his report, I become Afshar's interlocutor. He starts by saying that he will soon have to replace Fereydoun in New York, and asks my opinion about the choice of possible successors. I mention a couple of names, but as our conversation continues my thoughts turn inwards, and I begin to wonder whether at this late stage in the game it is at all important who represents Iran in New York, London or anywhere else.

Another one of those days, I think to myself, when again the only casualty has been what little remains of one's sense of national honour. While the Ayatollah is appealing to the masses in Iran to rise against the Shah, here are we in London, appealing to the British government. If the clock were turned back fifty years such an appeal would have been meaningful. Thirty years ago? Perhaps. But stripped of its imperial past Britain can no more determine the future of Iran today than we can of, say, Somalia. This country will, I hope, always remain a haven of sanity and civility, and the BBC will exercise its considerable moral authority, if for no other reason than that it retains its credibility. But that is surely about all. Even in economic terms, Britain is no longer a giant. Indeed, some might say that, were it not for North Sea oil, the future prospects for this country would look very grim indeed. Why then do we in Iran wish to attribute to Britain magical powers that the British themselves are the first to admit they no longer possess?

We cavil captiously at Callaghan's, or Carter's, every utterance on Iran, while the Ayatollah is contemptuously dismissive of them. And *he* is winning. Doesn't that prove the gigantic misapprehension with which we have viewed events throughout? The Shah's policies, undoubtedly honourable and benevolent in intent, have led to catastrophic consequences. Aspirations and animosities have been aroused on a national scale which the Government apparatus failed to recognise in time. Probably it can now neither satisfy the former, nor defuse the latter. The country is aflame with revolution. Whether any measure could produce order out of the present increasingly chaotic scene, is not for me to say . . . or even speculate upon, as I go through the diplomatic motions.

Enough of this ineffectual rambling.

Friday, December 15

Julian Amery has a letter in the *Daily Telegraph* calling Callaghan's remarks 'gratuitous' and 'a stab in the back', and the *Herald Tribune* reports the possible creation of a 'Crown Council', to which HIM would relinquish much of his authority. The Council, according to *IHT*, would consist of nine people, including two army officers and several respected politicians, including Entezam, Amini and Nahavandi, and would take over while HIM went on leave. Afshar says the report must be wrong 'because Nahavandi would be unacceptable'.

At the Embassy a message awaits me to call Petita Stilianopoulos. 'My news is bad,' she says when I speak to her, and is hesitant to convey it. I insist that she does. 'Gerardo Sanchez, the astrologer, has recognised the Shah from his birth date. Mercury is badly placed in the Shah's astrological chart, and one cannot be optimistic.' She says HIM will go on making concessions, but these won't be regarded as sincere 'because they are made in order to preserve him'. There will be elections in June, and by September the Shah will have left Iran for good, having been increasingly abandoned by his American friends. 'If he should insist on staying,' Sanchez has predicted, 'he will be killed.'

Saturday, December 16

The behind-the-scenes activities to find a political solution in Tehran are fully reported in the British press. According to Martin Woollacott of the *Guardian*, HIM has rejected the idea of even a temporary departure from Iran, observing that 'there can be no monarchy without a monarch'.

I receive a telephone call from the Queen of Jordan who, with her husband, is on a visit to London. 'This is Noor,' she says with arresting informality. 'I rang to see whether you were still here, and, if so, how you were.' They have been to Tehran. 'His Majesty was well, and Her Majesty was very strong, but one would have wanted to see a few more smiles.' She particularly wants to know whether I am bearing up well, whether the demonstrations have taken their toll, and what my state of mind is. Indelicately I tell her she is more solicitous and considerate in her exalted position than I remember her ever being before, and hear a gentle chuckle in acknowledgement from the other end of the line. She says she will arrange for us to meet while they are in London. I am overwhelmed by her enormous kindness.

In the afternoon some 800 members of the Confederation of Iranian Students put up a rowdy demonstration outside the Embassy, as about 400 policeman keep watch. Traffic has been diverted completely, with no cars allowed from Knightsbridge along Kensington Gore. As they reach the Chancery, four or five of the students try to break in, but are carried off into waiting vans by the police. They chant in Persian, 'Shah, we will kill you,' and 'Death to the Shah', while the slogan they are carrying in English, no doubt for the benefit of the British bystanders, is a more subdued 'Down with the Shah and his supporters'. The raised fist so visible in the Tehran demonstrations is much in evidence.

Sunday, December 17

In an article in the *Sunday Mirror* Woodrow Wyatt suggests that bobbies could provide advice on crowd control in Tehran. He telephones later to say that the suggestion is not an idle one, but one he had discussed with Lord Harris of Greenwich[1] and the Home Office is willing to help.

Noor telephones again, having dialled directly herself, to invite me to dinner tomorrow.

Monday, December 18

Afshar and a group of generally sympathetic MPs come to lunch. He turns up earlier than expected and insists on receiving the guests in the morning room, as was his habit when Ambassador, rather than upstairs as I had suggested. Peter Temple-Morris, Eldon Griffiths, Neville Sandelson, Andrew Faulds, Dennis Walters and Bryan Magee are the guests. Afshar presents his case well, and ends by complaining about the BBC, 'which, as far as we are concerned, is now as bad as Radio Moscow'.

At 8.30 precisely I present myself at 7 Palace Green. Five or six people are gathered in the drawing-room, including King Constantine and Queen Anne-Marie. I know King Hussein is appearing on the Panorama programme later, and suspect he is staying upstairs to watch the interview before coming down. Gus Shaker, a Cambridge contemporary and his wife Franca arrive, and Gus's brother Ghazi. Shortly afterwards the King's interview begins and the sound on the television set is turned up. Unlike HIM, King Hussein's image conveys sincerity, courage and humility, and his command of English is better than the Shah's. Towards the end of

[1] Minister of State at the Home Office.

288

the interview Fred Emery asks about Iran and the Shah's chances of survival. Rapidly blinking his eye-lashes, as he does at moments of acute concentration, the King replies: 'His Imperial Majesty has always been like a brother to me,' and adds that if the Shah was removed Iran would be in danger of disintegration.

Shortly after the interview Noor comes into the room. 'I guess you all know why we're late,' she says smilingly, and is followed by King Hussein. I thank him for his kind words about Iran and, with his new ambassador to London joining in, we engage in a conversation about the fate of Mr Bhutto.

Noor speaks to me about 'your old boss', and says his arrest 'is a weapon that cuts both ways'.

After dinner, which is frugal, we chat a bit longer, until King Constantine makes a move to leave. As I say goodbye to Noor, she says, 'You can always come here' if the need should arise. She is a most kind and generous soul.

Tuesday, December 19

There are reports on the news this morning of a 'mutiny' by a group of soldiers in Tabriz, where the military are said to have laid down their arms and handed over their weapons and vehicles to the demonstrators.

At 11.30 Sir Michael Swann, Chairman of the BBC, comes to Afshar's suite at Claridge's, and the next one and a half hours are devoted to singling out for Sir Michael's consideration instances, some genuine, others less so, of BBC bias and partiality against the Iranian régime. Sir Michael, a soft-spoken, pipe-smoking person of academic appearance, is understandably defensive.

As Ahmad Ghoreishi arrives to lunch with Afshar at 1, I return to the Embassy to see a cable from Zelli who, after speaking to the Prime Minister, wants to know whether Afshar agrees that Andrew Whitley should be expelled for his 'mutiny' dispatch. Afshar says Whitley should not be expelled before Swann has had a chance to reply to the numerous complaints lodged with him in the morning.

In the afternoon there are reports of the imminent formation of a civilian government in Tehran, headed by Gholam Hossein Sadighi, the seventy-three-year-old former associate of Mossadeq, whose cabinet would include people who have held no public office during the last twenty-five years.

Wednesday, December 20

The Public Prosecutor in Tehran has confirmed that some one hundred prominent Iranians did send out huge sums of money in the two months prior to the imposition of limits on such transfers. The sums transferred to banks outside Iran amount to 1.5 billion dollars.

There is a call from Bill Lehfeldt, an old US hand on, and in, Iran, who has just arrived in London from Tehran. When he comes to see me later that afternoon, Bill confesses generally to be optimistic for a number of reasons. The Government's tougher line is beginning to produce the desired effect, and the people are becoming increasingly fed up with the disruption to their daily lives. The 'mullatory', as he calls them, can't go on asking for increasing sacrifices from the people; and the emotional period of Ashura is over. He is not certain that HIM has regained his confidence, but believes that a coup by the military aimed at resisting further royal concessions to the mullahs ought not to be ruled out.

Thursday, December 21

Noor al-Hussein telephones to thank me for my flowers, and to remind me, yet again, that if ever I should be in need, or want help, I can go and see them in Amman.

Dr Fallah comes to lunch at PG. He says Entezam had finally been persuaded 'to lend his respected name' to the chairmanship of NIOC, so that 'things could return to normal'. He describes General Azhari as a simple, straightforward, honest soldier, with no knowledge of politics or economics, and no particular aptitude for public oratory, but as one who, perhaps because of his disarming sincerity, is trusted by the people. The hard-line generals, led by Oveisi, had opposed the allowing of the Tasoo'a demonstrations, but Amini and Entezam had prevailed upon HIM not to oppose them. The number of those taking part had come as a rude shock to HIM, and the orderly conduct of the demonstrators had been even more disturbing, belying as it did the claims of the generals that the masses were incapable of behaving responsibly, a point that had not been lost on the Americans. Amini had argued forcefully that the march could only be prevented by the slaughter of five thousand people, a tragedy that would be fatal to the monarchy. Both Amini and Entezam had been pressing HIM to disengage himself from day-to-day business, and give up much of his authority to a council of trusted elders, who could divert the torrent of abuse now aimed at HIM on to themselves. Amini had told Fallah that he was willing to step into the ring, risking his personal reputation and political career, and bringing upon himself the poisonous odium of the Shah's many enemies, in a final, courageous, self-sacrificing act of loyalty and dedication, to save the monarchy. But he reported that 'HIM was unwilling to make his well-wishers concessions which, under pressure, he was freely making to his enemies'. Yet Amini was still hopeful that a catastrophe could be averted.

Friday, December 22

Afshar leaves, at last, and Hossein, Mahdavi and I see him off.

Sanjabi has issued a letter publicly condemning Sadighi for trying to form a government of national reconciliation. 'It would be the negation of all your past,' he has written in a letter which has received wide coverage in the media.

I send a politely but strongly worded cable to Sanjabi, signing it 'The Supporters of the Iranian Constitution', accusing him of negating his own liberal-democratic convictions 'after only one meeting with the Paris-based divine', and urging him to support, rather than subvert, Sadighi's efforts. Copies go to Amini, Sadighi and one or two foreign correspondents in Tehran.

Saturday, December 23

A senior American official of Oil Services Company has been shot dead in an ambush in Ahvaz, and there have been demonstrations and shoot-outs in Mashad.

Sunday, December 24

Telephone and telex communication with Tehran are disrupted again. Some young demonstrators have tried to storm the American Embassy in Tehran. Cars have been set on fire and there has been much shooting.

Monday, December 25

The fall of the Azhari government appears imminent. Sanjabi has addressed a gathering of university students and urged them to keep a united front against the Shah. In his audience with the Shah twelve days ago, he now reveals, he had told HIM that small changes and minor concessions would not solve the problem. 'Only your departure will.' The crowd had roared its approval.

It is a wonderfully mild, sunny day; and there are, thank God, no papers.

Tuesday, December 26

There is a letter from Moinian to say simply that HIM had seen my report on the Zand/Afshar correspondence.

The Prime Minister has fallen ill in Tehran. Oil production is down to 500,000 barrels a day, and rioting and violence have continued in several parts of Tehran. A gloomy lunch with Farhad consumed in virtually total silence, as we both seem too preoccupied to allow ourselves the luxury of conversation.

Wednesday, December 27

Some sixty university professors, who are on strike, have been herded on to lorries and driven away by soldiers.

The 3 o'clock news speaks of 'the biggest traffic jam in the world' in Tehran, describing the scene as one of 'absolute chaos'. Pandemonium and hysterics are reported from Tehran airport as well.

In the evening, as I watch newsreel films of the rioting in Tehran on television, I reflect that we are witnessing nothing less than the death-throes of the monarchy.

Thursday, December 28

The fall in our oil exports has led to petrol rationing in South Africa, and soon perhaps in Israel. Khomeini has called for the observance of another day of national mourning on Saturday, while

292

a Majlis deputy by the name of Bani Ahmad has called for HIM's abdication.

As the violence continues in Iran, all is uncannily quiet at the Embassy. With communications with Tehran cut off, no news is transmitted, no instructions are received. An eerie lull pervades the air.

Friday, December 29

The 8 o'clock news speaks of the paralysis of industrial and commercial life in Tehran, and of President Carter's impending decision to send an aircraft-carrier to the Persian Gulf, presumably to frighten the natives.

But it's Hossein's call at 9 that rekindles the flame of speculation in my mind. Afshar has just spoken to him from Tehran to say there will be a change of Government within the next twenty-four to forty-eight hours, with hints that Shahpour Bakhtiar, the Number Two in the National Front, would head it. Afshar himself will not be in the new government. 'Things aren't as bad as one imagines they are from London,' he has told Hossein.

There are reports of sporadic shootings in Tehran, and the news at 11 says some government offices in South Tehran have been set on fire.

The telephone calls of sympathy continue, many of the callers being apparently under the impression that I am in the midst of feverish activity. 'You must be submerged in work,' suggests one kind caller. In fact, ironically, all is deathly quiet. Since the Foreign Minister's departure, not a single cable has been received from Tehran. The general paralysis of will there must have infected the Foreign Ministry as well.

I turn in my swivel chair so that I can look at the well-kept garden behind the row of houses in Princes Gate. A pile of golden leaves is being burnt at one corner of the garden. The sky is overcast, and the sun succeeds only occasionally in piercing the thick blanket of black clouds to show itself for a brief moment. My gaze wanders to the unprepossessing block on the right, in which so many Iranians own flats. A sudden downpour begins. How many more days will I occupy this desk, I wonder. And what afterwards? Do I return to an uncertain fate in an unimaginable Iran? Or do I remain in London to begin life as a political exile, a refugee from the vengeful clutches of my own compatriots?

The early afternoon news reports that, 'as a last, desperate gamble', HIM has asked Bakhtiar to form a government. There are letters of sympathy from Larry Collins and Lord Home, who writes: 'I pray that His Majesty may soon arrive in calmer waters.'

Both Reuters and ITV's Peter Snow ring to aks whether rumours now circulating in Tehran that the Shah is leaving Iran on President Carter's advice are true. I deny them categorically and hear the denial mentioned on ITV news.

There is a telephone call from a Jane Crane in Cornwall. I remember her name, though not her face, from her many years on the *Tehran Journal*. She invites me to go and stay, and then mentions a list printed in a Persian language paper, purporting to show the endless number of companies in which members of the Royal Family own shares. 'I always genuinely believed that the Royal Family were doing their best to improve the lot of the Iranian people,' she says. 'I defended them whenever and wherever I could. And now this!'

Khomeini has announced in Paris that Bakhtiar's government won't be acceptable to him and that only the Shah's departure can solve the crisis. Sanjabi, too, has dissociated himself and the National Front from the Bakhtiar initiative, insisting that Bakhtiar is acting in his individual capacity. Sanjabi is emerging as the Iago of the Iranian tragedy.

Saturday, December 30

The 6 o'clock morning news reports that the Shah's mother and a party of seventeen, including several children and two dogs, have arrived in Los Angeles aboard an Iranian Air Force Boeing 747. Bakhtiar's chances of forming a government are described as 'remote', and speculation that the Shah will shortly follow his mother have been vigorously denied by Ardeshir.

With astonishing swiftness, expectancy now replaces depression.

There is a cable from Afshar, classified 'Top Secret', to inform me that HIM, 'because he cannot, under the circumstances, entertain Her Majesty in the manner he would like to', has asked that her trip to Iran be postponed.

Later news reports speak of continued disturbances, of the burning of British and American cultural offices in Mashad and Ahvaz, and of Bakhtiar's possible expulsion from the National Front, pending a meeting of the Front's governing council.

Cyrus and Alireza come to dinner at PG. The worst part of being a refugee, Cyrus believes, would be 'having nothing to do'.

The 8 o'clock news reports that Bakhtiar has been expelled from the National Front. Cyrus says that of all the individuals whose names are being mentioned as suitable for forming a government, Sadighi is 'the most honourable'.

At 11 we hear that 'the Palace' has repeatedly denied rumours of HIM's impending departure. Bakhtiar's efforts to form a government have been stalemated, not only by the religio-political opposition, but by the condition that Ardeshir must be appointed head of the armed forces!

'He hasn't even done his military service,' observes Alireza, as we ponder whether HIM has taken leave of his senses.

A snow storm rages as I drop off Alireza at his Knightsbridge flat, and the temperature has sunk to below freezing. 'Tehran,' says a radio commentator reporting on the events of the day, 'is a city dying on its feet.'

Sunday, December 31

Bakhtiar has announced that he will persist in his efforts to form a government, and has attributed the split in the National Front to envy 'in certain quarters'. With news about Iran dominating the front pages, most papers speculate about HIM's impending departure. The *Telegraph* and *Express* in their editorials blast Khomeini's fanaticism – belatedly.

Ahmad telephones to say that yesterday in Mashad the mob hanged a number of people in the streets and burnt a tank, and today the military commander of the city has gone berserk and ordered the indiscriminate shooting of all demonstrators. He also says he understands the Empress and HIM's own children were on the plane that landed in Los Angeles yesterday. When I express scepticism about the Empress's departure, he rates the accuracy of his information as 'ninety per cent'.

The news at 1 o'clock confirms 'hundreds of casualties in Mashad', and says that 'at one point a tank drove straight into the demonstrators'.

In the early afternoon Ahmad calls again. 'A massacre has taken place in Mashad,' he says, 'and the dead number a thousand.' HIM, he adds, has summoned the military provincial governors to the Palace and described the situation to them as a war aimed at bringing about Iran's disintegration. He has reaffirmed his intention to stay, and urged the military governors to return to their posts with renewed confidence and to discharge their duty to their country. The new hard line Ahmad ascribes to the Empress's departure, 'though it's a bit late'. But he believes the military could still swing the situation.

I go to HP[1] to be alone a couple of hours, but no sooner have I arrived than Farhad rings to say General Jam wants to see me urgently. I return to PG and call the General, who comes over straight away. While out, he has been rung from Tehran by Moinian, by Moghaddam and by Bakhtiar, all with the urgent message that he should call back immediately. He wishes to send a message to Moinian to say he can be contacted care of the Embassy 'if HIM should want him'. 'But I am not going to call Bakhtiar,' he says.

He thinks he may be wanted for three possible posts – Minister of Defence, Chief of Staff, or membership of the proposed Regency Council. The first he will not accept, 'as it would be a simple administrative job, with no authority or power'. The second he would be most reluctant to accept, as HIM would be only offering it 'under duress and against his will, otherwise he wouldn't have left me in limbo for the past seven years'. And he doesn't wish to be a member of the Regency Council either. Whatever wrong HIM may have done him, he explains, he is still loyal to the Shah, and he wouldn't want to be associated with the sort of machinery that may be created to supervise the dissolution of the monarchy in Iran.

Jam says Bakhtiar will not last. Nor will Khomeini, and his band of ignorant supporters who lack organization or experience, and who will soon be pushed out by the communists.

I say it is not for me to offer advice, but while I understand and respect his reasons, he may feel that, at this most critical juncture in Iran's history, he has a duty to his country as well. Bakhtiar, whatever his motives or aspirations, may be the last barrier before a government of the mullahs, and if Jam's support can help Bakhtiar to survive, then, in my judgment, he ought to offer him that help.

Jam replies that Bakhtiar has no popular base, that his initiative is doomed to failure, and that it is only a matter of time before HIM goes and the clergy take over. Then, as if overwhelmed by the sadness of his own predictions, he stops speaking, and I see that he is struggling to control his emotions. 'His Majesty,' he says, after regaining his composure, 'should do what Alfonso XIII did. If the people don't want him, he should leave, without even abdicating. That would be the honourable thing to do.'

[1] My house in Holland Park.

I tell him that, whatever reply he wishes to make, the Embassy would, needless to say, be happy to transmit it to Tehran.

As I walk with him to the door, he turns to me as if suddenly struck by a thought, and asks: 'What will you do?'

'I shall go back to Tehran, if I can.'

After dinner I ring Saipa in New York. She sounds affectionate, and more resigned than unhappy. She says, emphasising the utmost secrecy, that HIM will leave as soon as Bakhtiar has succeeded in forming his government. 'A Regency Council will be established, and the Empress will remain to preside over it.'

'I thought she was in California.'

'No, she is in Tehran, and was crying when I spoke to her earlier.'

'Where would HIM go?'

'Jordan or Saudi Arabia.'

For the first time she professes to be very sorry for those who will be left behind in jails, and particularly mentions AAH. 'You will all have to come and live in New York,' she says.

It's New Year's Eve. In an hour or so, 1978 will end. It can't end soon enough, as far as I am concerned. It has been, beyond doubt, the most nightmarish of my forty-two years, with constant anxiety and endless uncertainty; a year of foundering loyalty, of fading courage, of massive self-doubt and of appalling self-recrimination.

It also marks the complete end of the style and manner of life that I have known and lived all my adolescent and adult existence. Gone forever will be the aura of élitist authority and importance which has glimmered, as if by divine right, round the heads of those of us who represented Iran's ruling classes for as long as I can remember. Suddenly and violently robbed of that power and privilege, the spectre of life as a stateless refugee looms ominously ahead.

Perhaps time itself will provide many of the answers. Tomorrow, I tell myself, is the first day of the rest of my life.

1979

Monday, January 1

The air traffic controllers have gone on strike, halting flights out of Tehran and causing still greater panic and confusion among the passengers desperate to get out.

I learn from Cyrus that, during the meeting of the governing council of the National Front, Sanjabi unleashed a barrage of venomous personal attacks on Bakhtiar, accusing him of having been hoodwinked by the Shah, and of allowing his boundless ambition to get the better of his life-long political principles. Henry Precht[1], to whom Cyrus had spoken, had employed the word 'tragedy' to describe what was going on in Tehran, Shaul Bakhash had told him from Tehran that it was now 'only a matter of time before HIM leaves'. The slogans in Tehran are undergoing a transformation from anti-Shah to pro-Tudeh, and lynchings and lootings have continued.

Later in the day I learn that Azhari has resigned. Ahmad's prediction, that I would probably outlive Afshar politically, has, for what it is worth, come true, I suppose. Bakhtiar will try to announce his government by Thursday, so that I have at least until then at PG. It is a bitterly cold day that starts 1979, and my first dramatic act of the year is to take my summer clothes over to HP.

From a coded cable of Jam's to Moinian, I see that he has quite firmly turned down the portfolio of Defence Minister in Bakhtiar's government on the grounds that he doesn't know Bakhtiar; that he doesn't believe Bakhtiar's efforts will succeed, and that he has family problems of his own in London.

Bakhtiar, meanwhile, has broadcast to the nation, appealing for help in the establishment of a liberal social democracy in Iran. It is an effective speech and a unique one, in that, for the first time at least in my memory, it mentions Mossadeq's name without mentioning the Shah's.

Cyrus, Alireza and Mina, Haleh and Farhad come to dinner at PG. On the news we see Their Majesties appearing outside their palace for a chat with foreign newsmen for the first time in two months. Yes, he will be going on vacation when the situation permits. No, he won't be going to St Moritz.

He looks lean and enfeebled; she, more aged. It is a brave but not totally convincing performance, and one that arouses sympathy. Our own dinner discussions afterwards reveal that tempers have grown short, nerves frayed.

[1] In charge of Iranian affairs at the State Department.

Tuesday, January 2

The Bakhtiar speech is massively covered by the papers and the radio. Though I yearn with every fibre of my being for him to succeed, I know in my heart of hearts that he won't. Had he been given the job two years ago, the appointment could have averted a revolution. But then it is inconceivable that two years ago it would have been offered him. As late as the summer of 1978 Amini was unacceptable to HIM, let alone Bakhtiar, who, in any case, sounds too good to be true. Already the mob in the street is calling for his death, labelling him an American puppet. When Bakhtiar goes, it will be left to a shoot-out between Khomeini and the generals.

Abbasgholi Bakhtiar, Shahpour's cousin, calls to say that he has been summoned back to Tehran from the States, where he has been seeing doctors about his son's eye injury. With no flights to Tehran, he wants to know whether we have any suggestions. He comes to the Embassy a bit later for a chat. He speaks of Bakhtiar as 'an exceptional man, an intellectual, a fighter and one who has suffered much'. He, too, is sceptical about Bakhtiar's chances, but says one must do what one can for one's country. 'Some people in Tehran,' he says, 'placed such high hopes on Afshar's visit to London. Did it achieve anything?'

I suppress a chuckle, as I recall the Court Protocol Officer's remarks to Ahmad, as he was about to call Brzezinski's office, wishing him 'God's protection'. When reason and reality predict doom, men place their hopes in miracles.

The midnight news reports an attempt by Iranian students to set fire to Princess Shams's house in Beverly Hills, where the Shah's 90-year-old mother is staying. King Constantine telephones late to ask if HIM is going to leave. I think so, I say, but haven't been told officially.

Wednesday, January 3

The Senate and the Majlis have jointly approved Bakhtiar's commission to form a government – a predictable outcome. The Shah's mother has been moved to a new and as yet undisclosed location, and violence has continued in Iran.

Bakhtiar has held a press conference in which he has said: 1) HIM will leave soon after the formation of his government; 2) Iran will no longer play the role of policeman in the Persian Gulf; 3) no more oil will go to Israel 'on religious grounds'. He also says,

302

'When the people of Iran appointed me to this position ...'

Moinian has spoken to General Jam on the telephone again, assuring him that HIM had made it crystal clear that his appointment to the cabinet now would be under completely different conditions from those prevailing seven years ago. Jam's refusal had not been accepted by HIM, who urged him to return. When Jam had pleaded the case of his drug-addicted son as a final excuse, Moinian had said: 'In that case, I'll put you on directly to His Majesty, and you can explain your reasons yourself.' Jam had demurred. A Lieutenant-General was on his way from Tehran to speak to him, and it now seems that he will go back to Tehran to judge the situation for himself.

Thursday, January 4

The *FT* has a leading article which speaks of the need for Bakhtiar to be seen to be operating independently of the throne. I cable it to Moinian, in the vague hope that the hint might be taken.

The 11 o'clock news says the Americans have denied asking the Shah to leave, though he would be welcome if he should wish to go to America. The Sanjabi faction of the National Front has called for demonstrations against 'traitors to the National Front who have collaborated with the illegal monarchy'. Meanwhile, to add to the confusion, an aide to Khomeini has stated that their future Islamic administration will include European-educated people, but not Iranian aristocrats like Sanjabi and Bakhtiar.

There is a front page article in the *Daily Express*, claiming that HIM has stashed a billion dollars safely away in banks outside Iran, and is now about to leave the country. I cable the relevant bits of the article to Moinian, adding that, since the Embassy's previous denials have caused HIM displeasure, would he now instruct me what to say.

The Persian Service reports that Generals Oveisi, Khosrodad and Rabii have resigned their posts and that Oveisi has left the country. Exit the hard-liners. AAH, to whom my thoughts turn again, must be in great danger.

At 9.30 there is a telephone call from a friend in Tehran. Mirfendereski is to be Foreign Minister in Bakhtiar's cabinet, he tells me. 'He would know my joy at his appointment,' I say, 'but I wish it had come under different circumstances.'

At midnight I call Saipa, who confirms the Mirfendereski appointment, adding, with complete forgetfulness of the humiliating manner in which they had been dismissed from their positions by her brother, that 'he and Jam are the only two people on our side in the Government'. Wistfully she goes on: 'But it's no use. What good is a Prime Minister who gives a press conference while standing under a portrait of Mossadeq?'

She says the British and the Americans have finally ousted the Shah. When I gently inquire by what method of deduction she had reached that conclusion, she replies: 'How else could all this have come about?'

When I ask why had General Gharabaghi, and not Jam, been made Chief of Staff, she replies it is because Gharabaghi 'is strong' while 'Jam is soft'.

'When will HIM leave?' I ask.

'He will leave in time, but not just yet,' she says, adding that there is still uncertainty about where he will go. She herself is in a hurry to go somewhere else, as her apartment is besieged by journalists who want to know whether the Queen Mother has moved in with her after fleeing Los Angeles.

Friday, January 5

Sanjabi and his National Front colleagues, who had called for a 'day of mourning and demonstrations' on Sunday, have had to tone down their appeal for one of 'mourning' only, because the clergy have not supported their call.

The BBC has an interview with Khomeini in which he sounds arrogant, intransigent, ignorant and nursing a massive grievance against the person of HIM.

Saturday, January 6

Bakhtiar presents his cabinet to HIM and Mirfendereski fills the post of Foreign Minister. I speak to Hossein, to Ahmad, to Cyrus, to Alireza, to Farhad. Suddenly everyone seems euphoric. HIM has spoken of 'the need for a rest' and, according to the Constitution, if he should go abroad a Regency Council will have to be formed. HIM's departure could actually defuse the crisis and increase Bakhtiar's chances in a holding operation, as Khomeini hasn't yet called for Bakhtiar's overthrow. We all agree that if, with the army's backing, Bakhtiar does manage to remain in office, and

if the situation deteriorates no further, the change to a constitutional monarchy would provide Iran with a society infinitely preferable
to that presided over by the Shah.

But will it hold?

There is a reply from Moinian to my cable on the alleged transfer
of a billion dollars. HIM has said that the report 'is a lie from top to
toe', adding: 'We have not one cent of money nor a house in
America.' I am instructed to deny 'these completely false allegations'.

In the evening we watch film of the presentation of the cabinet to
HIM. The ceremony is truly remarkable for what it doesn't show.
Gone are the gold-braided uniforms, the plumed hats, the dazzling
swords and the green and red sashes of Homayoun Orders. While
Bakhtiar bows deeply, neither he nor any of his Ministers kisses
HIM's hand. Overnight we have replaced the servile greeting of
foot-kissing by a respectable nod of the head, and everyone,
including the Shah himself, has gained in dignity as a result.

But my self-induced euphoria is soon shattered. In the evening I
learn that Khomeini has called Bakhtiar's government 'a conspira-
cy against the Iranian revolution', and called for a general strike on
Monday.

Perhaps it was all wishful-thinking after all.

Sunday, January 7

Some 10,000 people have demonstrated in Tehran, presumably in
response to the National Front's call for a march against the
Bakhtiar government. There has been more shooting.

The papers say that the Shah is going to leave on Wednesday,
and that the American administration has finally decided to
abandon its outright support for the Shah, giving him 'a private
burial'.

My usual collection of compatriots come to dinner, and as
always there is much heated discussion, with little chance of
success held out for the Bakhtiar government. References to HIM
at times become so scathing that I feel compelled to remind them
that we are still in the *Imperial* Iranian Embassy, enjoying the
hospitality of the *Imperial* Iranian Government.

Saipa rings from New York after dinner. Jam has finally turned
down Bakhtiar's offer of a government post, pleading his primary
loyalty to the Shah as the reason; and the Empress has said she will
stay behind to preside over the Regency Council after HIM's

departure 'even if they lynch me'. Saipa doesn't know when HIM is leaving, but confirms that he will, and agrees that he could not come back to Iran as King again. When I repeat to her Ahmad's observation at dinner, namely, that when the Shah has gone, 'Khomeini will return, and by Now Rouz we shall have an Islamic Republic', she lapses into a prolonged silence. She recovers, however, to insist on the good prospects there are for the Crown Prince to reign. She still doesn't know where HIM will go when he leaves.

Monday, January 8

In response to Khomeini's call, there have been massive demonstrations again. Bakhtiar, in an interview, has said that, for the first time in twenty-five years, the Prime Minister of Iran is running the affairs of the country; that anti-corruption trials will begin in ten days, and that 'it is a foregone conclusion some people will be executed'.

For the past few weeks an army of electrical technicians have been installing secret and highly sophisticated equipment on the roof of the Chancery to facilitate telephone conversations between the US and Iran. We have been told nothing about their activities, except for instructions to give them full cooperation. I now begin to wonder, with the Shah's departure imminent, whether the facilities are for the purpose of keeping HIM in contact with Tehran from wherever he may be in the States.

A certain General Huyser from NATO Headquarters has been in Tehran for the past few days for 'consultations', whatever that means, and 'to prevent the Iranian military from staging a coup d'état', according to the papers.

I lunch with John Graham at the Army and Navy Club. In a morbid way I find it quite funny that John should be wondering to whom he would have to present his credentials if HIM should leave by the end of the week. He says he understands from Tony's cables that HIM is scheduled to give a press conference on Wednesday. I say I know nothing about any such conference.

Sensing my unease, John delicately switches the conversation to Rhodesia, with which he has been so closely associated. A pleasant lunch in the company of an intelligent, sensitive man.

Back at the office I send my first cable to the new Foreign Minister. After referring to persistent press reports of constant American contact with, and support for, the Bakhtiar government, and alluding to the alleged activities of General Huyser, I say that such open reliance on foreign support will weaken the government's position. 'Your Excellency may therefore see fit to have some senior Iranian Government spokesman assert the unacceptability of foreign interference in Iran's internal affairs.' I add that the American Embassy could be given prior notice of the impending verbal attack on them, 'which would be a tactical manoeuvre, designed to enhance the government's chances of survival'.

I then refer to Bakhtiar's remarks about the outcome of the corruption trials, saying that, while I fully understand the need in the present difficult circumstances for 'utterances that would calm the public clamour', it would be preferable to say 'the accused will be tried according to the laws of the land, and the guilty given the maximum penalty under the law'.

Tuesday, January 9

An informed and poignantly written article in the *Guardian* by Martin Woollacott: 'Asked recently by a correspondent what had been his greatest error, the Shah replied in leaden voice: "To have been born." The Shah is neither a vicious man, although he has been responsible for much viciousness, nor a fool, although he has been lacking in wisdom.'

General Huyser has now openly expressed the Carter administration's support for the Bakhtiar government. In the *Mail* there are pictures of two people lynched for robbery and hanged from trees in some city in Iran, and 'Islamic courts' are rearing their heads everywhere.

There is a reply from the Foreign Minister to my cable of yesterday: 'Your proposals will be acted upon.'

I speak to Fereydoun in New York. Outwardly at least, his voice betrays no trace of emotion or nervousness. He spoke to AAH yesterday. The line had been tapped, so the exchanges had been limited. He says he has spoken to Vance about AAH, and wants me to be in touch with Martin Ennals.

Ahmad Ghoreishi telephones to say he has learnt that the Americans now say the Shah should leave, even if only temporarily, so that order may be restored. When I mention this to Saipa, to whom I speak a little later, she pauses a while, then says: 'So this is what they agreed to in Guadeloupe.'[1]

[1] Reference to the summit conference of the four leading Western industrial nations, then meeting on the island of Guadeloupe.

307

Wednesday, January 10

Khosro Eghbal rings from Paris. He is going to see Khomeini tonight, and intends to tell him that he is obviously out of touch with what is happening in Iran; that the dangers of Iran's disintegration are palpably real, and that his refusal to compromise, even with a post-Shah government, is going to take Iran into the communist orbit. Khosro says he will emphasize to Khomeini that, unlike those who now surround him, Khosro wants nothing for himself, but hopes merely for the continued existence of Iran as a country.

What does he think are his chances of success, I ask.

'Thirty per cent; maybe a little less.'

The news from Tehran focuses on Bakhtiar's continuing difficulties. General Khosrodad, according to rumours, has declared that if HIM leaves he will reduce Mashad and Qom to rubble before Khomeini's triumphant return.

Thursday, January 11

Bakhtiar has presented his cabinet to the Majlis. It is an admirable performance by the sound of it, in which he promises respect for human rights, the abolition of Savak, social democracy, observance of the Constitution, and a surprisingly liberal economic policy.

I see from the papers that Bakhtiar has threatened to resign if HIM should go back on his promise to leave Iran. Later in the day Cyrus Vance opines that the Shah should leave and a Regency Council should be established. Julian Amery and King Constantine ring to ask what I think of HIM's proposed departure. I say that, while I would have preferred HIM rather than Vance to announce that particular piece of news, and believe the Carter Administration guilty of perfidy in its relations with the Shah, nonetheless HIM's temporary departure may be no bad thing.

Friday, January 12

Dr Fallah rings to say that he has spoken to Khosro Eghbal in Paris. So frightened and alarmed had Khosro become by Khomeini's medieval imbecility, that he was now actually considering a return to Tehran to persuade the Shah to stay, at least for another couple of months, to allow a workable, sane succession to evolve. What do I think about HIM staying on for another couple of months, Fallah asks. I say that I don't honestly believe HIM's name can now be salvaged, and I would prefer him to go in order to give the monarchy a chance of survival. What I would ask Khosro to do is to urge Shariatmadari to break with Khomeini, and come out with a call for restraint, moderation and a spirit of compromise.

Later Khosro himself telephones. 'It was like speaking to a stone wall,' he says, 'I spoke for half an hour, and he just stared.'

I write a personal letter to the Foreign Minister, addressing him as 'My very dear Ahmad'. After expressing my delight at his appointment, and recalling the many lunches during which we would agonise over the rupture of his association with HIM, I come to my operative paragraph: 'My purpose in writing these lines to you at times of such anguish, is not to remind you of our long-standing friendship, or of my heartfelt devotion to you. It is, rather, to tell you not to allow our old friendship to stand in the way of asking me for anything that, in positive or negative terms, I may be able to do for you.' I assure him that he should feel free from any scruples he may harbour as far as my own position is concerned, and conclude by saying that his and Bakhtiar's success outweigh all other considerations.

I lunch with Alinaghi Alikhani,[1] Hossein and Farhad. Alikhani gives the Bakhtiar government no more than a five per cent chance of survival and believes HIM should leave at once to allow that percentage to rise. He thinks the revolution in Iran is a revolution of the middle classes, of school teachers and bank clerks, and of the best paid industrial work force in the country – the oil company workers. He thinks the peasants, the poor and the unemployed played no part in it. He is worried about the ultimate direction of events, and predicts that control will move from the clergy to the military, and from there to the left-wing militants. He describes Bakhtiar as a courageous man and the best of the National Front lot, 'but he is no Amini'. He adds: '*Il n'aime pas l'homme. Il aime l'humanité.*'

When I walk with him to the door, he asks what my own plans are. I reply that, in spite of all the risks, I would like to go back to Tehran so as not to be automatically lumped in people's minds with the more infamous of the Shah's associates. 'Don't go back,' he warns. 'The current joke in Tehran is about the fox who was hurrying out of town. Someone asked the reason for such haste. The fox said: "In that town they kill all foxes that have three balls."'

[1] A former Minister of Economy, then resident in London.

"But have you got three balls?" he was asked. "No," replied the fox, "but they kill you first and count your balls afterwards." '

Saturday, January 13

Hassanali Mehran, in London again, comes to lunch. Even though his name had not appeared on any list, he had had to obtain special permission from the office of the Prime Minister to be allowed out of the country. His description of the pandemonium at the airport, the aggressive, almost belligerent, attitude of the few remaining porters, the physical struggle to make one's way to the airline counter, the sly insinuations of those who look upon one as a potential fugitive, the conspiratorial gaze of one's co-passengers suggesting a bond of common guilt, and the shared impatience for a quick take-off, sound quite chilling.

He had seen HIM about ten days ago. Dejected, humbled, embittered, he had repeatedly asked what Khomeini had ever done for the Iranian people. His despondency at his apparent rejection by the workers and peasants for whom he had done so much seemed immeasurable.

One hundred thousand people have demonstrated at the now re-opened Tehran University, and Khomeini has announced the establishment of a Provisional Revolutionary Council, calling on the people to intensify their struggle without fearing the spilling of blood. Ardeshir has left for the United States to prepare, according to the BBC, for the Shah's arrival.

Sunday, January 14

The Regency Council has been formed. One or two old-timers of the Mossadeq era, Entezam, Ardalan the Court Minister, the Chief Justice, the Chief of Staff, the Presidents of the Majlis and the Senate, with the Prime Minister himself as Chairman, comprise its members. The newspapers speculate that HIM will leave by Thursday. Another week of agonising uncertainty lies ahead.

Monday, January 15

At my request George Jellicoe comes to lunch with me at PG. He says he has written to Bakhtiar 'simply to wish him well'. After a review of the exceedingly gloomy prospects ahead, I say that, with the Shah's departure imminent, it is increasingly likely that AAH will soon be brought to trial; and, equally, it is increasingly likely that he may not survive the outcome. I show George the appeal in *Le Monde* for AAH's release and ask whether it would be appropriate for some of AAH's British friends to launch a similar appeal.

Unhesitatingly, he says: 'Your wish is my command.' After a moment's reflection, he considers Alec Home to be 'the man who could bring everyone with him as the captain of the best eleven'.

The Senate has approved the Bakhtiar Government by a large majority, and rumours are again rife about the Shah's departure 'tomorrow'.

King Constantine telephones to say he has spoken to Their Majesties, and they were reluctant to speak about their plans, but they will leave tomorrow. The children have already gone to New Jersey. 'I felt as miserable as they did,' he says.

Later it is announced from Egypt that the Shah will fly to Aswan tomorrow, after giving a press conference in Tehran. So this, at last, is the end.

Tuesday, January 16

At 9.45 there is a telephone call from Tehran. It's Mirfendereski, the Foreign Minister. 'Haji Parviz,' he says, as he has always called me, 'take a pencil and write down what I say.'

'Yes, Sir.'

'It is exceedingly painful for me to terminate, for reasons that you will appreciate, your assignment as Ambassador to the Court of St James's. It is my personal opinion that, as one who without doubt has proved a most effective Iranian ambassador to Britain, the country is now more than ever in need of your valuable services. With deep regret, I want you to understand and to forgive.

Yours ever,
Ahmad Mirfendereski
Minister of Foreign Affairs.'

He would have cabled the text, but for the strike.

I assure him that I understand perfectly, and tell him that I have already written to ask him to put aside all considerations of personal friendship. I am given a month to say my goodbyes. The entire conversation lasts no longer than five minutes.

As soon as we hang up I send off a letter to the Foreign Office informing them of my departure 'before the end of January' and asking for appointments to bid farewell. I then call in Mahdavi and read him the Minister's message.

The press conference in Tehran has been cancelled abruptly, and we learn soon afterwards that the Shah and the Empress have left Iran. There had been a brief ceremony at the airport, with Bakhtiar, some army brass and a few members of the Regency Council present. Then, with tears streaming down his cheeks, the Shah had climbed the flight of steps into the plane, had sat behind the controls, and piloted the aircraft himself, taking with him, as his father had done, a handful of Persian soil as a symbol of his love for Iran.

The 3 o'clock news describes the mood in Tehran as a 'carnival atmosphere'. President Sadat has received the Shah in Aswan with much pomp and ceremony 'amid enthusiastic public acclaim'. How odiously fickle are the emotions of the masses.

Mahdavi comes in later in the afternoon to say that 'the Embassy staff' wish to make a gesture of solidarity with their revolutionary brethren in Iran by closing the Embassy for one day. From his tone I can't quite determine whether it is my permission which is being requested, or whether I am simply being notified. I tell Mahdavi that for the Embassy staff to have waited until the Shah's departure to demonstrate their revolutionary zeal does not increase my respect for their courage or loyalty. I tell him that *I* shall come to my office every day till the day I leave, and that no one is going to stop me. Nervous and crestfallen, he exits.

On reflection, I find that I am appalled by the manner of the Shah's departure. The ruse of the press conference was clearly intended to divert the attention of the media, and certainly such an occasion, with its noisy informality, and all the questioning that would only have further visibly frayed HIM's already shattered nerves, would have been most inappropriate as a last public appearance. But he could have made a dramatic television appeal, with as much *coup de théâtre* as he could have mustered, a final impassioned and emotional appeal to his people, reminding them that he was leaving to prevent the further spilling of blood, and exhorting them not to endanger the territorial integrity of Iran. Instead, this undignified, sneak exit. But ... does it really matter?

Wednesday, January 17

I learn from the 8 o'clock news that members of our UN Mission in New York have announced their solidarity with the Iranian revolution, and declared that Saipa is no longer head of the Iranian delegation to the UN.

Later, Radio Tehran reads out the names of nine ambassadors dismissed from office 'whose appointment contravenes the Foreign Ministry's regulations'. My name heads the list. The others are Bahrami in Paris, Fereydoun in New York, Ardeshir in Washington and the ambassadors to Rome, Canberra, New Delhi and Damascus.

The evening papers report my dismissal, photos and all.

Thursday, January 18

President Carter has appealed to Khomeini to support 'the legal Government' of Dr Bakhtiar, and expressed the hope that calm and stability will soon return to Iran.

I speak to Mohsen Goudarzi at the Foreign Ministry in Tehran and ask for a passport of 'whatever kind the regulations allow', and for two months' leave to begin on February 1.

The Embassy in Bonn has been taken over by 'representatives of the Islamic Government of Iran', who have held discussions, it seems, with an accommodating, compliant ambassador.

Later in the morning Michael Fitzalan-Howard, attired in morning dress, comes to bid official farewell, and to present me with signed photographs of the Queen and Prince Philip 'with the Queen's special regard for you'.

The one o'clock news broadcasts Khomeini's rejection of the Carter appeal in the form of a statement that calm and stability will be restored to Iran when outsiders stop interfering in Iran's domestic affairs. It is not for President Carter, he says, to pronounce on the legality of governments in Iran.

In the evening Shams, the cipher clerk, brings me confirmation of the Foreign Minister's telephone conversation of two days ago. Because of the continuing strike it takes the form of a post office telegram, and reads simply: 'Your assignment will end on February 19. You will transfer responsibility for the affairs of the Embassy to the most senior staff of the mission. Mirfendereski.'

Friday, January 19

The BBC says nearly two million people have marched in Tehran to support Khomeini's call for the creation of an Islamic republic on this day of Arba'in.[1] But Khosro telephones to report that he has spoken to someone in Tehran, who was cautiously optimistic about developments. Bakhtiar, he said, was gaining ground among the silent majority, who were becoming increasingly fearful both of Khomeini's intransigence and of the alliance of leftists whose ranks, now that the Shah had gone, were already beginning to crack. The army had stood firmly by Bakhtiar in dealing with disturbances in Dezful and Ahvaz.

With Hossein's keen business eye supervising, I close all the Embassy accounts, transferring signature rights to Mahdavi.

Letters and telephone calls from well-wishers innundate the office and necessitate much last-minute correspondence, a welcome respite from the gloomy and pointless speculation.

King Constantine and Julian Amery come to lunch at PG. The King has placed a call to Aswan, which comes through towards the end of lunch. He speaks to the Empress, who tells him they don't know how long they will stay in Aswan. 'We don't seem to be able to make our minds up,' she kept on repeating, Constantine says. She had also wanted to know what the news was, as there, ironically, they were confined to the BBC. She asked 'what the Ambassador was going to do'. The King is going to Aswan on Sunday to see them, and promises to telephone me when he is back.

'Tell them, if I may ask Your Majesty to act as courier, that my heart is with them,' I say, 'and if they should ever feel there is anything I can do for them, not to hesitate to ask. But tell them also that I shall never forgive His Majesty for his treatment of Hoveyda. It didn't save his throne, did it?'

There is a letter from Michael Weir:

'Dear Parviz,
I am deeply distressed to hear you are going. What a sad end to what, if I may say so, has been an outstandingly successful mission.

On top of personal regrets at losing a valued friend and colleague, one cannot but feel an acute sadness for your country at this perhaps uniquely critical moment in its history. I can only pray that Iran's historic character, spirit and integrity will survive through the trials ahead.

It is hard for an outsider to imagine the emotions you must be

---

[1] Fortieth day after the martyrdom of Imam Hossein, and another day of Shia mourning.

feeling at this time. You have my utmost sympathy, as well as warmest wishes for the future. It has been an uncommon pleasure to know and to work with you, and I would like to think the opportunity may come again.

Yours ever, Michael.'

Until I leave – and I shall count the days until I do – I shall have a distinctly uneasy sensation as long as I am residing at the Embassy. I feel somehow that my claim to be there has been invalidated, that I am an unwanted guest, a usurper, an illegal occupant. Each meal, each sip of wine, each glass of un-Islamic champagne, has lost its enjoyment. It was kind of the Minister to give me till February 19, but I simply couldn't bear it until then. I must leave as soon as I have said my official goodbyes.

Saturday, January 20

I spend the day packing. The gold-braided uniform, the white gloves, the ceremonial sword in its black velvet scabbard, the plumed hat, the decorations, already seem out of place, museum pieces evoking recollections of a bygone era.

What for many will be a joyful return to Iran from political exile will be for others the start of a life of endless wandering abroad in search of a safe haven or sanctuary. From now on, the diaspora will be predominantly Iranian.

The Shah – and those of us who, whatever our private reservations, publicly supported him to the end – got it terribly wrong; and the verdict of history, the judgment of posterity, will condemn us for the follies of our ways. Yet if the price for the Shah's errors had been confined to the overthrow of his dynasty, or even the abolition of the monarchy and the permanent exclusion from political life of all those who had served the Pahlavi régime, Iran itself might have been spared the terrifying fate that now awaits her. More than a dynasty, more than the monarchy, has been lost. The real tragedy is that the country will now fall into the clutches of the most bigoted and benighted clerical rule in its three-thousand-year history. The sanctimoniously hypocritical mullahs, with their ugly primitivism and sham religiosity, will now reign supreme, and those eternal universally valid values of civilization will be in permanent retreat. It will be a very very long time before the slide to cruelty and barbarism in the name of God can be stopped, let alone reversed. I know I won't be there to see it, and it breaks my

315

heart to admit it.

A letter from Ronald, the Embassy chauffeur:

'Dear Sir,

Because of the vast gulf which exists between us, both in status and academic qualifications, I have always remained a silent, and I trust, faithful servant, which of course is the way it should be, for no subordinate should ever exceed the bounds of his realm without the invitation to do so.

For that reason, Sir, I have always kept a discreet distance from approaching you, and will continue to do so for as long as I live. No Boss, before or after you can fill the gap that will be left in your passing.

In spite of friends, colleagues and acquaintances, no one really gets to know a person better than his own servants. His secretary, his butler, his maid, his chauffeur. These are the people who learn more about his personality than anyone else, for it is in their presence that he can be himself. There is no falsehood, no putting on a brave face for the sake of the company or the occasion.

They see him in pleasure and in pain, in high spirits and in low, but always in silence. Everything that constitutes his make-up, whether they approve or disapprove, is their own private observation. Yet in spite of this they remain loyal to him.

If I have ever appeared to be unsympathetic towards you by my silence, it was not constituted by my lack of interest in your personal problems, Sir, but because my position did not permit me to enquire or pry.

Whenever we visited doctors or specialists I have always desired to enquire after your welfare, but it was not my place to intrude.

When you parted company from Miss Spender and the newspapers had a 'Field Day' at your expense, I wanted to offer my condolences. But, now, more than ever, since I have learned the sad news of your departure from our midst, do I wish to express my own personal sadness at your relinquishment from the position of Ambassador to our Embassy. For beneath my own personal loss of a man I regard with great esteem, is the knowledge that all your efforts and years of dedication to your profession are to be wasted by an unkind quirk of fate that lies beyond your own control.

No human condition is ever permanent, Sir, the calm must always follow the storm in spite of what disruptions it may have left in its wake, and I am confident that a man of your qualifications and ability will survive to direct his initiative to some future (if unknown at this present moment) form of usefulness in society.

Although, I fully appreciate that such sentiments are of little value at this present time.

Forgive my frankness, or the extension of my right to penetrate the realms of your privacy with outbursts of 'Home-Spun' philosophy, but I could not let this hour pass without offering some comment of my own feelings for both yourself and the situation, however uncalled for they might be.

For all the kindnesses that you have extended towards me during our short relationship together, Sir, I would now like to thank you.

In the same token I would like to apologize for any mistakes or misunderstandings on my part that may have caused you annoyance or displeasure at their time of occurrence. I have always tried to do my best, but owing to the human factor there must have been several occasions where I failed miserably.

It only remains for me to wish that Health, Wealth and Happiness will be your constant companions in the distant and unforeseeable future.

Serving you has been my pleasure. Losing you will be my loss.

I say that with tears in my eyes, and I don't give a damn if it sounds sentimental.

GOOD LUCK! Sir,

Sincerely, respectfully and obediently yours,

Ronald.'

I must be losing control. An irrepressible rush of tears blurs my vision as I reach the end of his letter.

Sunday, January 21

Goudarzi rings from the Ministry to say that Mirfendereski has agreed to give me 'any sort of passport you choose to have', but he recommends an ordinary one, which is what I wanted in the first place. I am also given two months' leave.

Khomeini has announced he will go back to Tehran on Friday.

Cyrus Ghani telephones to say Dante should have added one more category to his description of people in hell – the unemployed.

Before his departure from Tehran, it is now reported, HIM had been asked why didn't he urge his supporters in Iran to come out into the streets and demonstrate *for* him, as de Gaulle's supporters had done on the Champs-Elysées. 'The trouble,' HIM had replied, 'is that my supporters *are already* on the Champs-Elysées.'

Monday, January 22

Students have broken into the Embassy in New Delhi and attacked the Consulate in Bombay.

Farhad leaves for the US, promising to keep in touch. He says he has made up his mind to return to Tehran as soon as the situation permits: 'There is no reason why I should go on living the life of a refugee.'

Mahdavi telephones to say there is a circular from the Ministry with instructions that all pictures of the Royal Family should be removed from public display, but kept safe in a place where they would be protected from any disrespect. I book my departure, to Rome, for Friday.

HIM has gone to Morocco. Rumour has it that he had been so infuriated by Carter's call to Khomeini to show restraint that he will now not go to the US. Clashes have continued in Tehran, mostly between Khomeinists and communists. Seyyed Jalal Tehrani, Chairman of the Regency Council, who went to Paris to see Khomeini, has had to resign his post before the Ayatollah would receive him.

Tuesday, January 23

The Shah will *not* go to the States after all, says the BBC. The Americans, according to Ardeshir in a *NY Times* interview, don't really want him there, and Ardeshir believes that, if HIM did go to the US it would mean his abdication – in fact, if not in name – and also that if one day he were to return, the CIA would inevitably be given credit for his restoration.

I speak to Fereydoun, who tells me AAH is preparing himself for his trial. In the afternoon Mahdavi comes to see me. He says he, and the four counsellors at the Embassy, would like to come and see me off at the airport when I leave on Friday.

Bazargan has called on Bakhtiar to resign, and the Embassy in Paris has been broken into by students.

George Jellicoe and Michael Stewart come for a drink, to meet Farid and Farideh Hoveyda (cousins of AAH), and to see what could be done in the way of placing an appeal for AAH's release in the papers at the appropriate psychological moment.

I write Mirfendereski a handwritten confidential memo, informing him that I have, in a secret fund in my possession, over £20,000 of government money and would he tell me what to do with it.

Wednesday, January 24

The military have occupied Tehran airport with troops and tanks, and no planes are allowed in or out. A Khomeini aide in Paris has declared that as long as one airport remains open in Iran the Ayatollah will return.

After lunch with a group of distraught compatriots, I spend the afternoon making goodbye telephone calls to many who had called to express sympathy. Then I speak to Mother in Tehran. She says relatives and a few other intimates whom she has consulted all believe I should stay away for a while. Then, perhaps to soften the blow, she says: 'Even if there were no other considerations, there is no electricity.' She is adamant about wanting to stay herself. 'There are so many like me,' she says, 'only, if a traveller is coming this way, perhaps you could send some candles.'

News reports in the afternoon announce Tehran airport has reopened, and a spokesman for the military has referred to 'a misunderstanding'. Khomeini is returning after all, it seems.

Thursday, January 25

At 9.30 I go to the Foreign Office to make my goodbyes. Ivor Lucas meets me at the entrance, and we proceed to Michael Palliser's room. The unpredictability of the course of events in Tehran is discussed, and I learn that, because of the prevailing chaos at Tehran airport, the plane carrying John Graham had been diverted to Kuwait, where he now is, awaiting a chance to resume his journey to Tehran when he can. Sir Michael walks with me to the Foreign Secretary's room, and we shake hands. I am determined that the occasion should be free from even the faintest hint of sentimentality.

I next see David Owen. The British government, he says, has decided for the moment not to make any comments on the situation in Iran, but he personally would stand by a recent statement he had made, to the effect that the mullahs could well be succeeded by the communists. I agree, and say it is difficult to be optimistic. Handshakes again, as I take my leave.

On to Michael Weir's, where he extends his good wishes for Hoveyda and myself, and expresses the hope that we may meet one day in Cairo. And finally a brief chat with, and a warm farewell from, Roger du Boulay.

After lunch Mahdavi calls to say that, despite all precautions,

319

some thirty people have taken over the Consulate, and have presented a list of demands which include renaming the Embassy to that of 'The Islamic Republic of Iran', a call for the abolition of the monarchy, and the resignation of 'Bakhtiar's illegal government'. Later he and six of the Embassy staff come for a discussion of the demands, and I see that one of the Consulate employees is militantly siding with the invaders. It is agreed that the invaders should be persuaded to leave peacefully, and the promise given that their demands will be transmitted to Tehran for consideration. If this approach should fail, then the police should be asked to evict the occupiers.

My farewell cocktail party for the Embassy staff is less than a total success, as many of them are engaged in heated discussions with the Consulate occupiers and so cannot attend.

Friday, January 26

Today I leave, after two years, seven months and twenty-two days as HIM's ambassador to London. By a curious, possibly portentous coincidence, my assignment began, and ended inauspiciously. There was Amirteymour's death on arrival; and now, as I leave, the Shah has departed, the monarchy is endangered and Iran is in the grip of revolutionary turmoil. Who could have foreseen these momentous traumas three, or even two years ago, and the sad ending to it all?

Yet the intervening period between arrival and departure will remain in my mind as the most fascinating, instructive, agonising, frustrating and, at many a moment, enjoyable time of my life. And now, inundated as my thoughts are with worry and anxiety, I feel no regret and even less bitterness. Indeed, my sentiments at this moment are those of gratitude and appreciation for the kindness, friendliness and civility which were such constant features of British attitudes towards me.

A somewhat awkward, silence-filled, emotional final parting from Lizzie; and more telephone calls to last-minute well-wishers.

Jessica Douglas-Home is my last visitor. 'Like Charlie, who is so full of energy and enthusiasm about life', she says, I, too, 'will be all right'.

I shout my goodbye to Rosa, the housekeeper, from the stairway, to avoid a potentially lachrymose farewell, as had been the case with Josey, the Embassy cook. But Ballal's black cheeks are covered with tears as Jessica and I walk past him; then goodbyes to

Abbas and Manuel, an embrace from Jessica and on to the airport.

Ivan May of the Foreign Office Protocol Department is already at the airport lounge, as are some newspaper reporters and photographers, and we are asked to pose and shake hands.

A little before six, as two uniformed policemen accompany me to the aircraft, I say a final goodbye to Ronald, board flight BA506 and fly out to a new life.

EPILOGUE

The note I sent Mirfendereski, Bakhtiar's Foreign Minister, about the £20,000 in my possession never reached him. Khomeini returned to Tehran to triumphant acclaim on February 1, declared Bakhtiar's government illegal, and on February 5 appointed Mehdi Bazargan Prime Minister of the Provisional Government of the Islamic Republic of Iran. As violent demonstrations continued, Bakhtiar struggled to assert the legitimacy of his office, vowing not to give in to the threats of 'the primitive Ayatollah'. But the army generals on whose support his position entirely rested, and who were being counselled by General Huyser, Carter's emissary, not to mount a coup, began to show signs of deep division. Leaderless, confused and demoralised, one faction under General Khosrodad and the Imperial Guard favoured a massive military crack-down, while another under General Gharabaghi, the Chief of Staff, leant towards accommodation with Khomeini.

On Friday, February 10, the Imperial Guard attacked an Air Force base which had declared in support of the Ayatollah. The defenders, young Air Force technicians, opened the barrack arsenal to the local population and the fighting escalated dramatically. However, the following day General Gharabaghi, fearing that the Imperial Guard was about to stage the expected coup, issued a statement announcing the 'neutrality' of the armed forces and ordering the troops to return to barracks. The fate of the Bakhtiar government was thus sealed and Bakhtiar himself fled into hiding.

For the next two days Tehran was in the grip of revolutionary insurrection. Army headquarters and Savak buildings became prime targets for the now armed revolutionaries, and any semblance of civil or military authority vanished completely. In the prevailing pandemonium some of those supposed to be guarding the Shah's former associates – themselves mostly Savak agents and fearful for their own lives – took to their heels. Thus, on the morning of Sunday, February 11, AAH, who was then being held at a Savak guest house in the village of Shian, east of Tehran, found himself abandoned by his former guards. Paradoxically, his gaolers had also been his protectors, and now, as the mob roamed freely, he was without either.

His regular liaison with the outside world was his doctor cousin, Fereshteh Razavi, a courageous and resourceful woman who acted as his personal physician as well. AAH telephoned her in the morning to describe his new circumstances, and she in turn sought the advice of a few trusted friends. The possibility of escape was considered and almost immediately rejected by him as impractical. Time was of the essence, as the villagers of Shian, always curious about the mysterious compound in their midst, were already fingering the locked gates of the guest house. The sudden with-drawal of the army had allowed no time for planning and, since his face was too well-known not to be instantly recognised, AAH decided that he should turn himself in. Fereshteh telephoned Dariush Foruhar, one of the leaders of the National Front, who contacted Khomeini's headquarters. Within the hour several revolutionary guards and a couple of mullahs appeared at Feresh-teh's house and together they drove to Shian. The road to the village passed the Imperial Guard headquarters at Saltanatabad, which was then being ransacked. The convoy was stopped every few yards and allowed through only after the mullahs had identified themselves and explained their mission. AAH was driven first to the National Front offices, and was later in the day moved to the Alavieh School in south Tehran where Khomeini had set up his headquarters. As he himself must have known, it was for him the beginning of the end.

On March 15, news was given of his trial at Tehran's Ghasr prison, the charges ranging from spying for the West to waging war against God and his emissaries. Photographs showed him wearing what appeared to be a black leather jacket with a huge cardboard placard bearing his name hanging round his neck. Possibly as a result of international pressure, which included a plea to the Bazargan government from the four surviving former British Prime Ministers that Hoveyda's life be spared – the outcome of George Jellicoe's creditable efforts – his trial was suspended for a while; but it was resumed secretly on April 6, and on the following day Hoveyda's execution was announced. It seems virtually certain that no defence of his, however convincing or well presented, would have made any difference to the outcome of his trial. Nonetheless, it may be noted from the transcripts of the proceedings that appeared in the Persian press that AAH maintained that his hands were stained with neither blood nor money. It also emerges that, throughout, he retained his dignity. By his own account,[1] Ayatollah Khalkhali had acted as the presiding judge at the trial, while the actual execution – two bullets fired into the neck and shoulder – was carried out by another cleric, one Hadi Ghaffari, who is at the time of writing a member of the Islamic parliament.

On the same day that AAH turned himself in, a band of armed revolutionaries set out for the Jamshidieh barracks where many of the Shah's former ministers and officials were being held. Although the commander of the compound had earlier sent the soldiers on leave and had told the 200-odd inmates they were free to depart, some soldiers from the Imperial Guard and a number of Savak

[1] See V.S. Naipaul's *Among the Believers*, pp 40 and 56.

agents decided to resist the onset of the mob, and shooting broke out. In the ensuing mêlée many, including Majidi, the former Budget Bureau Director, Mahdavi, the ex-Commerce Minister, Homayoun, Information Minister in Amouzegar's cabinet, and Nahavandi, once head of the Empress's Bureau, succeeded in getting away. After months in hiding, they eventually made their way out of Iran. Others who were recognised were not so lucky. General Nassiri, the former head of Savak, was savagely tortured by the mob. Along with General Khosrodad, and the military governors of Tehran and Esfahan who were arrested elsewhere, he was spreadeagled on the roof of the Alavieh School and machine-gunned to death on February 17.

Mayor Nikpey, whose visit to London I had seen welcomed by the traditional syncopated handclapping at the Mansion House dinner two years earlier, was also recognized and detained. Khalatbary, the kindly and soft-spoken Foreign Minister, was arrested a few days later. He was found guilty of not having opposed the sale of Iranian oil to Israel. Both he and Nikpey, along with eight other prominent civilians, faced the firing squad on April 10. The executioners were specifically instructed to aim their machine-guns from the knee up.

Of the Shah's former Prime Ministers, Hoveyda alone was destined to be executed. Ali Amini, now the elder statesman of Iranian expatriate politicians, lives in Paris, as does Shahpour Bakhtiar. Amouzegar, Sharif-Emami and General Azhari are all in America.

Princess Ashraf lives mainly in New York, as do Fereydoun Hoveyda and Hushang Ansari. Ardeshir Zahedi left Tehran a few days before the Shah's departure and is based in Montreux, while Afshar lives mostly in London.

My brother Farhad now has a pediatrics consultancy in Los Angeles. Of my personal friends, Hossein Eshraghi, Alireza Arouzi and Mohsen Tayebi are resident in London. Cyrus Ghani makes seasonal migrations between London and New York. Afsaneh, AAH's secretary, lives with her French husband in Paris, as do Cyrus and Parvine Farmanfarmaian. Ahmad Ghoreishi is a lecturer at some college in San Francisco.

Sanjabi, the National Front leader who succeeded Mirfendereski as Foreign Minister, read the private note I had addressed to his predecessor about the money in my possession, and by cable requested that I pay it into the account of the Embassy in London, my sole act of compliance with the wishes of the government of the Islamic Republic. Mirfendereski himself was arrested in March 1979 and detained for seven months. He was released in October of that year, but after the abortive American attempt to rescue the hostages in April 1980 was about to be re-arrested when he fled to Turkey via Kurdestan. He, too, now lives in Paris.

Some of my Embassy colleagues were dismissed, a few stayed on and many returned to Tehran. I have lost track of most of them, but those with whom I am in contact I have not named out of consideration for their safety.

As for myself, my wish is for Iran to survive as a country, and for me to see the day when a measure of what are commonly regarded as humane civilised values comes to prevail over the lives of its beleaguered people.

INDEX

Atlantic Richfield, 71
Avery, Peter, 67, 184
Azar, Lieutenant General Bakhshi, 119
Azhari, General, Prime Minister, 252, 266, 283, 290, 292, 327; resignation, 301

Baez, Joan, 134 and n.
Bahais, the, 214, 218, 224
Bahrami, Major, 108, 157–8
Bahrami, Shapour, 240, 313
Bakhash, Haleh, 125
Bakhash, Shaul, 301
Bakhtiar, Abbasgholi, 302
Bakhtiar, Agha Khan, 254
Bakhtiar, Shahpour, 91, 256, 297, 301, 302, 306, 307, 325, 327; attempts to form Government, 293–6, 301; expelled from National Front, 295; Government formed, 302–5, 308; and anti-corruption trials, 307; U.S. support, 307; Prime Minister, 309–14, 318, 320, 325; flees into hiding, 325
Ball, George, 279, 282, 283
Baraheni, Reza, 41, 79, 88
Barber, Lord, 249
Barnetson, Lord, 71, 181 and n.
Bayulken, Secretary-General of CENTO, 68
Bazargan, Mehdi, 181, 186, 246, 258, 318; and allegations of torture, 200–2; appointed Prime Minister by Khomeini, 325, 326
BBC, 21, 28, 38, 71, 80, 93, 106, 111, 125, 134, 141, 152, 157, 158, 160, 165, 178, 194, 209, 212, 218, 227, 229, 236–7, 239, 243, 244, 271, 272, 276, 277, 279–81, 286, 288, 289, 310, 314, 318; *Panorama*, 39, 76–8, 288; World Service, 129, 153, 178, 215, 239, 261, 282; Persian Service, 152, 154, 166–8, 173–4, 184, 187, 234, 236–7, 242, 248, 252, 253, 256, 262, 268–71, 284, 303; Radio 4 programmes on Iran, 182, 191; and Khomeini, 237, 242, 266, 304; and the mullahs' edict, 277–8
Begin, Menachem, 147, 185
Behbahanian, of Court Ministry, 188, 190
Behnam, Cyrus, 13, 19, 21, 25, 94

Berlin, Isaiah, 86, 145, 152, 154
Berrill, Sir Kenneth, 67
Bessell, Peter, 262
Bethell, Lord, 75 and n., 184
Beveridge, Lord, 120
Bhutto, Zulfigar Ali, 17, 165, 208, 289
Birley, Ann, 52, 61, 71
Blain, Professor, 52
Blanch, Lesley, and her biography of the Empress, 58–9, 92–3, 160, 196, 202, 204
Bloom, Claire, 151
Borchgrave, Arnaud de, 121, 123
Borchgrave, Dominique de, 73
Bossom, Sir Clive, 34
Bowker, Lady, 276–7
Boxer, Mark, 85
Bozorgmehr, Kiumars, 158 and n.
Brandt Commission, 183
Brewster, Kingman, U.S. Ambassador, 146
Brezhnev, L.I., warns against interference in Iran, 261
British Cultural Festival, Iran (1977), 31, 33
British Institute Library project, Tehran, 290
British Parliamentary delegation to Iran, 158, 159, 170, 185, 189–90, 199
Brown, George, *see* George-Brown, Lord
Bruce, David, 87 and n.
Brzezinski, Zbigniew, 277, 302
Bulloch, John, 86, 167n.
Butler, Adam, 172 and n., 184
Butler, William, 186

Cadbury, Belinda, 24, 140
Callaghan, James, 22, 74, 117, 152, 286; support for the Shah, 231, 236, 238; Queen's proposed visit to Iran not to be regarded as support for the régime, 281–4, 286
Calnan, Dr. C.D., 69
Cambridge University, 267
Cameron, James, 236
Campos, Robertó, Brazilian Ambassador, 185–6, 204
Carrington, Lord, 33, 34, 202, 204, 245, 249
Carter, President Jimmy, 23, 29, 33, 79, 82, 97, 123, 133, 134, 142, 161,

demonstrators, 277–8
Mulley, Fred, 54
Murray, Len, 94

Nahavandi, Hushang, 96 and n., 194, 208, 209, 287, 327
Naipaul, Shiva, 161–2, 326 n.
Najafi, Minister of Justice, 270
Najm-el-Molk, 270
Namibia, 165, 167
Nasr, Seyyed Hossein, 277; and BBC, 270, 278–80
Nasser, President, 159
Nassiri, General, head of Savak, 18, 84, 243, 255; removed, 186, 187; murdered by mob, 327
National Front (Iran), 123, 126, 168, 173, 179, 186, 209, 217, 218, 239, 246, 248, 249–51, 258, 260, 285, 293–5, 301, 304, 305, 309, 326, 327; refusal to join coalition, 251; split, 295, 303
National Iranian Oil Company (NIOC), 2–4, 48 n., 79 and n., 96, 125, 148–9, 151, 162, 283, 290
NATO, 13, 106; and the Shah, 267
Nehru, B.K., Indian High Commissioner, 105
Nehru, Jawaharlal, 86
New Left Review, 91
New Statesman, 131, 138, 140, 162, 222
New York Review of Books, 40, 41
New York Times, 20n., 260, 261, 318; interview with the Shah, 199
Newens, Stan, 21, 74–6, 81, 201, 231
Nicolson, Harold, 215
Nikoukhah, Farhad, 98
Nikpay, Gholam Reza, Mayor of Tehran, 28 and n.; executed, 327
Niloufar, Princess, 241
Noor, Queen of Jordan, 287–90
Norris, General, USAF, 116
Nossiter, Bernard, 17, 115
Nowshahr, Shah's residence on the Caspian, 18, 98, 100, 212

Observer, The, 62, 71, 131, 183n.; article on Iran, 166
Ogilvy, Angus, 36, 195–6
Oil and oil policy, 2–3, 8, 48, 49, 90, 243; oilworkers' strikes, 248, 255, 258, 259; army takes over installations, 247, 248; loss of

production, 282, 292
Oman, BBC transmitter off, 271
Omran, Adnan, 24
OPEC, 48–9, 58, 59, 243; Doha Conference, 48 and n., 49; Stockholm Conference, 90; Caracas Conference, 132
Oppenheimer, Richard, 226
Organisation for Social Services (Iran), 235, 261
Orwell, George, 31, 32
Orwell, Sonia, 30–2
Oskoui, Dariush, 225
Oveisi, Colonel Ahmad, 191, 193
Oveisi, General, 226, 259, 290, 303
Owen, Dr. David, 40–1; Foreign Secretary, 61, 68, 80–3, 117, 128, 130, 153, 163, 166–8, 187, 189, 236–7, 239, 258, 281, 285, 319; support for the Shah, 244, 248, 256, 265–6, 284
Oxford, 14, 16, 65; Ashraf Pahlavi Library, 14, 86; Wadham College, 14–15

Pace, Eric, 20 and n.
Pahlavi Foundation, 208, 225, 251, 253, 256
Pahlbod, Mehrdad, 145, 229
Pakistan, 68, 104 and n., 105, 208
Pakravan, Saideh, 77
Palestinians, the, 139, 144, 185
Palliser, Sir Michael, 319
Pallister, David, 131
Palmer, Tony, 120
Pan-Iranist Party, 194, 229
Parsons, Sir Anthony, Ambassador in Tehran, 17 and n., 18, 65, 83, 101, 103, 107, 110, 117, 149, 152, 157, 194–5, 235, 238, 248, 253, 256, 258, 266, 267, 285, 306
Parsons, Lady, 103, 194, 267
Perinat, Marquis de, Spanish Ambassador, 77, 260
Peron, Ernest, 24
Pezeshkpour, Pan-Iranian leader, 194, 229
Philby, Kim, 86
Phipps, Colin, 158, 201 and n.
Phipps, Diana, 39, 40, 54, 85, 87
Pinay, Antoine, 270 and n.
Pincher, Chapman, 34–5, 92, 94, 104 and n., 152, 245

342

70–1, 80
White Revolution, 3, 97
Whitehorn, Katharine, 71
Whitelaw, William, 184
Whitley, Andrew, 93, 137, 215, 245,
    248, 272; proposal to expel him
    from Iran, 266, 271, 289
Widdecombe, Gillian, 88
Widlake, Brian, 71
Wilsher, Peter, 79, 80
Wilson, Sir Harold, 82, 121, 152, 154,
    159, 183, 262
Wilson, William, 21
Wimbledon, 198
Woollacott, Martin, 194, 199, 287, 307
World Football Cup, 129, 187
Worsthorne, Peregrine, 62, 63; article
    by, 66
Wright, Sir Denis, 24 and n., 25, 65,
    196, 204, 280
Wyatt, Verushka, 182
Wyatt, Woodrow, 182, 288

Yamani, Sheikh, 90
Yaseri, Hassan, 79
Yeganeh, Mohammed, 65 and n.
Young, Andrew, 189
Young, Gavin, 62

Zaed al Nahyan, Shaikh, Ruler of
    Abu Dhabi, 27
Zahedi, Ardeshir, Iranian
    Ambassador in Washington, 22
    and n., 26, 33, 65, 88, 93, 115, 120,
    121, 137, 143–5, 147, 155, 187, 198,
    203, 226, 236, 241, 247, 262, 270,
    274, 294, 295, 310, 318, 327;
    dismissed, 313
Zahir Shah, Mohammad, ex-King of
    Afghanistan, 161
Zand, Siamak, allegations on ITV,
    259–63, 292
Zelli, Manuchehr, 200, 289
Zia-ul-Haq, President of Pakistan,
    165